Exploring Language Change

D1461913

'This book provides a brilliantly student-friendly account of language change, with an unusual and innovative emphasis on deliberate, intentional changes. A range of case studies and the authors' lively and readable style makes complex linguistic developments accessible without over-simplifying. The material on revitalisation versus revival, and on invented languages, is inspired!'
April McMahon, *University of Edinburgh, UK*

This book explores the phenomenon of language change, with a particular focus on the social contexts of its occurrence and its possible motivations, including speakers' intentions and attitudes.

Using wide-ranging case studies presenting new or little-known data, Jones and Singh draw a distinction between 'unconscious' and 'deliberate' change. The discussion of 'unconscious' change considers phenomena such as the emergence and obsolescence of individual languages, while the book also includes detailed discussion of 'deliberate' change, traditionally marginalised in favour of explorations of the 'unconscious' variety. The sections on 'deliberate' change focus on issues of language planning, including the strategies of language revival and revitalisation movements, and also include a detailed exploration of what is arguably the most extreme instance of 'deliberate' change: language invention for real-world use.

As a student-friendly text which covers a wide variety of language situations, it also makes a clear, but often ignored, distinction between concepts such as language policy and planning, and language revival and revitalisation. The innovative case studies which permeate the text demonstrate that real-life language use is often much more complex than theoretical abstractions might suggest.

This book will be extremely useful to students on a variety of courses including sociolinguistics, historical linguistics and language policy and planning.

Mari C. Jones is Senior Lecturer in French at the University of Cambridge and Fellow in Modern and Medieval Languages at Peterhouse, Cambridge. **Ishtla Singh** is Lecturer in English Language and Linguistics at King's College London.

Exploring Language Change

Mari C. Jones and Ishtla Singh

Routledge
Taylor & Francis Group

LONDON AND NEW YORK

First published 2005
by Routledge
2 Park Square, Milton Park, Abingdon, Oxon OX14 4RN

Simultaneously published in the USA and Canada
by Routledge
270 Madison Ave, New York, NY 10016

Routledge is an imprint of the Taylor & Francis Group

© 2005 Mari C. Jones and Ishtla Singh

Typeset in Sabon by RefineCatch Limited, Bungay, Suffolk
Printed and bound in Great Britain by
The Cromwell Press, Trowbridge, Wiltshire

British Library Cataloguing in Publication Data
A catalogue record for this book is available from the British Library

Library of Congress Cataloging in Publication Data
Singh, Ishtla.
    Exploring language change.
        p. cm.
    By Ishtla Singh and Mari Jones.
    Includes bibliographical references.
    1. Language change.   2. Language obsolescence.
    3. Language planning.   4. Language revival.
    I. Jones, Mari.   II. Title.
P142.5565 2005
417'.7—dc22   2005000408

ISBN 0–415–31774–6 (hbk)
ISBN 0–415–31775–4 (pbk)

To April McMahon, with warmest thanks for her inspiration and support

Contents

Introduction

When we, the authors, initially met as graduate students in linguistics, we were working in areas which at first glance seemed to have very little, if anything, in common: Mari's thesis focused on language obsolescence in Wales (UK) and Ishtla's on the emergence of an English creole in Trinidad (the Caribbean). As we soon discovered, however, our respective topics often took our work in similar directions and indeed, were ultimately unified by an underlying but significant thread; namely, a consideration of *language change* – a phenomenon which has long been recognised in linguistic research and which continues to be extensively studied today. Indeed, the concept of language change – and of its importance – is one which pervades many modern linguistic approaches. Since the nineteenth century for instance, it has provided the fulcrum for various larger theories of Language: the Neogrammarians formulated what they believed to be universal laws about the regularity of sound change (as well as the concept of *analogy* as a sporadic regulator of the effects of change); Structuralist linguistics hypothesised that a (perhaps universal) need to maintain balance and symmetry in a system was often a driving factor in change; and a significant amount of work in the Generative school of linguistics has concentrated on determining the fundamental locus of change (in this perspective, at the innate unconscious level) and its processes. The concept of change has also become fully integrated into general sociolinguistic and historical linguistic approaches: work in both areas is typically constructed around considerations of variation, change and its linguistic and sociocultural effects from both synchronic and (particularly, of course, in the case of historical linguistics) diachronic perspectives.

It is noteworthy, however, that despite what seems to be a ubiquitous acceptance of language change as a phenomenon which *exists*, is intrinsic to all linguistic systems and which is therefore often an important consideration in linguistic description, it is by no means a 'done deal': our understanding of change, its mechanisms and effects is far from complete or settled. This should not, of course, be taken as a failing or disadvantage: the very wealth of available (and continuously changing) language data plus the ideological shifts that have taken place within linguistics have meant that the study of change itself has remained mutable and, importantly, imbued with the potential for further discovery as we learn more about language systems and their speakers, a quality that can only be viewed positively in academic scholarship.

We should perhaps note here that we do not claim to have made any new discoveries in the field of language change. The fact that its boundaries are not yet definitively 'set', however, has given us scope to bring together theories and ideas about, as well as aspects of, change which are not always examined in conjunction. In particular, we have looked at change as it relates to notions of *language birth* and *language death* – our two respective fields which, as implied earlier, have the potential to be treated (and have been so) as dichotomous – but have also introduced an additional dimension to our discussion; namely, a distinction between 'unconscious' and deliberate change. This has seemed to us to offer an interesting and perhaps novel perspective on change, birth and death: the three are typically discussed in the general context of 'unconscious' change, but processes which aim to influence or change linguistic behaviour (such as strategies of revival and language invention) necessarily involve a significant measure of speaker awareness of language death, birth and, arguably (if we push the metaphor to its limits), *rebirth*.

The structure of the book reflects this division between 'unconscious' and deliberate change and, incidentally, in so doing maintains a distinction between established theories of change and their 'application' in more recent fields of study. Thus, our first four chapters explore the traditional dichotomy between internally and externally motivated change (Chapters 1 and 2 respectively), as well as their potential diachronic effects, *language birth* (Chapter 3) and *language death* (Chapter 4). As we will see, the boundaries between what appear to be very different types of change (as in *internal/external*) and their effects in what eventually become distinct (socio)-linguistic phenomena (such as *birth/death*) are in fact often blurred. To take a simple example, processes of change such as convergence (typically characterised as externally motivated) may have the same linguistic result as parallel development (which may be internally motivated). Similarly, contact (usually discussed in relation to externally motivated change) can trigger processes of change which, given the appropriate circumstances, may result in either the obsolescence of a speech variety or the emergence of a new one.

Chapters 5, 6 and 7 consider instances in which conscious attempts have been made to influence the form (and often the status) of a linguistic variety. Chapter 5 contextualises this discussion with an exploration of language policy and language planning. Chapter 6 considers processes and issues involved in language revival (which may take place after a language has *died* or ceased to be spoken), and Chapter 7 looks at specific deliberate attempts at language invention (*birth*) and examines the linguistic and sociolinguistic reasons which may underlie the success of these systems, or lack thereof, with speech communities.

Discussion in each chapter is anchored in case studies, which have been selected with two main purposes in mind. First, the range of data neatly illustrates the fact that language change ('unconscious' and deliberate) is common cross-linguistically, and also allows for the presentation and discussion of less well-known cases alongside those that may be much more familiar to the reader. This has also had an ideological advantage for us, in that it has facilitated inclusion of data from languages such as creoles which are typically marginalised in what might be termed mainstream discussions of language change. Second, and as will become clear throughout the following chapters, the chosen case studies have also provided a springboard for 'problematising' issues in, and approaches to, language change. They therefore, quite simply, help illustrate the fact that in many instances, sociolinguistic and linguistic processes of change are not easily definable, discrete and static entities.

We therefore hope that the following chapters will provide you, the reader, with a useful mixture of established theoretical overview, new data and new perspectives on their combination. For your interest, we have appended to the Bibliography a list of useful web sites which you might like to consult for further information on some of the topics covered. The web sites were all accessible in June 2005. Finally, we would like to note that although the following chapters have attempted to present theory and data in an accessible manner, we have assumed some (albeit elementary) prior linguistic knowledge and familiarity with the International Phonetic Alphabet.

Abbreviations

1pl	first person plural (pronoun)
2pl	second person plural (pronoun)
3	third person marker
A	adjective
AAVE	African American Vernacular English
ADEA	Association for the Development of Education in Africa
EAM(s)	evidence act morpheme(s)
EPIC	English Plus Information Clearinghouse
ESG	East Sutherland Gaelic
G	genitive
H	high (code, in a diglossic situation)
HCE	Hawai'ian Creole English
HFC	Haitian French Creole
IALA	International Auxiliary Language Association
IAL(s)	invented auxiliary language(s) (our abbreviation)
L	low (code, in a diglossic situation)
loc	locative marker
(m.)	masculine (gender)
ME	Middle English
MPE	Melanesian Pidgin English
N	noun
NIP	National Institute of Pedagogy (Republic of the Seychelles)
NP	noun phrase
O	object
OE	Old English
OFS	older fluent speaker (of East Sutherland Gaelic)
OHG	Old High German
ON	Old Norse
OSV	object-subject-verb (word order)
OVS	object-verb-subject (word order)
PG	Pennsylvania German
PIE	Proto-Indo-European

pl	plural
Post	postposition
Prep	preposition
S	subject
SAM(s)	speech art morpheme(s)
SOV	subject-object-verb (word order)
SS	semi-speaker (of East Sutherland Gaelic)
sub	adverbial subordinator
SVO	subject-verb-object (word order)
top	topic marker
UEA	Universala Esperanto-Asocio
UG	Universal Grammar
UGC	Unesco General Conference
USA	United States of America
V	verb
VOS	verb-object-subject (word order)
VP	verb phrase
VSO	verb-subject-object (word order)
YFS	younger fluent speaker (of East Sutherland Gaelic)

1 Internally motivated change

1.1 Introduction

In 1712, Jonathan Swift stated in his *Proposal for Correcting, Improving, and Ascertaining the English Tongue* that language change, which he associated specifically with 'linguistic corruption' and generally with social decline, was a process that should be kept in check: 'I see no absolute Necessity', he stated, 'why any Language would be perpetually changing' (1712: 15). Swift's comments were made with the standardisation of English in mind, but his antipathy to change and its alleged negative linguistic and social dimension is one which often found popular expression (see, for instance, Milroy and Milroy's (1999) discussion of the 'culture of complaint' in relation to English) and which was also perpetuated, until relatively recently, in scholarly perspectives. Indeed, with respect to the latter, it is perhaps fair to say that in principle, theories and understanding of change have undergone as much transformation as the data linguists have sought to describe, as ideologies and perspectives have themselves shifted. We will not attempt here to trace an entire history of linguistic thought in this area but the following brief and selective discussion should serve to illustrate our point.

In the European linguistic tradition, observation of change effectively began in the late eighteenth century, when work into reconstructing language families (or genetic linguistics) was underway. Initial discussions of change, however, were necessarily limited in this early period, comprising either unsystematic and fragmentary catalogues of changes in the languages being researched, or 'the rather directionless pursuit of individual forms down the branches of the family tree' (McMahon 1994: 18). Language itself was often metaphorised as a biological organism – an entity that underwent birth, maturity, decay and death (see, for instance, Schleicher 1863 (in Koerner 1983)); and change was typically (and negatively) viewed as the mechanism that effected loss of linguistic 'vitality' and signalled decline. A heavily inflected language such as classical Latin, for example, was considered to be at the height of its 'maturity', or in its Golden Age (a perspective due more to the reverence with which classical civilisation was viewed in many parts of eighteenth-century Europe than to any innate linguistic quality) whereas its Romance descendants such as French and Italian (with comparatively reduced inflectional systems) were seen as poorer and degraded relations which had 'lost' valuable linguistic material.

Early explanations of change were also rooted not in direct observations of languages and their speakers, but instead in ideas of divine intervention and human acclimatisation: the biblical story of the Tower of Babel, for example, was often cited as a motivating factor for change, as were the supposed effects of 'climate, diet or race on language . . . for instance, frication of stops might result from speakers moving into mountainous regions, where the thin air made it harder to catch one's breath and the exertion of running up and down mountains promoted heavy breathing' (Meyer 1901; cited in McMahon 1994: 18).

By the late nineteenth century, however, perspectives on linguistic change had themselves undergone transformation. The Zeitgeist had embraced science as a legitimate pursuit and, concomitantly, the notion that all aspects of existence were underpinned by the operation of logic and the maintenance of order. Unsurprisingly, this approach was adopted by the dominant contemporary school of historical linguistic research – the Neogrammarian[1] – through which change began to be studied in a more structured, scientific way and, importantly, with primary explanatory emphasis on language itself, instead of on alleged external causal factors such as geographical region.

Such principles have remained important in studies of change, albeit sometimes undergoing a measure of modification. Thomason and Kaufman (1988: 1), for instance, point out that for over a century, mainstream historical linguistics has continued to differentiate between change that occurs because of 'innate' factors (*internal* or *internally motivated*), and that which is due to catalysts such as contact (*external* or *externally motivated*) – a distinction that has become largely accepted and used in the literature (although see discussion of Mufwene (2001) below). However, the measure of importance accorded to each has shifted somewhat: traditionally, historical linguistics concentrated solely on determining the motivations for and mechanisms of internal change, which was considered the more 'normal' and, indeed, primary of the two. Thus, historical linguistic techniques developed in the nineteenth century such as comparative reconstruction (which, in essence, uses available data to work backwards to unrecorded linguistic ancestors) were initially based on an assumption that 'virtually all language change arises through intrasystemic causes' (Thomason and Kaufman 1988: 1). Similarly, later twentieth-century schools of linguistics such as the Generative (see Section 1.5) based theories of diachronic change on assumptions of 'normal transmission'; that is, intergenerational transmission unaffected by external factors. As we will see, the Generative school also focused explanations of change on shifts within speakers' innate *grammars* or language systems.

By default, external factors such as contact have therefore often been viewed as relatively unimportant: witness Welmers' view that external influences 'are insignificant when compared with internal change . . . the established principles of comparative and historical linguistics, and all we know about language history and language change, demand that . . . we seek explanations first on the basis of recognised processes of language change' (1970: 4–5; in Thomason and Kaufman 1988: 1).[2] However, from at least the second half of the twentieth century (cf. Weinreich 1953; see also Chapter 2), acknowledgement has gradually been made of the fact that a language's 'external life' – its social contexts of use and shifts in its communities of speakers for example – plays a significant and 'normal' role in the changes it undergoes. Consideration of external motivations has therefore been increasingly incorporated into modern historical linguistic and sociolinguistic accounts of change.

As a final, and recent, example of how perspectives on studying and accounting for change have shifted, we will briefly look at some of the ideas in Mufwene's current work in *language ecology*, which in part argues against the traditional distinction between internally and externally motivated change (the following discussion is simplified for explanatory purposes). Mufwene (2001) argues that the early trope of *language-as-organism* still pervades discussions of change, and its use tends to obscure certain 'realities' about both the nature of language itself and the actuating factors that underlie linguistic change. For instance, it is arguable that the language-as-organism metaphor encourages us to envisage (and therefore represent) language as a holistic entity that all members of a speech community share and make use of in exactly the same way. However, we know from relevant studies that this is not accurate: 'variation in the production of sounds, in the expression of concepts, in the encoding of meanings etc.' (Mufwene 2001: 148) is actually a constant in any given speech community. The notion of a shared 'communal language' is therefore a convenient abstraction, an assumption of 'a collective mind that is an ensemble of individual minds in a population' (Mufwene 2001: 2). However, each 'individual mind' possesses, in Chomsky's (1986) terms, an *I-language* (internalised language) or idiolect, which is that speaker's particular system of a language. Idiolects in a speech community are not identical, but they typically share enough properties to allow for successful communication. A language is therefore 'an aggregating construct, an extrapolation from individual idiolects assumed to share a common ancestry and several structural features' (Mufwene 2001: 150) or, to use another biological metaphor, a *species*: 'like a biological species defined by the potential of its members to interbreed and procreate offspring of the same kind, a language can be defined as "a population of idiolects that enable their hosts to communicate with and understand one another"' (Robert Perlman, personal communication to Mufwene, 1999; quoted in Mufwene 2001: 150).

In this perspective, change occurs because of inter-idiolectal contact among speakers. This creates a mental 'feature pool' in which variants compete and from which speakers select, thus becoming 'the default causation for change' (Mufwene 2001: 15), an idea that arguably brings us closer to 'the real actuation question', namely 'why certain instances of variation become changes while others don't' (McMahon 1994: 248).[3] Thus, for Mufwene, the traditional distinction between internally and externally motivated change is one which really only has social salience, since *all* change is ultimately motivated by speaker contact.

A distinction between internal and external motivations has, however, continued to be observed in discussions of, and debates about, the nature of linguistic change; and we will attempt to illustrate both in this and the following chapter. We begin with examples and explanations of internally motivated change.

1.2 Locating internally motivated change

It is arguable that the use of the term *motivated* in explanations of change appears to assume that it is possible to access the initial reasons *why* a change might begin. Given, however, that language ultimately exists in the mind of the speaker, who is mostly unaware of his or her innate linguistic knowledge, this is highly unlikely if not downright impossible. In cases of change designated as externally motivated, the phrase has a measure of aptness in that it is possible to pinpoint contributory contextual factors such as contact (although again, we do not know exactly *how* social factors translate onto the innate linguistic landscape), but in those where no correlation to external events has been or can be made, the linguist can only hope to discern tendencies or patterns of change once they are under way. Explanations of internally motivated change therefore, necessarily tend to describe and theorise processes of change or the mechanisms by which change can occur, and to hypothesise about their possible motivations. As we will see later in this chapter, such actuation hypotheses, although useful, are also sometimes inevitably problematic.

In general, explanations of internally motivated change locate processes either in what we might call the language system, or in a more individualised context which we might loosely term 'native speaker creativity'.[4] The former type of explanation focuses on how change works within, and sometimes across, particular components of a language such as its phonology or morphology, while the latter describes change in terms of processes in which the (individual and abstract) speaker engages as part of an ongoing adaptation of their language to their needs. We look at system-based accounts of change in Sections 1.3, 1.5 and 1.6, which present instances of sound change (the Great Vowel Shift), syntactic change (word order in Icelandic), cross-componential change (grammaticalisation of the future in Urdu), and at 'native speaker creativity' in Section 1.8 (derivational productivity in Haitian French Creole).

As an initial illustration of both types of explanation, however, we can briefly consider certain Neogrammarian explanations of sound change, an area that this school worked on almost exclusively. The Neogrammarians proposed that certain regular[5] changes in pronunciation occurred because of speakers' needs for ease of articulation. Thus, the pronunciation of a word such as 'handbag' as [hæmbæg], which results from assimilation (where a sound is made similar or identical to another in its phonetic environment) occurs because it is supposedly easier for individuals to pronounce bilabial nasal [m] + bilabial plosive [b] than alveolar nasal [n] + [b]. For Neogrammarian scholars such as Hermann Paul, such processes, despite beginning in physical articulation, impacted on speakers' internal language systems (or I-languages) since they could generate a shifted mental 'target' pronunciation for a speech community. At the same time, the Neogrammarian school also worked on the assumption that regular sound change occurred simply because it had to in language systems; it operated slowly but with 'blind necessity' (McMahon 1994: 20) independently of speakers' will. This meant not only that speakers were in a sense powerless to stop a sound change from unfolding but also that they could not foresee what impact such a change could have on other areas of a language's system. A sound change could, for example, have grammatical consequences, such as causing similarity of form between items that were once grammatically distinct: witness late Old English (OE) nouns such as *lufe* 'love', for instance, where final inflectional -*e* could signal either singular accusative, dative or genitive. In the Neogrammarian perspective, the 'grammatical residue' of a sound change was partially sorted out after the event, typically through a process known as *analogy*.[6] The slow, inevitable and 'independent' (from speakers' awareness) nature of sound change was crucial to its unfolding: as McMahon (1994: 20) points out, 'it was thought that if speakers knew a sound change was in operation and might have undesirable consequences for the grammar, they would try to stop it.'

We now turn to our first case study which looks at a Structuralist, system-based explanation of a particular sound change in the history of English – the Great Vowel Shift. As we will see, the Structuralist school, which succeeded that of the Neogrammarians, focused on considerations of structure and function in their explanation of internally motivated change.

1.3 Case study: symmetry and function in the Great Vowel Shift

Structuralism was based on the ideas of Ferdinand de Saussure, a Swiss linguist initially trained in the Neogrammarian school. Between 1907 and 1913, he gave a series of lectures on general linguistics, a reconstruction of which was published posthumously as the *Cours de linguistique générale* and in which the principles of Structuralist thought, which would later be adopted not only in linguistics but also in literary critical theory, were outlined. We will not detail these here but will instead note the concepts which are necessary to an understanding of the Structuralist explanation of the Shift.[7]

One of the most important tenets of Saussure's approach lay in a distinction he drew between *langue* and *parole*. The former comprises speakers' 'innate knowledge of the systematic correspondences between sound and meaning which make up our language (including the knowledge of what utterances are possible . . . and what utterances are not)' (Andersen 1988: 24). *Parole*, on the other hand, refers to the outward manifestation of *langue* in the individual's use of both spoken and written language. Saussure proposed that the main aim of linguistic study was ultimately to arrive, through examination of *parole*, at an understanding of *langue* – the abstract systemic essence of a language in which its units and rules were ordered. This structured system was seen as one in which components were ordered contrastively and relationally. For example, Saussure drew attention to the associative relationships that appear to exist for speakers among sets of words or sounds, such as the *paradigmatic*, which involve the possibility of alternative elements at a single structural point. Thus, the initial consonants in [hɪt], [sɪt], [pɪt] are paradigmatically related; as are adjectival alternatives such as *happy, sad, wonderful* and so on in a sentence such as *Jim is a ____ man*. The notions of contrast and relativity are also present in Saussure's explanation of how sound and meaning combine in a language. He postulated that speakers of a language link a form or *signifier* (the spoken or written word) with a concept, or the *signified*, into a *linguistic sign*. Once established, the link seems indivisible but is, in fact, essentially arbitrary – there is no reason beyond convention, for example, that a signifier such as *dog* should be tied to the concept that it is. Importantly, Saussure also stipulated that signs were ultimately only meaningful when considered in the context of their place in a language system. A significant component of the meaning of a sign such as *red*, for example, is derived from its contrastive relationship with others in the colour spectrum; that is, from the fact that it is 'not-blue', 'not-black', 'not-green' and so on. Thus, just as the idea of language-as-organism was fundamental to pre-Neogrammarian scholars, so too was that of language-as-system to the Structuralist school; and crucially, *system* in which contrast and relationship functioned meaningfully in maintaining order and symmetry. Language was therefore 'un système où tout se tient' (Meillet 1912), 'a system in which everything has its place'.

Given the Structuralist belief in the primacy of *langue*, it is not surprising that much of their work concentrated on the internal workings of and, specifically, the internal motivations for, change in this underlying system. It is important to note, however, that this focus was not completely divorced from a consideration of external factors that could catalyse and influence the direction of linguistic change. Thus if a 'gap' existed in a component of the underlying system (thus threatening symmetry), filling it might well be prompted by a factor such as language contact. Thus the pre-eighteenth-century English fricative system comprised voiceless and voiced pairs such as /f/~/v/, /s/~/z/ and /θ/~/ð/. The voiceless /ʃ/, however, had no voiced counterpart. This gap was later filled by /ʒ/, which arose from the combination of [z] + [j] in the pronunciation of French loanwords such as *leisure*.

Similarly, Structuralist thought acknowledged that a change in pronunciation, for example, could upset the innate symmetry of the contrastive relationship among a particular set of sounds, prompting 're-adjustment' in order to restore balance. In principle, this encapsulates the Structuralist explanation of the Great Vowel Shift – a set of changes in the pronunciation of southern Middle English (ME) long vowels which seems to have begun sometime in the fifteenth century. Figure 1.3 provides a simple, diagrammatic representation of the Shift, which affected both front and back long vowels.[8]

Figure 1.3 reflects the assumption that the long vowels exist in a linked system which is therefore affected in its entirety by any movement or change. In this perspective, it is therefore possible to argue (as has been done by Martinet (1952)) that the symmetry of this system was initially threatened by the diphthongisation of the high front and back vowels /i:/ and /u:/, which left 'gaps'. This simultaneously triggered movement in the rest of the long vowel system in order to restore symmetry. The mechanism of this movement is typically referred to in the literature as a 'drag chain' (first proposed in Martinet's *chaîne de traction* (1952: 11)): the lower long vowels were progressively raised or 'dragged' upwards as the high vowels diphthongised.

However, another possible internal motivation for change may have arisen from considerations of function. Martinet (1952) postulated that systems in which each sound has its own distinctive acoustic and articulatory space, with a wide 'margin of safety' between them, function most efficiently for speakers in their maintenance of meaningful contrasts. Sometimes, however, that safety margin is breached, causing sounds to fall together (or

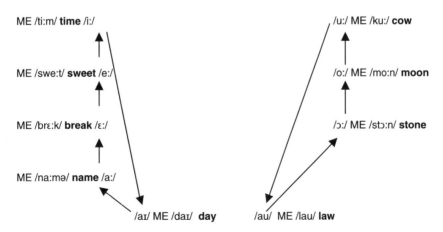

Figure 1.3 The Great Vowel Shift

undergo *phonemic merger*) and consequently, words to become hom-ophonous. Such mergers could therefore potentially cause communication difficulties if they occurred frequently and with phonemes that carry a high functional load.[9] Merger was therefore a process that systems might try to avoid. With this in mind, it could be argued that if one phoneme in a linked system began to encroach on the phonological space of another, it would trigger a domino effect of crowding and movement among components. Alternatively therefore, the mechanism of the Shift may have been a *push chain* (Martinet's *chaîne de propulsion* (1952: 11)), which began with upward movement of the lower vowels. In order to avoid merger, the next highest vowels shifted in the same direction, and the process was repeated until margins of safety were restored (with different vowel realisations in affected lexical items).

We should note that considerations of structure and function are not mutually exclusive in the Structuralist understanding of internally motivated change. As we have just seen, explanations invoking function are predicated on the assumption of structural symmetry. In addition, data from some English varieties suggest that both drag and push mechanisms (and, by extension, considerations of both structure and function) may have been involved in the Shift. For example, whereas the ME pronunciations of words such as *mouse* and *house* shifted to /maus/ and /haus/ in southern Early Modern English dialects (in accordance with the diphthongisation of the high front and back vowels), northern dialects continued to preserve an older /mu:s/ and /hu:s/ (which can still be heard in some modern Scots dialects). It has been proposed that the reason for this lies in the fact that ME /o:/ had fronted to /ø:/, leaving a 'gap' in the back vowels. Thus, the pronunciation /u:/ remained in words such as *house* and *mouse* because there was no /o:/ to 'push' it towards diphthongisation. However, articula-tion of the other vowels did move, which is generally taken as a good indica-tion that the Shift may have initially begun with /ɔ:/ (and with the front vowels, /ɛ:/) which 'pushed' into the territory of /o:/ where it was present, and 'dragged' the lower vowels up to fill the resultant 'gaps'.

We will return to the Structuralist explanation of change at the end of this chapter.

1.4 Drift

Another system-based explanation for internally motivated change is encapsulated in the notion of *drift*. The term seems to have first appeared in Sapir's 1921 work, *Language*, in which drift is characterised as being both a social and linguistic mechanism that drives language change. Importantly, social drift and linguistic drift are distinct and independent processes, but the operation of one, Sapir argued, is sometimes predicated on the occur-rence of the other. For instance, Sapir's (1921 [2000]: 1–2) discussion of the emergence of dialectal difference hypothesises that, within any language, variation at the individual level is typically kept from 'rising to dialectic importance' by the silent 'consensus of usage' within a speech community. However, language populations do segregate into groups, and sometimes 'two or more groups of individuals . . . become sufficiently disconnected to drift apart, or independently, instead of together'. This social drift erases the previous norm-enforcing 'consensus of usage' and leaves the way open for the establishment of independent dialectal norms. These new norms emerge as a result of the operation of linguistic drift, which occurs 'on its own account' and moves each developing dialect 'further and further away from its linguistic fellows' (Sapir 1921 [2000]: 3). For Sapir, this co-occurrence of social and linguistic drift characterises a cyclic process of language change in which all dialects continue to split into subdialects and also to diverge, eventually resulting in mutually unintelligible languages.

Sapir's postulation that the operation of linguistic drift is autonomous and not necessarily catalysed by social drift is noteworthy: he stated that even if 'there were no breaking up of a language into dialects' and a language therefore remained a uniform entity, it would still undergo drift and ultimately be transformed into a new language. This, Sapir argued, was because drift carried language through time 'in a current of its own making' (Sapir 1921 [2000]: 2). This current, however, was purposeful – linguistic drift 'has direction' (Sapir 1921 [2000]: 4):

> only those individual variations embody it or carry it which move in a certain direction, just as only certain wave movements in the bay outline the tide. The drift of a language is constituted by the unconscious selection on the part of its speakers of those individual variations that are cumulative in some special direction.
>
> (Sapir 1921 [2000]: 4)

Sapir stated that drift causes speakers to 'move' language in three important directions, the most primary of which is towards the use of invariable (meaning 'uninflected') words. This in turn drives the other two tendencies of drift towards the reduction of case inflection and the fixing of word order respectively. As we will see in Section 1.9, this idea that it is the ultimate achievement of particular language states that subconsciously impels change is somewhat problematic, raising it does questions about what McMahon (1994: 330) identifies as teleology of purpose and function. Indeed, Sapir's idea of drift seems to imply that there are universal 'laws' or even 'metaconditions' (Lakoff 1972) of change for languages. If these do in fact exist, at the moment they prove to be extremely elusive, and research has been most successful in identifying not laws, but *tendencies* that languages might follow (and are therefore under no obligation to follow). This allows for a more generalised interpretation of drift as an umbrella term for certain, possible directions of change.

Two such directions of drift which appear to occur cross-linguistically are change in word order and grammaticalisation. We will look at instances of each in Sections 1.5 and 1.6 respectively.

1.5 Case study: word order change in Icelandic

Word order in a language is typically ascertained through examination of the basic, unmarked[10] order of three central constituents: subject (S), verb (V) and object (O). This is taken to reflect an innate or underlying ordering which has become established in the syntactic component of the language system. On this basis, languages may be categorised as belonging to one of six permutations: SVO (for example, English, Swahili), VSO (Welsh, Scots Gaelic, Pacific languages), SOV (Basque, Turkish, Japanese), VOS (Malagasy), OVS (Hixkaryana) and OSV (Apurinã). Greenberg (1963) proposed that the ordering of S, V and O in individual languages is accompanied by other structural properties, for example, the ordering of elements such as determiners and adjectives relative to nouns, nouns relative to prepositions and postpositions, and auxiliaries relative to main verbs. His data (drawn from about thirty languages, the majority of which were SOV, SVO and VSO) indicated that languages in which V precedes O have certain properties in common, as do those in which O precedes V. Further and later research appeared to confirm this (see, for instance, the modifications of Lehmann (1973) and Vennemann (1974, 1975)). As a consequence, the six syntactic types have been collapsed into two general categories (VO and OV), in which certain universal tendencies are thought to hold. The majority of these tendencies are implicational, meaning that the presence of one property in a language implies the presence of another. Thus, languages which are OV tend to have postpositions and nouns (N) that are preceded by genitives (G) and adjectives (A), whereas those that are VO seem to have prepositions and nouns followed by adjectives and genitives (see 1.5.a). Overall, this classification system enables the establishment of a word order typology for languages. In other words, it allows for a taxonomy through which certain properties of a language can be described and compared cross-linguistically.

1.5.a Word order typologies

VO	Prep	NG	NA
OV	Post	GN	AN

Analysis of historical data has shown that word order does not necessarily remain unchanged through time. It is therefore possible to construct a diachronic typology of changes for languages which experience this kind of drift. Thus Delsing (2000), using corpora from the latter half of the thirteenth century onwards, argues that Swedish, now a VO language, was once OV. During the transitional period between the two types (fourteenth to sixteenth centuries), both OV and VO structures coexisted but by the middle of the seventeenth century, VO appears to have been settled on as the basic clausal structure.

It is important to note, however, that such studies are not purely descriptive: given that word order classifications reflect certain syntactic properties, research is typically also directed towards trying to ascertain the mechanisms that have effected change at this particular underlying level. Studies such as Sigurðsson's (1988) and Rögnvaldsson's (1994) – which we will consider below – have therefore attempted to explain word order change (in this context, in Icelandic) within theoretical frameworks that facilitate such an approach, such as that of Generative-based diachronic syntax.

The Generative school of linguistic thought (which, for many, has become synonymous with the name Noam Chomsky) first came to prominence in the 1950s with work on synchronic syntax (and later on phonology and sound change). One major, indeed perhaps the most major, innovation of the Generative approach lay in its conceptualisation of the nature of the language system and of how speakers acquire language. In essence, on the strength of two particular observations – namely, that certain types of structures and properties appear to be common cross-linguistically and that 'normal'[11] children seem to quickly acquire the ability to produce novel, well-formed utterances from an early age despite a high level of inadequate adult linguistic data (including speech errors, hesitations, incomplete sentences) in their environment – Chomsky proposed that all humans are born with an innate universal grammar (UG), a genetically inherited outline of universal language properties. Children each learn their native language by listening to the data around them, abstracting away from its 'imperfections' and feeding language-specific details into their pre-set UG. From this, they each build a rule-governed, internalised mental grammar, which gives them native-speaker *competence*, allowing them to understand and produce well-formed utterances ad infinitum. As in previous schools of thought, Generative theory has traditionally been most interested in the nature of this underlying innate grammar and the rules by which it operates. Actual language *performance* (which is the outward reflection of innate competence) has been of interest only in so far as it provides data through which the workings of the internal grammar can be glimpsed. It therefore follows that the Generative approach to language change focuses on change at the level of this internal grammar.

Early Generative work on diachronic syntax compared synchronic and successive grammars that had been constructed for the language in question and attempted to demonstrate that surface changes were due to changes in underlying syntactic rules: 'these could be added or lost, their form or order could alter, and children could construct a different, simpler grammar from their parents'' (McMahon 1994: 108). Later refinements to this approach allowed for the emergence of models such as that of *government and binding*, or *principles and parameters*. This was predicated on an assumption that the internal grammar is divided into a set of interacting modules, each of which has its own principles. Other principles are not module-specific and operate throughout the grammar. All of these principles are part of the speaker's genetic linguistic inheritance, as are various innate parameters, which each language learner sets in accordance with incoming language data. The setting of parameters is often metaphorised as the setting of a switch: a child hearing a high frequency of sentences in which the object precedes the verb, for instance, will set his or her parameter switch to OV.

We now turn to Rögnvaldsson's (1994) Icelandic data (note that the discussion here is simplified for explanatory purposes). Modern Icelandic is a VO language, whereas Old Icelandic (typically taken to be the language of the thirteenth and fourteenth centuries) appears to have had a much freer word order. Consider the Old Icelandic data in 1.5.b (adapted from Rögnvaldsson 1994: 2).

1.5.b Word order in Old Icelandic

i *Lýtinguraf Sámsstöðum mun hafa vegið hann og bræður hans*
  Lyting of   Samsstadir will have killed him   and brothers his
  'Lyting from Samsstadir will have killed him and his brothers.'

(Brennu-Njáls saga)

ii *En   ekki   mun   eg   þenna   mann   séð   hafa*
   But   not   will   I   this   man   seen   have
   'But I believe I have not seen this man.'

(Laxdœla saga)

iii *þorgilsi   hafði   gefin   verið   öxi   góð*
    Thorgils   had   given   been   axe   good
    'Thorgils had been given a good axe.'

(þorgils saga og Halfliða)

iv *Ekki   vildi   eg   þér   mein   hafa   gert*
   not   would   I   you   harm   have   done
   'I wouldn't want to do you any harm.'

(Gunnars þáttur þiðrandabana)

The properties considered in 1.5.a imply that, in noun phrases (NP), modifiers or *operators* such as G or A consistently appear on one side of the noun head or *operand* (either GN or NG, for instance). The same principle is thought to hold for verb phrases (VP): modifiers or operators such as auxiliaries and object NPs also consistently appear on one side of the verb head (operand). Thus, OV languages have modifier-head (operator-operand) order while VO languages have head-modifier (operand-operator) structure.

Sentence 1.5.b.i displays VO order in the sequence *finite verb–auxiliary/ modal–main verb–object* ('will have killed him and his brothers'). This has become the norm in modern Icelandic. Sentence 1.5.b.ii displays OV word order (*finite verb–object–main verb–auxiliary/modal*: 'will . . . this man seen have'), and 1.5.b.iii–iv, what Rögnvaldsson calls 'mixed word order'. Thus, 1.5.b.iii has *finite verb–main verb–auxiliary–object* order ('had given been axe good'): the main and auxiliary verbs are in the order typical of OV structures (cf. 1.5.b.ii), but the object is in final position, as in a VO structure (cf. 1.5.b.i). In 1.5.b.iv, the word order is *finite verb–object–auxiliary–main verb* ('would . . . you harm have done'). Here, the verb order is typical of VO structures (cf. 1.5.b.i), but the object precedes the auxiliary and main verbs, as in OV sentences.

Generative studies on Old Icelandic data have largely assumed that the basic and underlying word order was VO (or operand-operator), and that this had resulted from a very early change from ancestral Proto-Norse OV. Sigurðsson (1988), for example, claims that Old Icelandic was uniformly VO in its *deep* or underlying structure, but that extensive leftward movement of modifiers such as objects (as well as others such as adverbial phrases and non-finite verbs) gave rise to different word orders on the surface – 'both what looked like pure OV-order and also several types of mixed OV–VO order' of the kind in 1.5.b (Rögnvaldsson 1994: 13). Sigurðsson (1988) therefore argues that the Proto-Norse grammar (see 1.5.c below) was replaced by an alternative grammar in early Icelandic (which predates the oldest preserved manuscripts):

1.5.c Grammars of Proto-Norse and early Icelandic

Proto-Norse grammar	Early Icelandic grammar
Basic OV	Basic VO
(VO achieved by rightward movement of modifiers/operators)	(OV achieved by leftward movement of modifiers/operators)
	(adapted from Rögnvaldsson 1994: 12)

Rögnvaldsson (1994: 13) takes issue with this perspective, pointing out for example, that OV structures, 'pure' and 'mixed', continue to appear extremely frequently until well into the eighteenth century, centuries after the typological shift proposed by Sigurðsson: a factor which seems somewhat at odds with an assumption of VO basic order. Rögnvaldsson's own textual research (as well as that of Hróarsdóttir 1995, 1996) indicates instead that the frequency of OV order began to drop significantly in the first few decades of the nineteenth century, and that 'OV order does not seem to occur in the texts of people born after 1800' (1994: 14). Indeed OV order is considered ungrammatical in modern Icelandic.

It would seem then, that one of two conclusions is possible. We either assume, following Sigurðsson (1988), that the Old Icelandic VP was head-modifier (basic VO order) with extensive leftward movement of modifiers or that, on the basis of textual data, it was head-final (basic OV order) with extensive rightward movement of modifiers. Both, however, involve a series of complicated movements of some constituents (and not of others) in the generation of both 'pure' and 'mixed' structures: a state that Rögnvaldsson finds unsatisfactory. He therefore proposes a 'third way', postulating that the Old Icelandic VP was variably head-initial or head-final (that is, allowing both OV or VO order). Thus, for speakers, 'the choice could have been (more or less) free' (Rögnvaldsson 1994: 4).

In essence, Rögnvaldsson argues that the parameter for basic word order remained unspecified for a long time in Icelandic. In other words, generations of children born into this speech community were constantly and consistently faced by 'pure' and 'mixed' OV and VO structures, making it difficult to 'set the switch' for basic word order. In addition, Rögnvaldsson argues that if processes such as *stylistic fronting* (which appears to have occurred often in textual data, particularly relative clauses, as in *sveinninn heilsar **þeim** vel er komnirvoru*, 'the boy greets **them** well that have come') also occurred frequently in actual speech, the resultant increase in OV structures may well have 'complicated' the data. Rögnvaldsson (1994: 24) therefore concludes that

> . . . during the centuries when OV and VO orders co-occur, both with considerable frequency, language learners could not fix the value of the head parameter, which thus remained unspecified, which in turn led to the continuing generation of both OV and VO orders. Only when a great majority of sentences came to have VO-order, language learners began to fix the value of the parameter, and OV-order became extinct in a relatively short time.

Of course, this raises the question of why OV would have begun to disappear in the first place, after such a long stable coexistence with VO. Rögnvaldsson speculates that the fact that the great majority of all clauses had surface VO order may have eventually triggered a parameter setting (although this in itself raises the question of why, if this was the case, it did not happen earlier). He also suggests that factors such as a drop in the frequency of stylistic fronting (which indeed is rarely used in modern Icelandic) and the perhaps concomitant increase in the use of an expletive subject *það* may also have increased the occurrence of VO structures, thus making it easier for language learners to set the relevant parameter in the direction of VO. This however, remains to be borne out or modified by further research.

We have so far concentrated on change at one particular level: the phonological in Section 1.3 and the syntactic in Section 1.5. There are, however, (internally motivated) processes of change which are not so 'confined' in their effect. One such is grammaticalisation, which is explored in Section 1.6.

1.6 Case study: grammaticalisation in Urdu

Meillet (1912: 131) described grammaticalisation as 'le passage d'un mot autonome au rôle d'élément grammatical' ('the shift of an independent word to the status of a grammatical element'). Thus, words with full semantic content such as nouns, verbs and adjectives become part of grammatical categories such as auxiliaries, prepositions and adverbs and, in turn, may undergo further grammaticalisation into affixes. Such changes of category are typically accompanied by other developments, such as a change in phonological form as well as *semantic bleaching*, or loss of semantic content. Grammaticalisation is thus the 'cross-componential change par excellence' involving change in more than one element of a language system (McMahon 1994: 161).[12]

A good and current example of these processes can be seen in what appears to be a case of grammaticalisation in the tense-mood-aspect system of Hawai'ian Creole English (HCE). Velupillai (2003), who has recently carried out extensive fieldwork in this area, postulates that HCE speakers express futurity in two main ways: either with auxiliary verb *go(i)n(g)/ gonna + main verb* constructions (1.6.a.i–ii), or through the use of *bumbye* (1.6.a.iii–iv):

1.6.a Future marking in Hawai'ian Creole English

(i) I *gon take this over there now . . . I come back, I gon take some over there first.*
'I'll take this over there now . . . I'll come back, I'm going to take some over there first.'

(ii) *This gonna be the part as the part you gonna pound on the board.*
'This will be the part, that's the part you will pound on the board.'

(iii) *Bumbye the baby ma-ke die dead.* (from Yamanaka 1993; cited in Velupillai 2003: 63)
'Eventually the baby will die.'

(iv) *This cigarette goin kill you . . . bumbye the stick poke you the stick kill you.*
'These cigarettes will kill you . . . eventually those sticks will poke you, those sticks will kill you.'
(adapted from Velupillai 2003: 56–7; 63)

While all the examples indicate events that will take place at some future point in time, Velupillai (2003: 62) argues that *bumbye* also 'seems to contain an element of remoteness'. This combination of remoteness and certainty is particularly evident in 1.6.a.iv, where the speaker expresses both the certainty of the addressee's death by smoking (*goin kill*) and the fact that while it may not happen in the near future, it is inevitable. Velupillai (2003: 63) states that the meaning of *bumbye* can only be adequately translated into English through the use of remoteness adverbials such as *eventually*, and also notes that *bumbye* and *go(i)n(g)/gonna* are not interchangeable: if we were to alter the second half of the utterance in (iv) to *the stick gon poke you the stick gon kill you*, the sense of remote futurity would be lost to a more immediate sense of certainty.

Finally, it is noteworthy that Velupillai's informants found combinations of *bumbye* with adverbials such as *next year* and *when I retire* acceptable, but rejected those with *in a minute* and *tomorrow* (both implying a more immediate future). Velupillai's argument that *bumbye* is performing a particular type of 'grammatical work' in HCE therefore seems highly plausible.

In terms of grammaticalisation processes, it is likely that *bumbye* has been derived from English *by and by*. If this is the case, it has definitely begun to undergo phonological reduction and, if Velupillai is right, semantic bleaching, in its movement from adverbial phrase to remote future marker. Velupillai (2003: 63) is at pains to point out, however, that if the data is in fact showing evidence of grammaticalisation, it is still at an early stage of the process, primarily because 'the sense of grammatical remoteness seems to be more of a tendency than a rule'. We would therefore expect that if *bumbye* follows a grammaticalisation cline, it will gain a more frequent, 'consistent domain' (Velupillai 2003: 63) of usage and will very likely continue to undergo morphophonemic reduction. It remains to be seen whether Velupillai's hypothesis will be borne out.

Another example of grammaticalisation can be seen in the development of future marking in Urdu. In their discussion of tense and aspect marking in modern Urdu, Butt and Geuder (2003: 14) compare the current system to that of its ancestor Sanskrit, which expressed such properties via a complex inflectional system. In modern Urdu, this has been 'lost and replaced by a mixed periphrastic and inflectional system'. For example, past, imperfect, perfect and progressive forms of a main verb are inflected only for number and gender and their accompanying auxiliaries (typically the verb *to be*), either for person and number, or for number and gender. Butt and Geuder (2003: 14) provide the data in 1.6.b, using third-person singular forms of the verb *maar* 'to hit' (the *-aa* suffix indicates masculine gender and singular number).

1.6.b Third-person masculine singular forms of the verb *maar* 'to hit'

Past	*maaraa*
Imperfect	*maartaa* + Aux *be*
Perfect	*maaraa* + Aux *be*
Progressive	*maar rahaa* + Aux *be*

Future forms of the main verb are not combined with auxiliaries, however, and are inflected for number, person and gender, as can be seen in 1.6.c (the inflections are separated from the main verb and each other for ease of identification). The vowel inflection that occurs immediately after the stem and before -*g*- (-*ūu*-, -*ēē*- and so on) indicates person agreement, -*g*- itself marks future, and *ii/aa* ~ *ũ/ee* indicate gender/number agreement.

1.6.c Future conjugations of *maar*

	Singular	Plural
First person	*maar-ūu-g-ii/aa*	*maar-ēē-g-ũ /ee*
Second person (*tum*)	*maar-oo-g-ii/aa*	
aap (polite *you*)		*maar-ēē-g-ũ /ee*
tuu (rude *you*)	*maar-ee-g-ii/aa*	
Third person	*maar-ee-g-ii/aa*	*maar-ēē-g-ũ /ee*

(after Butt and Geuder 2003: 14)

The future inflections evidence two instances of grammaticalisation. First, the future marker -*g*- appears to have its ancestry in the Sanskrit verb *ga*, 'to go', specifically, the past participle form *gatah*. As Sanskrit verbs underwent inflectional reduction, *gatah* increasingly came to fulfil an auxiliary function, experiencing both the phonological reduction and semantic bleaching that marks the grammaticalising 'split' from the original lexical verb. Butt and Geuder (2003: 6) point out that the semantic bleaching was accompanied by a process of metaphorisation, through which the original meaning of physical movement embodied in *gatah* became understood as a future marker (incidentally, a common cross-linguistic occurrence for verbs of movement). This new auxiliary (a form of which they cite as the Prakrit **gao*) continued to undergo grammaticalisation, eventually developing into the modern affix form. Butt and Geuder do not include examples of this diachronic development apart from one sentence which dates from the nineteenth century. In this utterance, an emphatic particle *hii* has been inserted between the person inflection and the future marker -*g*-:

> *maan-ee-hii-g-ii*: 'heed'-3rd person singular-emphatic-future-feminine = '(She) will see reason'

This use of the emphatic particle is today only marginally possible, which indicates that cohesion between the main verb and the affixes has been increasing and that crucially, the 'grammaticalisation process is still underway' (Butt and Geuder 2003: 15).

Finally, the second instance of grammaticalisation concerns the inflection for person agreement. It appears that these may ultimately have developed out of an auxiliary verb *hoo* (/ho/), 'to be', which would have continued to accompany lexical verbs even in periphrastic constructions with the *go* auxiliary. The similarities between the person inflections in the verb conjugation in 1.6.c and in the modern present-tense conjugation of *hoo* (in 1.6.d) appear to bear this out.

1.6.d Present conjugation of *hoo* 'to be'

	Singular	*Plural*
First person	*h-ũu*	*h-ε*
Second person (*tum*)	*h-oo*	
aap (polite 'you')		*h-ε*
tuu (rude 'you')	*h-ε*	
Third person	*h-ε*	*h-ε*

(after Butt and Geuder 2003: 15)

In both cases, grammaticalisation appears to have followed, in principle, the route postulated by Meillet. In the case of the future marker, it has been possible to trace a complete grammaticalisation cline, from full autonomous verb to auxiliary to affix; whereas with the inflections for person, we are able to observe the process from about the halfway stage from auxiliary to affix (it is highly likely that auxiliary *hoo* developed out of an original, lexical verb). In addition, both cases show evidence of semantic bleaching and phonological reduction which, as stated earlier, appear to be typical of the process.

1.7 Native-speaker creativity

So far, we have considered examples of change in which explanation has focused on the workings of the language system. However, as stated at the beginning of this chapter, certain changes have traditionally been explained through closer reference to the unconscious linguistic processes of the language speaker. Limitations of time and space prevent a detailed examination of all such changes here, but we will illustrate the point with a brief discussion of lexical change; specifically, lexical creativity, in Section 1.8.

Before doing so, however, it is worth noting that although each subsystem of a language undergoes internal processes of change distinctive to it (so that the lexicon 'experiences' *compounding* and *derivation*, for example, and meaning *specialisation* and *generalisation*), they are also subject to ones which supersede componential boundaries. Two such processes, which we will briefly look at here, are the operation of *analogy* and of *reanalysis*.

As intimated in Section 1.2 (and explained in Note 6), the concept of analogy was initially developed in the field of historical linguistics, specifically in reference to explanations of sound change in Neogrammarian theory, where it was conceptualised as a 'kind of housekeeping device, which resignedly picks up at least some of the mess made by the more impetuous sound change as it hurtles blindly through the grammar' (McMahon 1994: 70). The fact that analogy also has salience at the grammatical level, however, has meant that it is sometimes invoked as a primary factor in morphological change, typically operating through processes such as *analogical extension* (the application of a morpheme or of a relationship between morphemes beyond its original usage) and *analogical levelling* (the 'smoothing out' of irregularities in a paradigm). A good example of the operation of analogical extension can be seen in the system of number marking in English. While the majority of modern (standard) English plural forms carry inflectional -*s*, number marking in ancestral OE was quite different, with individual classes of nouns carrying distinctive inflections marking case, gender and number. Thus, the plural form of a word like *stone* (OE *stān*; masculine gender) was *stānas* in nominative case and *stānum* in the dative; but the plural nominative form of *ship* (OE *scip*; neuter gender) was *scipu*, and that of *love* (OE *lufe*; feminine gender) *lufa*. By the end of the ME period, the majority of such different inflections had disappeared but the OE -*as* (later ME -*es*) of nouns such as *stānas* was retained, and -*s* became reinterpreted as the only plural inflection for this particular class of masculine-gendered nouns. Through analogical extension, this -*s* was generalised to other noun classes which had originally formed plurals very differently (such as those to which *love* and *ship* belonged), but which had lost their particular inflections. Today, this -*s* continues to be extended to new nouns entering the language: witness *dotcommers*, *blurbs*, *Audis*. The operation of analogical extension is also sometimes referred to as *proportional analogy*, or *four part analogy*, since speakers appear to invoke a kind of four-element equation in their analogical argument, as in:

> *computer : computers = dotcommer* : X
> X = *dotcommers*

It is worth noting here that although analogy creates regularity, it is in fact irregular in its application (see Note 6). Despite the productivity of -*s* plurals, English still retains nouns which not only do not conform to this pattern but also display no intention of doing so: witness the continued vitality of 'irregular' forms such as *teeth*, *oxen* and *sheep*.

Analogical levelling is a process which essentially affects paradigms of inflected words, such as verb conjugations. A sound change (or series of sound changes) can affect certain forms in a paradigm, subsequently creating allomorphs, or morphological alternations, in what is essentially the same word. In some cases, it appears that analogy erases this diversity. Consider, for instance, the conjugation of the Old English verb *cēosan* 'to choose' in 1.7.a. Regular sound changes affected the pronunciation of the final stem consonant in these forms: -*s*- in *cēosan* became voiced because of its intervocalic position after an unaccented syllable, and another sound change known as rhotacism turned [z] to [r] in certain contexts. The related Old High German (OHG) forms also ended up in a similarly irregular paradigm because of sound changes:

1.7.a Conjugations of 'to choose' in OE and OHG

	OE	OHG
	OE	*OHG*
Infinitive	*cēo[z]an*	*kiu[s]an*
Past singular	*cēa[s]*	*ko[s]*
Past plural	*cu[r]on*	*ku[r]un*
Past participle	*(ge-)co[r]en*	*(gi-)ko[r]an*

Analogical levelling has, however, since made the semantic relationships both within and between these paradigms much more transparent in modern English and German: in each language, speakers have chosen one alternant and applied it throughout, thereby erasing the variation (see 1.7.b).

1.7.b Conjugations of 'to choose' in modern English and modern German

	Modern English	*Modern German*
Infinitive	*choo[z]e*	*kü[r]en*
Past singular	*cho[z]e*	*ko[r]*
Past plural	*cho[z]e*	*ko[r]en*
Past participle	*cho[z]en*	*geko[r]en*

Both extension and levelling are considered systematic and regular types of analogy: they occur quite frequently, operate in the contexts of established patterns and paradigms, and can affect a fair number of forms. Analogy can, however, also be applied sporadically, as can be seen in instances of *back formation* and *folk etymology*. Back formation is a process of word formation in which a historically invalid base is derived from what is mistakenly thought to be an affixed form. English, for example, makes use of an agentive suffix -*er* in the derivation of nouns from verbs, as in *teach* > *teacher*; *sing* > *singer*. Through analogy with this pattern, English speakers, assuming that one-time loanwords *editor*, *burglar* and *sculptor* include this suffix, have back-formed verbs such as *edit*, *burgle* and *sculpt*.[13] In instances of folk etymology, a word or phrase which is difficult for a native speaker to interpret (usually because it is foreign in origin) is 'readjusted' through analogy with more familiar patterns. Thus French *asparagus* became the English dialect form *sparrow grass* and one of the stopping places for the fifteenth-century *Infanta of Castile* as she made her way through London to meet her first husband Prince Arthur was named, in her honour, *Elephant and Castle*.

   As the above examples indicate, both back formation and folk etymology involve the joint operation of analogy and reanalysis. Reanalysis can however occur without analogy, as can be seen in Lightfoot's (1979) explanation of a particular syntactic change in the history of English: the emergence of modals (*can, may, will, shall, must, could, would, should, might*). The OE predecessors of these forms were *pre-modals*, a set of lexical verbs which shared many of the syntactic and morphological properties of other verbs. Lightfoot proposed that sometime between OE and the end of the ME period (*c.* 1500), certain developments in the use of the pre-modals increasingly isolated them from other verbs. One such early isolating factor, for example, may have been the seeming inability of pre-modals to take *to*-infinitive forms. Old English verbs in the infinitive generally carried an inflectional suffix -*an*, as in *singan* 'to sing'. However, many verbs also had a *to* infinitive as well (as in *to singenne*), with the meaning 'in order to X'. While OE texts evidence the co-occurrence of non-pre-modal main verbs with this inflected infinitive, there are no attestations of it with a preceding pre-modal. This is possibly because such constructions were regarded as ill-formed utterances: the fact that OE pre-modal *will* actually meant 'want', makes utterances such as **ic wille to singenne* ('I want in order to sing') ungrammatical (as opposed to *ic wille singan* 'I want to sing'). During the late OE period, the infinitive inflection -*an* began to disappear and *to* correspondingly became more frequently used as the regular infinitival marker (thus meaning that *to* infinitives lost their particular sense of 'in order to X'; see also the earlier discussion of semantic bleaching). However, the constraint on *pre-modal + inflected infinitive* appears to have remained in ME, and pre-modals continued to take what were historically -*an* infinitives which no longer carried the latter inflection (as in *I will sing* vs. **I will to sing*). Another isolating development lay in the fact that all OE preterit-present verbs (or verbs whose historically past-tense forms are used to signal present time reference) became obsolete during the transitional ME period; all, that is, apart from the pre-modals, which had also belonged to this category in OE. Finally, pre-modal forms such as *sculde* 'should', and *wolde* 'would', which had originally signalled past time reference in OE, lost this particular property (witness modern English *I should see her next week*); and all pre-modals appear to have stopped being used with nominal objects (as in **I must tomato soup*) by the end of the ME period. As we can see, these developments still have salience in modern modal usage.

Thus, by the sixteenth century, pre-modals had lost many of the properties they had originally shared with other verbs and indeed, no longer 'behaved' like their one-time counterparts. As a result, Lightfoot proposed that a 'radical reanalysis' took place, in which 'these exceptional forms were reinterpreted as members of a new category, Modal' (McMahon 1994: 118). In the tradition of Generative grammar (see Section 1.5), this reanalysis was argued to have taken place at the level of speakers' innate grammars, and to have caused certain 'surface' changes which, as McMahon (1994: 118) states, were manifested more or less simultaneously. These include loss of infinitive forms (**to may, *to shall*) and of non-finite forms (**they are musting go, *they mayed have gone*). Finally, Lightfoot argued that reanalysis was also responsible for developments such as the fact that only modals (and auxiliary *be, have, do*) can invert with subjects in the formation of questions (*May I see that?, Have I seen that?* vs. **See I that?*) and take a following negative marker (*He wouldn't say that, I don't think so* vs. **He sayn't that*).

Analogy and reanalysis are therefore processes in the unfolding of which the individual speaker is perceived as playing a significant role. As mentioned earlier, linguistic subsystems also each undergo distinctive language-internal processes of change which, in some explanatory frameworks, are discussed in the context of 'native speaker creativity'. Section 1.8 provides an illustration of this in an outline of the processes involved in internal lexical change.

1.8. Case study: lexical derivation in Haitian French Creole

In Chapter 2, we will see that one of the ways in which languages productively increase and change their lexical stock is through externally motivated processes such as *borrowing*. However, languages also experience internal creativity as speakers turn existing word stock into new morphemes. It is worth noting here, before looking at some of the processes through which this is achieved, that speakers of a language will apply these self-same processes to borrowed material, or loanwords.

In terms of lexical creativity, speakers generate new words (or in some cases, new usages of words) through processes such as back formation, which we have already discussed, and *conversion*, in which words come to be used in new parts of speech additional to their initial categorisation (as in *pretty* (adjective): *a pretty house* > (adverb): *that's pretty awful*). Conversion also covers cases of the generic use of originally proper nouns, as in the use of the brand-name *Hoover* as a general term for vacuum cleaners (*get the hoover from the cupboard*), as well as instances of their use as verbs (*I'll hoover the bedrooms*; 'she googled her blind date' (from the name of the search engine *Google*). An extremely productive source of new words cross-linguistically is *compounding*, whereby two or more words are put together to create a new lexical item (as in *pickpocket, smartcard, content-rich*). English also has numerous examples of compounds which incorporate elements ultimately derived from loanwords: witness formations such as *submarine* (Latin *sub* 'under' + Latin *marin-* 'sea'), *telephone* (Greek *tele* 'far' + Greek *phone* 'voice'). Some compounds are also termed 'hybrid' in the sense that they combine elements from different languages: the second component of *television*, for example, was borrowed from Latin, and the first of 'gentleman' derives from French *gentil* (*man* is English in origin). Speakers also make use of processes such as *clipping*, in which a shortened form of a word is derived from a longer version (*phone* from *telephone*; *pram* from *perambulator*) and *blending*, whereby elements of two words are 'glued' together (*Bollywood* from *Bombay* + *Hollywood*; *electrocute* from *electricity* + *execute*). Speakers can also make acronyms function as full words: *AIDS* (Acquired Immuno-Deficiency Syndrome), *SARS* (Severe Acute Respiratory Syndrome), and *FBI* (Federal Bureau of Investigation) are all now treated as independent nouns. In addition, native speaker creativity allows for the fact that some new words are simply made up: *blurb*, for example, was originally an invention by Gelett Burgess; and J.K. Rowling's *quidditch*, now included in the *Oxford English Dictionary* and even used as a proper noun,[14] was made famous by the Harry Potter book series.

Another major cross-linguistic process of language-internal creativity, which we will now illustrate with examples from Haitian French Creole (HFC), is *derivation*, or the creation of new words via the use of derivational morphemes. We have chosen this data partly to vary the emphasis so far in this section on English examples (which are numerous in the literature) but primarily to demonstrate (as in our earlier example of Hawai'ian Creole English) that internal processes which are typically discussed in relation to 'established' languages are also to be found in systems such as creoles, whose genesis in sociocultural and linguistic contact has sometimes detracted attention from this fact (see DeGraff 2001 for a full and illuminating discussion of this point).

DeGraff (2001: 54) states that since the mid-seventeenth century (and at the very least, until the late twentieth century), the majority of descriptions of morphological processes in creoles have become 'repeated variations' on particular themes. There is, for instance, the theme of *incipience*, in which creoles are viewed as new languages which lack the properties that characterise 'older', 'mature' languages. They are therefore sometimes referred to as 'younger' and 'less advanced' languages (see Seuren and Wekker 1986: 66, 68). Another related, and indeed, perhaps even resultant theme of incipience is that of *(near) absence*, in which it is assumed that creoles make use of few or no morphological processes: '[M]orphology is essentially alien to creole languages' (Seuren and Wekker 1986: 66); '[I]t is logically impossible for [Haitian] Creole to manifest [derivational] processes' (D'Ans 1968: 26). Another important theme is that of *lapidescence*, which is related to (near) absence. In this view, creoles are morphologically unproductive because affixes inherited from the source language have been fossilised in the borrowed words of which they are part and are therefore unanalysable for creole speakers: '[Derivation] plays only a minor role in the creation of new words [in Haitian Creole]' (Valdman 1978: 148; DeGraff's translation, cited in DeGraff 2001: 56). For the purposes of this case study, we will focus on the claim of lapidescence for HFC, which is based on the assumption that 'morphologically complex words in French were adopted in the incipient Creole as morphologically simplex words that have since remained permanently unanalysed' (DeGraff 2001: 56).

DeGraff illustrates his counterargument to this perspective with reference to HFC words ending in *-syon*. Creolists such as Valdman (1978), Hall (1953) and Lefebvre (1998) have maintained that HFC nouns with this ending that have French counterparts (as in HFC *adorasyon*, French *adoration* 'adoration'), are unanalysed loanwords from the latter language. In other words, HFC speakers allegedly do not interpret *-syon* as a productive noun-forming suffix but instead as part of the word stem. While it is difficult to prove that such words are not borrowings from French, other HFC data strongly indicates that the assumptions of unanalysed words specifically, and of unproductive morphology generally, are erroneous. For instance, DeGraff (2001: 63) notes that HFC has 'scores of X*syon* words that are morphologically and semantically related to their respective stem X' (1.8.a lists a selection of examples). If we assumed that Valdman et al. are right, we would not only have to accept that HFC borrowed relatively vast numbers of such pairs (which seems unlikely), but also that HFC speakers could not, and can not, discern the transparent pattern of derivation in what is actually a large and consistent database. It therefore seems much more plausible to accept that HFC speakers use -*syon* productively to derive abstract nouns from verbs.

1.8.a -*syon* forms in HFC

admirasyon 'admiration'	cf. *admire* 'to admire'
diskisyon 'discussion'	cf. *diskite* 'to discuss'
edikasyon 'education'	cf. *edike* 'to educate'
imigrasyon 'immigration'	cf. *imigre* 'to immigrate'
pinisyon 'punishment'	cf. *pini* 'to punish'

(after DeGraff 2001: 64)

Further evidence bears this out: HFC speakers also make use of X*syon* forms which are not attested in French (see 1.8.b):

1.8.b HFC -*syon* forms not attested in French

dekoupasyon 'dividing wall, screen'	cf. *dekoupe* 'to cut up, to carve'
eklerasyon 'enlightenment'	cf. *eklere* 'to enlighten'
levasyon 'education, upbringing'	cf. *leve* 'to educate, to rear'
pansyon 'anxiety'	cf. *panse* 'to think'
vivasyon 'conviviality'	cf. *viv* 'to live'

(after DeGraff 2001: 65)

It is worth noting that some such HFC formations have been dismissed by Valdman as 'pseudo-French'; in other words, as the hypercorrect product of HFC speakers who have little or no knowledge of French. He therefore views them not as creations of a productive derivational process in HFC but rather, as 'nonexistent derivatives formed by adjoining occurring French suffixes to the "wrong" HC stems' (Valdman 1988: 75).[15] DeGraff (2001: 63) argues however, that Valdman is here confusing etymology and morphology: while it is true that much of HFC morphology ultimately has a (seventeenth- to eighteenth-century) French etymology, the morphological system of the creole (which is actually spoken by a monolingual majority) functions independently of French, as is evidenced by the presence of X*syon* 'Haitianisms'. Indeed, the simple fact that X*syon* forms such as those in 1.8.b have been created and are used by HFC speakers is enough to evidence that they emerge from a productive derivational process. As a further and final example of the fact that HFC does indeed make use of productive derivational processes, DeGraff (2001: 66) notes that speakers derive verbs from X*syon* nouns through the addition of a verbal suffix *e(n)/ne*, as can be seen in 1.8.c:

1.8.c Verb derivation from -*syon* forms in HFC

estasyone 'to park'	cf. *estasyon* 'station'
keksyone 'to question'	cf. *keksyon* 'question'
koleksyone 'to collect'	cf. *koleksyon* 'collection'
komisyone 'to commission'	cf. *komisyon* 'commission'
pansyone 'to think, ponder'	cf. *pansyon* 'thought, anxiety'

DeGraff (2001) discusses the productivity of other HFC derivational processes in much more detail than we can provide here. However, this brief discussion should have served to illustrate specifically some of the 'productive morphological processes' located in 'the minds/brains of [HFC] speakers' (DeGraff 2001: 65) and to exemplify generally the kinds of language-internal derivational processes unconsciously used by individual speakers cross-linguistically.

1.9 Discussion

The examples and discussion of internally motivated change in this chapter are by no means exhaustive, but should serve to illustrate some of the major processes that have been identified in this area. As stated at the beginning of this chapter, and as has become evident throughout our discussion, many explanations of internally motivated change have necessarily focused on describing and theorising the processes and mechanisms through which change takes place, such as drag and push chains, grammaticalisation, reanalysis, derivation, parameter setting and so on. As we have also seen, the focus on processes and mechanisms has not precluded varying degrees of discussion of – and conjecture about – actuation, particularly (but not exclusively) in relation to what we have called system-based explanations of change. Neogrammarian explanations of sound change, for example, cited motivating physical factors such as ease of articulation, while Structuralist discussions emphasised the need to maintain symmetry and function within a system. The purposeful drift of a language down 'a current' that it shapes itself has also been proposed as the governing factor of change.

While it may well be that some or all of these factors have in principle some measure of validity, they all individually lack complete explanatory adequacy. For instance, ease of articulation locates the actuation of sound changes such as assimilation in human physiology. This does not, however, have full explanatory force: assimilation processes seem to occur only in some words and not as consistently and universally as we might expect of a physiologically based change. Thus, to return to our example at the beginning of this chapter, although assimilation occurs in the pronunciation of a word like 'handbag' ([nb] > [mb]), it does not inevitably follow that all instances of [nb] in all relevant languages will undergo the same process. Similarly, the Structuralist explanation of changes such as the Great Vowel Shift also raises questions: the alleged need to maintain symmetry and effective function in a system may well be an important factor in change, but it really only applies once change is underway. It does not actually address the issue of why, in this case, initial movement of the vowels began in a system that was already symmetrical and functionally effective.

The explanatory notion of drift has also not been a straightforward issue, particularly because it has carried, in certain discussions, implications of purposeful, independent activity on the part of a language. This is evident in Sapir's (1921 [2000]) initial discussion: although he explicitly states that language is a human creation ('language exists only in so far as it is actually used – spoke, heard, written and read' (Sapir 1921 [2000]: 4)) and that all change begins in individual variation, he also argues that the goal-directed movement of drift happens independently of speakers' will. Language therefore has 'a power to change of its own accord' (Sapir 1921 [2000]: 4); an ability to logically determine the changes it 'needs' to undergo – incidentally, an idea that also surfaces in the Neogrammarian theory that sound change occurs with 'blind necessity'. This personification of language as a rational organism is extremely difficult, if not impossible, to accept, and is arguably an instance of biological metaphor taken to an illogical extreme. In addition, the assumption of purposeful movement towards a particular end raises a host of questions about such 'goalhood'. First, it implies that the linguistic goals of drift must be useful or advantageous in some way, but it remains unclear how this is to be assessed both without the benefit of formal and objective criteria for measuring 'linguistic usefulness', and without (given that such assessment necessarily takes place after the event) invoking the criticism of circularity of reasoning. The assumption of goal-directed activity also persuades us to assess languages in terms of their distance from these alleged 'useful' goals, 'plunging us . . . into the muddy waters of assessing some languages as better than others' (McMahon 1994: 329). Finally, there is an issue in the identification of these goals: we might, for example, be able to observe what seems to be a line of changes, but this in itself is not enough to determine where an alleged goal lies. In terms of a set of sound changes, for instance, 'the end-point may not be significant . . . the starting-point may be more relevant, in that one sound change operates, and subsequent changes will tend to proceed in more or less the same direction' (McMahon 1994: 331).

Despite such issues, this teleological notion of drift has continued to be invoked, and to be problematised. Thomason and Kaufman (1988: 9), for example, define drift as 'tendencies within the language to change in certain ways as a result of structural imbalances'. It remains unclear, however, how a process such as grammaticalisation, for example, resolves or even emerges from 'structural imbalances', whatever they may be. This idea of drift and imbalance can also be found in earlier work, such as that of Lehmann (1973) and Venneman (1974), who proposed that the driving force behind word order change, for instance, was the 'goal' of typological harmony or consistency – a 'natural and preferred' state of complete conformity to the properties of either VO or OV languages (see Section 1.5). If a language experienced typological inconsistency, then drift towards a resolution of that state was therefore inevitable. Again, this perspective raises quite a few questions. For example, if the preferred language state is one of consistency, it is not clear why and how 'imbalance' or inconsistency is ever allowed to develop. Another issue lies in the not-insignificant fact that a huge proportion of the world's languages do not exhibit complete typological harmony, which seems an odd state of affairs if consistency is the favoured option. English, for example, is SVO but NA, and Persian is OV but has had all the other related properties of a VO language for a few thousand years. It could be argued that these languages are in a transitional phase between types, with a slow but sure movement towards once again restoring typological harmony. This perspective, however, seems unsatisfactory on two counts. First, it means that we have to classify the majority of languages as being in an 'unnatural' transitional phase, an uncomfortable and somewhat counter-intuitive position, not least because allegedly inconsistent languages either continue to thrive as they are or, if they do undergo change that can be interpreted as movement towards typological harmony, change extremely slowly. Second, such a stance implies that once typological drift is triggered in a language by the threat of inconsistency, that language, to paraphrase Sapir (1921 [2000]), makes its own current and uses it determinedly throughout the centuries, despite changing generations of speakers, to reach a predetermined end: an anthropomorphic conclusion that we have already discounted as dubious. Overall, we do not yet know enough about the world's languages to be able to determine exactly what consistency (and hence, inconsistency) entails, apart from the fact that it does not seem to be 'a perfect state towards which all languages eternally struggle' (McMahon 1994: 149).

Thus, drift as used in a teleological or goal-directed sense is not particularly satisfactory as an explanation of what motivates linguistic change. A more general interpretation of drift, however, such as that employed in this chapter, where it labels tendencies rather than obligatory rules, seems to be more useful in explaining processes of change that languages may follow.

A final and general issue that we need to consider in the context of explanatory adequacy is the traditional separation of internal and external motivations. As we stated in the introduction to this chapter, contemporary studies of language change tend at the very least to acknowledge that consideration of extralinguistic factors is important in constructing an accurate idea of how change unfolds, even if their primary focus is on a process that might be considered internally motivated: see, for example, Smith's (1996) discussion of the Great Vowel Shift, which examines systemic processes in the context of social contact between different groups in sixteenth-century London. Studies such as Smith's also allow important questions about transmission, or about how change spreads and is adopted in a speech community, to be addressed, something which explanations based solely on internal motivations cannot, by their very nature, examine. As we have seen throughout this chapter, the idea that 'change can never be necessary directly for system-internal reasons' (Hróarsdóttir 2001: 23) has not always been a given, especially in the early historical linguistic tradition; and this focus away from speakers as social beings who interact, in the truest sense of the word, *sociolinguistically*, has perhaps been one of the primary reasons ultimately behind the inadequacy of certain internally motivated explanations. This is not to detract from the usefulness of work which has concentrated solely on internal motivations, but simply to underline the complementary nature of both types of explanation in understanding catalysts of change, how they might unfold and, importantly, how they might spread and take hold. As Smith (1996: 111) states,

> the explanation of the triggering of a given linguistic change depends on an understanding of many interacting extralinguistic and intralinguistic processes. A single explanation for the triggering of change is not enough; as in the physical or biological, the multi-factorial causation of events needs to be an accepted part of the methodology.

We turn now to an examination of the other half of the story – externally motivated change – in Chapter 2.

2 Externally motivated change

2.1 Introduction

In the previous chapter, we considered examples of linguistic change that occur due to internal restructuring within a language, without influence from any other linguistic variety. Such change (which, as we saw, is usually referred to as internal or internally motivated change) seems to be an inherent tendency of all living languages and occurs irrespective of the language's social context (see, for example, Thomason 2001; Winford 2003). In this chapter, we will consider a different type of language change, which is generally termed *external* or *externally motivated* change. As its name implies, this type of change may be contrasted with internal change in that it occurs due to the influence of another language.

The question of why languages change at all has preoccupied linguists for a long time. As we saw in the previous chapter, one of the earliest attempts to solve this problem was made by the Neogrammarians in the late nineteenth century. Although the Neogrammarians' views (that all regular sound change was internally motivated) were highly influential at that time, they were not the only ones to be voiced – for example, Hugo Schuchardt was one early advocate of language contact as a source of linguistic change, claiming 'I have maintained that of all the questions contemporary linguistics must tackle, none is of greater importance than that of language mixing' (1884: 3; our translation).

However, Schuchardt's position with respect to language contact appears to have been rather a lonely one. Other influential linguists of the day were clearly opposed to this type of explanation. For example, Müller's view was that 'There are no mixed languages' (1861: 86; our translation) and Whitney claimed that 'Such a thing as a language with a mixed grammatical apparatus has never come under the cognisance of linguistic students: It would be to them a monstrosity; it seems an impossibility' (1867: 199).

And yet, language does not exist in a vacuum. By virtue of being spoken, its development is continually being influenced by its speakers and so, as we saw in Chapter 1, abstracting away from the individual and concentrating only on the internal structure of language cannot account for the whole picture. Indeed, the second half of the twentieth century, in particular, saw a growing realisation that contact does play a significant role in language change. Indeed, thanks to ground-breaking works such as Uriel Weinreich's *Languages in Contact* (1953), which examined the effects of contact on different areas of a language (phonological, grammatical and lexical), the role of contact in language change has gained in prominence so that, by today, we find contact-induced change described as 'in no way exceptional' (Giacalone Ramat 1992: 327) and even 'commonplace' (Jeffers and Lehiste 1979: 138).

This chapter therefore complements the previous one by considering externally motivated change. As we will see, this type of linguistic change is commonly found in situations where one or more languages are in contact and its extent is governed by the degree and nature of the contact. In Chapter 4, we will see that externally motivated change is also common in situations of language obsolescence, where there is usually an asymmetrical dominance relationship between the languages in competition and where interference from the dominant language causes change in the obsolescent language. However, as this chapter will show, externally motivated change is by no means exclusive to cases of language obsolescence and can also occur in so-called 'healthy' languages. Moreover, in Chapter 3, we will see how contact between languages may even give rise to language birth.

2.2 Borrowing

Lexical *borrowing* is a frequent by-product of language contact and may be broadly defined as the incorporation of foreign words into a speaker's native language. Few linguistic communities have been able to exist without contact of some kind with other peoples – usually through commercial or economic relations. The result of this is that their language will also have been in contact with one or more other languages and will almost inevitably bear some hallmark of this. That being said, contact does not automatically precipitate lexical borrowing: in a study of the Vaupes region of Brazilian Amazonia, Aikhenvald (1996) illustrates how the one Arawakan language of the region has undergone dramatic structural interference after the model of the Tucanoan languages of the same area, but the stigma attached to lexical interference has meant that this has occurred without any lexical borrowing taking place. Similarly, although trilingual in Tewa, Spanish and English, the Tewa-speaking people of Arizona show very little borrowing from the other two languages in their Tewa (Kroskrity 1993). Cases such as these, however, are very much the exception and, in fact, most languages may be viewed as a sort of potted history of their speech communities, indicating the contact the latter have had with other speech communities during their history. In fact, the number of borrowings a language makes at a specific point in time can serve to illustrate the importance of the contact between the two speech communities at that time (or at least how influential the foreign speech community was vis-à-vis that of the borrower language). For instance, from Table 2.2.a, adapted from Guiraud (1965: 6), we can see that Italian influence was prevalent in French society in the sixteenth and seventeenth centuries but that this influence then waned and was replaced by a growing amount of influence from English from the eighteenth century onwards.

The phenomenon of borrowing is one which has been extensively studied in historical linguistics and, as such, we will devote the rest of this section to a discussion of what appear to be its main processes and mechanisms. We begin with a brief consideration of the apparent reasons why languages borrow.

One of the most common reasons for one language to borrow from another is when it needs to refer to notions and things that have been newly introduced to its speakers. The Italian word *pizza* for example only entered English when the food to which it refers was adopted by English speech communities. Similarly, *glasnost* was borrowed from Russian to express a policy of openness and frankness in Soviet political life that came in the wake of the Gorbachev era and represented a concept that had hitherto been unfamiliar to the English speech community. Maori *haka* was borrowed to denote a specific ceremonial dance performed by members of a New Zealand sports team before a game. This type of borrowing, then, is due to a 'deficiency' in the native vocabulary – termed a *referential* (or *lexical*) gap – and is by no means a recent phenomenon: during the Industrial Revolution, French borrowed a great deal of terminology from English (such as *rail*, *wagon* and other railway terms) to denote objects which were introduced from Britain at this time.

2.2.a Lexical borrowings in French

Century	12th	13th	14th	15th	16th	17th	18th	19th
Arabic	20	22	36	26	70	30	24	41
Italian	2	7	50	79	320	188	101	67
Spanish			5	11	85	103	43	32
Portuguese				1	19	23	8	3
Dutch	16	23	35	22	32	52	24	10
Germanic	5	12	5	11	23	27	33	45
English	8	2	11	6	14	67	134	377
Slavic	2			1	4	6	11	10
Turkish	1			2	13	9	6	14
Persian	2			2	1	5	3	1
Hindu					1	4	8	5
Malaysian					4	10	6	5
Japanese/Chinese					36	25	21	7
Greek	8	4	5	3	1	2		
Hebrew	9	1	2	5	2	2	1	1

However, a referential gap is not the only possible motivation for lexical borrowing. Prestige is also important. In many situations of language contact, one language may be perceived to be more prestigious than another, and the latter may often undergo borrowing from the former in order to enhance its status. This can occur even if the less prestigious language already has an indigenous word for the relevant concept. For example, in the sixteenth century, Italian was considered to be the language of culture and refinement within Europe, which made it a prime source of borrowing for other European languages. For instance, the French word for 'soldier' (*soldat*), which was borrowed at this time from Italian (*soldato*), despite the existence indigenous French *soudart*. The borrowing occurred for reasons of prestige and resulted in the coexistence in French of two words with the meaning 'soldier', with the indigenous term existing alongside the borrowing. *Soudart* eventually dropped out of usage.

When borrowing takes place for reasons other than the existence of a referential gap, indigenous loanwords frequently coexist for a time. Not all doublets survive (as seen in the case of *soldat* and *soudart* above) but where both words do remain, one of the pair often undergoes a slight change of meaning. In some cases, the indigenous term comes to refer to a more concrete concept, and the borrowed term takes on a more abstract or specialised meaning. For example, the adjective originally corresponding to the English noun *king* was *kingly*. In the ME period, however, the adjective *royal* was taken from French as a prestige borrowing. The conflict between these doublets was resolved by *royal* becoming the usual productive adjective corresponding to the noun *king*, with the meaning 'originating from, connected with, a king or line of kings' and *kingly* taking on the more specialised meaning of 'having the character, quality or attributes of a king'. However, it is not always the original term that undergoes modification of its meaning, as can be seen in the case of the verb *cleaner*, which was borrowed into Jersey Norman French[1] from the English *to clean* despite the existence of the indigenous term *netti*. These doublets, too, underwent a refinement of meaning so that in Modern Jersey Norman French, *netti* has retained the basic meaning of 'to clean', whilst *cleaner* has specialised its meaning to refer to the annual ritual of spring cleaning (Le Maistre 1947: 11).

Although borrowing is extremely widespread, not all loanwords are destined to be incorporated into the borrower language. Many are only transitory and disappear in the space of a relatively short time. Why, then, are some borrowings so short-lived and yet others relatively long-lived? The question is quite a complex one, but, simplifying slightly, we can isolate three main reasons. In the first place, a borrowing is likely to be retained if it denotes an object for which no other word exists in the borrower language (as in the word *pizza*, mentioned above). Second, borrowings will also be accepted if they are perceived to be fashionable and up to date by their users; so, for example, words borrowed from US English will remain in a language up until the point that its speakers no longer consider the USA as a model to emulate. Finally, borrowings will remain in a language if the indigenous equivalent is seen as more cumbersome – take the example of the English loan *scanneur*, which 'saves' five syllables over its French indigenous equivalent *radiomètre à balayage*.

As new concepts and objects are introduced into a speech community, words are needed to denote them. As it is easier to borrow a word than to invent one, in some 'modern' domains borrowings may be relatively frequent. In some speech communities, however, borrowings may be perceived as problematic. This is often the case in obsolescent languages, where the fact that the language is recognised as threatened seems to make speakers more self-conscious about them than might otherwise be the case. (English, for example, contains hundreds of loanwords and acquires several more each year, but this generally passes without comment.) Dorian reports how the use of English borrowings in obsolescent East Sutherland Gaelic is a 'touchy matter' (1981: 101). In such contexts, those trying to protect the language may even seek to find other words to replace the loanwords, such as in the following examples taken from Breton (2.2.b), where terms felt to be too obviously reminiscent of French are replaced with words felt to be more intrinsically Breton in nature:

2.2.b Breton 'replacements' for French borrowings in modern Breton

French borrowing	*Breton replacement*	
konfitur	kaotigell	'jam'
photographie	luc'hskeudennerezh	'photography'
secrétaire	skriverezerez	'secretary'

However, the replacement of borrowings by indigenous terms also occurs in 'healthy' languages. The French government, for instance, has attempted to stem the already steady flow of English loanwords into French by passing legislation such as the *Loi Bas-Lauriol* (1975), which made French compulsory in commercial and advertising contexts, in work contracts and in the context of information given to consumers either by private firms or public bodies and the *Loi Toubon* (1994) which further reinforced the implementation of French terminology on penalty of fines or, in the worst case, imprisonment. In order to reinforce such legislation it has been necessary to establish commissions to create new terminology to replace the borrowings (*voyagiste* and *baladeur* are two such examples, which, in recent years, have started to replace *tour operator* and *walkman*). This newly created terminology has now been made compulsory in all governmental documentation, contracts, education and in all other state institutions. Borrowings are similarly discouraged in Iceland, as it is thought that the use of non-native words might distance speakers from native Icelandic culture. Lexical gaps are frequently filled by Old Norse words being revived with a new meaning.

Such a mindset is not new: after the defeat of Germany in the Thirty Years' War (seventeenth century), for example, many locally organised clubs emerged dedicated to restoring what they saw as the 'purity' of the German language by eliminating all borrowings. Not all of the proposed replacements caught on, but it was at this time that *Gewissensfreiheit* – in a neat illustration of the link between language use and national identity – came to be used for the first time in place of *liberté de conscience* ('freedom of conscience') (Hock 1991: 414–15).

Another issue that has received (linguistic) consideration is the question of how languages borrow. Picoche and Marchello-Nizia (1991: 338–9) reduce the process of borrowing to three stages. The first stage is when a word from one language is used in an utterance of another language in order to create a somewhat exotic effect. At this stage, the word is not a borrowing, but rather what they term a *xenism*. An example of a xenism used in an English sentence would be *At the harbour, we went for a sail in a gulet*, where *gulet* is the word for a type of Turkish sail boat, which has no real equivalent in English. Since neither the concept not the word exist in the English-speaking world (using the term *sail boat* in its place, for example, would conjure up a completely different image), the xenism is used to denote the foreign object in a way that adds 'local colour' to the utterance.

Borrowings differ from xenisms in that, unlike the latter, both the foreign term and the referent become integrated into the speech community – either in terms of a new, concrete object or else as a new concept that has been introduced into the speech community. Xenisms are not considered to be part of the borrower language, whereas borrowing is seen to have taken place when a term is no longer considered as foreign. In other words, when a speaker of language A uses a foreign term, not as a fortuitous reference to language B but because he or she has heard it used by others in speech acts of language A, then from a purely descriptive point of view, the term may be considered as having become an integral part of language A.

The second stage in the integration of a borrowing is adaptation. This makes the borrowing look more like an indigenous word of the borrower language and can involve both phonology and morphosyntax. If a word is adapted phonologically, its pronunciation is brought in line with the phonological system and sound patterns of the borrower language, with the phonemes of the borrowed word replaced by the closest indigenous sounds of the borrower language. For example, some south-east Asian languages have borrowed Indic words, replacing the 'foreign' retroflex consonants (characteristic of Indic but absent from their respective phonological inventories) by 'indigenous' non-retroflex apicals (Deshpande 1979: 258). If a borrower language has certain phonological rules, then borrowings that have the potential to contravene these will be modified accordingly. For instance, loanwords into German are typically made to conform to its phonological rule of devoicing word-final stops. Thus English *trend* has become German [trɛnt]. Loans into Japanese are adapted to conform to its CVCV syllable structure, hence English 'tractor' is pronounced [turakutura] (McMahon 1994: 206).

In morphosyntactic integration, loanwords are reanalysed (see Chapter 1) to conform to certain grammatical patterns in the borrower language. For instance, English nouns which are borrowed into languages which have grammatical gender are made either masculine, feminine or neuter: *football* > *el fútbol* (masculine) (Spanish); *factory* > *y ffatri* (feminine) (Welsh); *poster* > *das Poster* (neuter) (German).

Plural marking can also be affected during the morphosyntactic integration of a borrowing. For example, English has borrowed the word *formula* from Latin, which has a plural *formulae*. Some speakers advocate keeping the original plural form for the borrowing, while others tend to form the plural in the English way, by simply adding an orthographical -*s* (*formulas*). The original method of plural marking has been entirely abandoned in the case of the Italian word *pizza* (plural *pizze*), which has become *pizzas* in English.

Sometimes, a word may be plural in the donor language but be reinterpreted as singular in the borrower language. For example, *macaroni* is plural in Italian, but since in French most plural nouns end in orthographic -*s*, speakers have reinterpreted this noun as singular and created a plural form *macaronis*. This has also happened with the word *sportsmen*, which has been reinterpreted as singular in Russian as the language does not make use of umlaut as a method of plural formation.

Reanalysis of a word (see Chapter 1) happens quite frequently during the adaptation of a borrowing. McMahon (1994: 207) mentions how the English expression *keep left*, used in Swahili in the adapted form *kiplefiti* as the word for 'roundabout', has been reanalysed as *ki-plefiti* due to the fact that some Swahili nouns can have a *ki-* prefix in the singular. This gives the corresponding plural *viplefiti* 'roundabouts'. Similarly, *madigadi* (from English *mudguard*) and *maching oda* (from English *marching order*) fit into the Swahili class of nouns which have *ma-* as their plural prefix. In Swahili, the prefix is absent in the singular of this class of words, hence the forms *digadi* 'mudguard' and *ching'oda* 'marching order'.

As well as being adapted phonetically and morphosyntactically, a borrowed word may be adapted semantically. Initially the word will be borrowed with one particular meaning. However, once the borrowing is completed, just as any word in the language may take on a new meaning, the borrowing may also acquire one or more new meanings in the borrower language that will not be acquired in the donor language. For example, in French, the noun *match* has a much wider use than in English, and can be used for any sort of sporting competition. This, then, is further evidence in support of the fact that, once borrowed, a word is no longer subject to influence from the donor language.

When no modification occurs, the borrowing is said to be adopted or imported. Examples of such 'wholesale' borrowing from English would be words such as *chic* (from French) and *macho* (from Spanish), where the words are pronounced in more or less the same way as they would be in their donor languages. Adoption may occur especially in cases where the new language comes to be known quite widely throughout the speech community. For example, in Asiatic Eskimo the pronunciation of Russian loanwords borrowed in two distinct periods differ from one another. The first set of borrowings, made in the pre-Soviet period, have undergone quite extensive phonological adaptation. The later borrowings, however, were made during the Soviet period, when Russian was taught in schools and was therefore known more extensively throughout the community. These show less phonological adaptation, as can be seen in 2.2.c:

2.2.c Phonological adaptation of Russian borrowings in Asiatic Eskimo

Russian	*Earlier borrowings*	*Later borrowings*	
bljudce	pljusa	bljutca	'saucer'
čaj	saja	čaj	'tea'
tabak	tavaka	tabak	'tobacco'
pačka	paska-q	pačka	'bundle'

(after Thomason and Kaufman 1988: 32–3)

The third stage in the integration of a borrowing is what Picoche and Marchello-Nizia (1991: 339) term its *naturalisation* by more considerable transformations, such as when the borrower language starts to form derivations from the borrowing that do not exist in the donor language. At this point, therefore, the borrowing develops independently of the donor language and is treated like a fully fledged lexical item of the borrower language. For instance, the Spanish noun *wisquería* (a bar specialising in whisky) has been formed on the basis of the borrowing *whisky*, even though English, which originally supplied the borrowing, has no similar derivative (see also Section 1.8).

It is worth noting that although, in theory, any word may be a potential candidate for borrowing, the fact that words cannot be used in isolation but rather form part of an overarching structure (namely the utterance) means that some categories of words seem to be borrowed more easily than others. Whitney (1881) suggested a hierarchy of: *nouns–other parts of speech–suffixes–inflections–sounds* which was elaborated further by Haugen (1950) into: *nouns–verbs–adjectives–adverbs–prepositions–interjections*.

In general, it seems that nouns are the most frequent lexical items to be borrowed, possibly because they are the easiest items to integrate, since their importation has relatively few repercussions on the morphology and syntax of the borrower language. Verbs are less common, due to difficulties of integration (they have to be given morphology in order to be conjugated). But most difficult of all are the so-called grammatical words (such as prepositions), which are hardly ever borrowed. Of course, the purpose behind the borrowing clearly also has a bearing on which types of word are most commonly borrowed, and since loanwords are most often used to fill a referential gap, it is not surprising that nouns are much more frequently borrowed than other parts of speech.

Finally, we may consider the question of whether lexical borrowings are recognisable as such once they have become integrated into a language. It is in fact often possible to identify a word as a borrowing thanks to one of the principles recognised by the Neogrammarians, who were mentioned at the beginning of this chapter and referred to in Chapter 1. We saw that the Neogrammarians recognised that all languages change over time and that changes affecting a particular sound or sounds in a particular phonetic environment, at a given point in time and within a specific speech community will operate regularly and without exception. Borrowings entering the language after this time will therefore often stand out from a language's indigenous words due to the fact that they will not have undergone these changes.

For example, as a result of a sound change known as the Second Germanic Consonant Shift, the initial [p] of words in Germanic languages becomes [pf] in standard German. This happened whether the word in question was indigenous or borrowed, hence, English *plant* – German *Pflanze*; English *plight* – German *Pflicht*. Knowledge of this sound change enables us to tell, therefore, that modern German words such as *Pilger* ('pilgrim') (from Latin *peregrinus* – which begins with a [p]) must be a borrowing, as it shows no evidence of the sound change described above.[2] Furthermore, as we know that the sound change ceased operating in about the seventh century, we also know that the word *Pilger* must have been borrowed after that time. This gives us a crude method for dating the emergence of borrowings in a language.

Another means of establishing whether or not a word has been borrowed is by looking at comparative data. If a word in a particular language family has easily identifiable *cognates* (defined neatly by McMahon (1994: 2) as 'words which show regular and repeated correspondences of a particular sound in one language to another sound or sequence of sounds in others, along with similarity in meaning') in languages that are also members of that family, then it is unlikely to be a borrowing. For example, if we compare the word for 'horse' in Spanish (*caballo*) with other Romance languages, we find the following, as seen in 2.2.d:

2.2.d Examples of words for 'horse' in Romance languages

French	*cheval*
Italian	*cavallo*
Occitan	*caval*
Catalan	*cavall*
Sardinian (Nuorese)	*cabaddu*
Romansch (Upper Engadinish)	*chavagl*
Ladin	*chavà*

The words for 'horse' in these different Romance languages are undoubtedly cognates, and have derived from the same source (Latin). However, if we consider the word for 'goose', our results are rather different, as seen in 2.2.e:

2.2.e Examples of words for 'goose' in Romance languages

French	*oie*
Italian	*oca*
Occitan	*auca*
Catalan	*oca*
Sardinian (Nuorese)	*occa*
Romansch (Upper Engadinish)	*ocha*
Ladin	*ocha*
Spanish	*ganso*

This time, we can see that although most of the languages share a cognate form, Spanish has a completely different word. Based on this evidence, therefore, it is likely that the Spanish term is a borrowing (in fact, it comes from Germanic *gans*, which has yielded words such as *Gans* (German) and *goose* (English) in the modern Germanic languages).

Although we have concentrated so far on the introduction of lexical items through borrowing, it is important to note that the lexis is not the only area of a language that can be affected by this phenomenon. For instance, as discussed above, not all lexical borrowings are adapted phonologically into the borrower language. This may occur especially in cases where the new language comes to be known quite widely throughout the speech community. If the phonological inventories of these two languages differ, unadapted borrowings may sometimes become a source of new phonemes for the borrower languages. For example, due to the influence of English, French has acquired the /ŋ/ phoneme, via words such as *le smoking, le parking* and so forth. At present, however, the phoneme is only present in borrowings. Campbell (1998: 72), however, reports that the clicks borrowed into some Bantu languages from the neighbouring Khoe and San languages of southern Africa are now also used in native words.

Morphological borrowing may also occur. Thomason and Kaufman (1988: 219) describe an instance of this phenomenon in Asia Minor Greek whereby Turkish personal suffixes are added to Greek verbs in some Cappadocian dialects. For example, the first (1pl) and second (2pl) persons plural past-tense forms *kétunmistik* 'we camped/lodged' and *kétunstiniz* 'you camped/lodged' contain the Turkish inflectional suffixes *-ik* (1pl) and *-iniz* (2pl).

There are also attested cases of syntactic borrowing. Karaim, a Turkic language spoken in the Baltic area, has created a new pattern for deriving compound nouns by borrowing Slavic word order (*noun +*

noun-plural-genitive) (Csató 2002). Compare the Turkish structure in 2.2.f with that of Karaim in 2.2.g:

2.2.f Turkish
kadin   doktoru
Noun   Noun-possessive
'female doctor of it' ('gynaecologist')

2.2.g Karaim
sawuxturuwču   t'iš'lar'n'in'
Noun   Noun-plural-genitive
doctor   tooth-plural-genitive
'doctor of the teeth' ('dentist')

In the latter's new syntactic pattern, the plural form of the genitive attribute follows the head noun, which does not carry any morphological marker. Here, therefore, both the order of the two nominal elements (i.e. with the modifier following the modified) and the non-Turkic use of the plural in the second element are borrowings from Slavic. Moreover, as the genitive is only used in Turkic in possessive construction, it is clear that the Slavic use of the genitive in derivation has also been borrowed here.

In the above examples, it has been relatively easy to identify the external source of the change in question. However, this is not always the case. In some instances, it is possible for foreign elements to be incorporated into a language without its speakers being aware of them. This phenomenon is known as *calquing*, or *loan translation* (Weinreich 1953: 51) and is very frequent when two languages are in a situation of high contact, with one language usually serving as a model for the other. Calquing occurs when the foreign elements are incorporated into the borrower language but are first translated into it morpheme for morpheme (or word for word in the case of an expression). The result of this is that despite the fact that the calque is nonetheless a borrowing, since it is composed entirely of indigenous elements, it does not seem at all 'foreign' to its speakers.

Calques are by no means recent phenomena. A frequently cited example of this type of change comes from the early days of the Christian church. In the Bible, the Hebrew word *ml'k* 'messenger' was often used in the sense of 'angel'. Since there was no word for 'angel' in Greek, the translators of the Bible copied the polysemy of the Hebrew term by using the Greek *angelos* 'messenger' with the meaning of 'angel'. From the Greek, the word passed into Latin as *angelus*, which has subsequently become *angel* (Welsh, English), *angelo* (Italian), *ange* (French), *Engel* (German) and so forth in different modern European languages.

A more recent example of this phenomenon may be seen with the noun *skyscraper*: a compound word which originated in English and which is completely transparent in meaning – conveying the image of a building so tall that it scrapes the sky. This word has been calqued into several European languages giving: *rascacielos* (Spanish), *gratteciel* (French), *grattacielo* (Italian), *Wollenkratzer* (German) and *nebo skrjób* (Russian). Since, in all cases, the component parts of this word (*sky* and *scraper*) have been translated into the language in question, in the absence of comparative data from other languages, it is impossible for native speakers of any of these languages to tell that the word they are using is a borrowing.

Calquing is not restricted to content words. In Jèrriais (the Norman French of Jersey), we find examples of prepositions being used in contexts with which they were not traditionally associated. As can be seen in 2.2.h, these clearly represent calques from English.

2.2.h English calques in modern Jèrriais
I tchit bas 'He fell **down**'
J'chèrchis pouor 'I looked **for** it'
J'comprends des mots dans l'Espangno 'I understand some words **in** Spanish'
(Jones 2001: 122–7)

Syntactic calques can also occur. For instance, some second-generation German Americans who speak quite fluent German replace colloquial standard German constructions such as *Wie heisst du?* (lit. 'How are you called?') with *Was ist dein Name?* (lit. 'What is your name?') on the model of English (Jeffers and Lehiste 1979: 141).

Like borrowing, calquing typically increases the greater the contact between two languages. Fowkes (1945: 247) notes that although seven examples of loan translations were found in the first fifty pages of the early eighteenth century work *Gweledigaethau y Bardd Cwsc*, calques are even commoner in modern Welsh literature. An example of an English calque in Welsh, which today would be considered totally acceptable, is the expression *cwympo mewn cariad* 'to fall in love', where all the constituent elements are Celtic, although the expression itself is a clearly a loan translation.

Calquing therefore represents a relatively insidious form of borrowing. It is a form of externally motivated change that can affect both the lexis and the syntax of a language but that appears largely undetectable at first glance due to the fact that it is the meaning rather than the form of the foreign item which is borrowed. The next section considers another type of externally motivated change where evidence of contact is not immediately apparent, namely the phenomenon known as linguistic *convergence*.

2.3 Convergence

As we have seen, lexical borrowing occurs when two languages are in contact in the same speech community. We have seen that, in fact (as with

English and French) the donor language does not need to be widely spoken as a native language for borrowing to take place, as there is no need for bilingualism to occur. Once adopted, a borrowing may or may not be long-lived.

Convergence, by contrast, is an example of externally motivated change that can be seen as a mirror image of lexical borrowing in so far as it affects only syntax – leaving the lexis intact – and requires a certain amount of long-term bilingualism before it can take place. Moreover, unlike lexical borrowing, equal status is enjoyed by all languages concerned, for if one were to be perceived as socially dominant, it is likely that the situation of bilingualism needed to give rise to convergence would come to an end. Convergence typically involves two or more languages of similar prestige (termed *adstratal* languages) spoken in the same territory, and the area in which the convergence occurs is termed a *convergence area*, or *Sprachbund*. The languages involved in the convergence may belong to the same family or may be completely unrelated. A Sprachbund originates due to the fact that individuals in this area typically use two or more of these different linguistic varieties on a regular basis. This often leads to some grammatical features of one language being adopted by another and vice versa, which results in the modification of the grammar of both languages spoken within the Sprachbund. If these languages are also spoken outside the Sprachbund, evidence of the convergence can be seen clearly by comparing the form of the language spoken inside the Sprachbund with that spoken outside this area.

We will now examine two very famous – and highly contrastive – examples of convergence areas, namely the Balkans (in Europe) and Kupwar (in India).

2.4 Case study: the Balkans

The Balkans convergence area involves Greek, Albanian, Romanian, Bulgarian, Serbo-Croatian and Macedonian. These are all Indo-European languages but they belong to different subfamilies: Greek is classed on its own, as is Albanian; Romanian belongs to the Romance group; Bulgarian and Serbo-Croatian are Slavonic languages. Some linguists also include non Indo-European Turkish (Ural-Altaic) and Hungarian (Finno-Ugric) in this convergence area.

Due to the fact that all these languages belong to different families, it is not surprising that they shown some differences in structure. However, it is possible to highlight certain areas where they converge and show the same structural patterns, in this case, referred to as 'Balkanisms'. For instance,

(i) As seen in 2.4.a, some of the languages in question have a post-posed definite article:

2.4.a Post-posed definite article in Romanian, Bulgarian and Albanian

Romanian	*lup* 'wolf'	*lupul* 'the wolf'
Bulgarian	*trup* 'body'	*trupat* 'the body'
Albanian	*djal* 'boy'	*djal-i* 'the boy'

This occurs whether the word itself is indigenous (as in 2.4.a) or borrowed (as in 2.4.b):

2.4.b Post-posed definite article in borrowed words in Romanian, Bulgarian, Albanian and Macedonian

Romanian	*mecanicianul*	'the mechanic'
Bulgarian	*mexanikut*	
Albanian	*mekaniku*	
Macedonian	*mexaničarot*	

(Trudgill 1983c: 175)

From the examples above, it can be seen that although these languages all share the same structure, in each case the morpheme expressing the definite article differs according to language. In other words, although these languages are converging structurally, they remain distinct in terms of the building blocks they use for these structures (i.e. their morphology and lexis). As these languages are not spoken outside the convergence area, it is not possible to compare the structure they have within the Sprachbund with an extra-Sprachbund form. However, we can compare the structure of a language such as Romanian with that of other Romance languages, as languages derived from the same source often share structural features. For example, as a Romance language, Romanian uses Romance morphs for both the definite article and the noun of *lupul* (cf. French *le loup*, Spanish *el lobo*). However, as Romance is characterised by pre-posed definite articles, we can see that the Romanian structure has undergone change.

(ii) Another syntactic example concerns the replacement of infinitival constructions with a subordinate clause introduced by a conjunction and followed by the subjunctive, as illustrated in 2.4.c:

2.4.c Replacement of infinitival clauses in Romanian, Bulgarian, Albanian and Modern Greek

Romanian	*da-mi sa beau*	'give me that I drink'
Bulgarian	*daj mi da pija*	
Albanian	*a-më të pi*	
Modern Greek	*dòs mou nà piõ*	

(Bynon 1990: 247)

These can be contrasted with related non-Sprachbund languages that use an infinitival structure (French *je veux boire*; Spanish *quiero beber* 'I want to drink').

(iii) The future tense of many Balkan languages is formed on the basis of the auxiliary meaning 'to want', as seen in 2.4.d:

2.4.d The use of 'to want' as a future auxiliary in Romanian, Albanian and Serbo-Croatian

Romanian	*o să scriu*	'I will to write' > 'I want to write'
Albanian	*do të shkruaj*	
Serbo-Croatian	*pisa-ću*	

(Hock 1991: 496)

Again, if we compare Romanian to other Romance languages, we find that most of the latter form the future tense on the basis of the auxiliary 'to have' (French *j'écrirai*, Spanish *escribiré*, Italian *scriverò*).

(iv) An example of convergence in the morphology of the Balkan languages is provided by the case-mergers undergone by some members of this group. As 2.4.e illustrates, there has been a merger of the dative and the genitive in both Bulgarian and Romanian:

2.4.e Case-mergers in Bulgarian and Romanian

Bulgarian	*na starlkut*	'to the old man'/'of the old man'
Romanian	*omuloi*	'to the man'/'of the man'

(McMahon 1994: 218)

(v) Turning now to phonology, we find that a mid-central vowel, such as *schwa*, has developed in Romanian, Albanian and Bulgarian (McMahon 1994: 218).
(vi) Romanian has developed a series of palatalised consonants under the influence of Bulgarian (Petrovici 1957).
(vii) In the domain of lexis, we find that in the Balkan languages, the numerals from eleven to nineteen often take the form of 'one on ten', 'two on ten' and so forth. This is illustrated in 2.4.f:

2.4.f The numeral 'eleven' in Romanian, Bulgarian and Albanian

Romanian	*un-spre-zece*
Bulgarian	*edin-no deset*
Albanian	*njëm-bë-dhjetë*

(viii) Finally, in Balkan languages, we find many examples of idioms that are word-for-word equivalents of one another. As illustrated in 2.4.g, all the languages render 'may God punish you' by their equivalents of the phrase 'may you find it from God'.

2.4.g 'May God punish you' in the Balkan languages

Romanian	*s-tĭ-o-afli dila Dumnidaŭ*
Albanian	*e ģetš nga Perɛndìa*
Greek	*a pò tò theò tobrés*
Bulgarian	*ot Boga da mu se naměri*
Serbo-Croatian	*da ot Boga nadješ*

(Weinreich 1953: 50)

Bynon also mentions the example 'to eat oneself with somebody', which is used in many of the languages for 'to quarrel' (1990: 247). Similarly, the phrase 'to eat someone's ears' is used to mean 'to make a frightful noise' and 'to remain without a mouth' is used for 'to kill oneself'.

In these examples, too, we can see that although the ordering is shared by different Balkan languages, the linguistic components are indigenous to the language concerned. Thus, it is only by comparing the features across different languages that any form of interference is discernible.

On the basis of written evidence, it seems that the Balkan Sprachbund was already in existence in at least the seventeenth century. It has been suggested that the main unifying force at its origin was the influence of Byzantine civilisation and, in particular, the Greek church. Greek can, in fact, be identified as the model on which some of the shared structures are based (such as the loss of the infinitival constructions) and Sandfeld (1930: 213) felt that in many cases these features developed within post-Classical Greek and then passed into other languages at different periods. However, this explanation, with Greek as the model behind the changes, does not account for all the converging features: for example, the most famous Balkanism, the postposed definite article, does not occur in Greek, and neither does Greek have the distinctive Balkan form of numerals between eleven and nineteen. Joseph (1983) even maintains that the loss of infinitival structures cannot be attributed unequivocally to Greek and that it may have represented a central innovation begun in Macedonian, Bulgarian and Greek and spread partially to the languages at the margins of the Sprachbund, such as Romanian, Serbo-Croatian and Albanian. Hock suggests that the structure of the '-teen' numerals may be attributable to Slavic (1991: 496). He also believes that the convergence area may even have been larger in the past than it is now (1991: 497). Indeed, Hock and Joseph (1996: 416) discuss several 'Balkanisms' also apparent in Germanic and thereby suggest the existence of a late Roman imperial convergence area, in which the Germanic peoples were an important ingredient. They believe that, in the modern period, the link between the Balkans and the Germanic languages has been disrupted by several divergent linguistic developments and that this has had the effect of disintegrating the bilingualism responsible for earlier convergence.

The Balkan Sprachbund, although well studied, has not as yet been fully explained. Not all the languages show all of the contact-induced developments and, as is often the case with convergence, it is not possible to identify any one language as the model for all the changes. Nevertheless, it is clear that contact has led to the languages spoken in the Balkans converging structurally to a significant degree.

2.5 Case study: Kupwar

The Kupwar Sprachbund contrasts with that of the Balkans in that it is a far less extensive geographical area. As we saw above, Kupwar is a village in India (lying at the border of the Indian states of Maharashtra and Karnataka) and has a population of just 3,000. Four languages are spoken in Kupwar – Urdu, Marathi (which are both Indo-Aryan) Kannada and Telugu (which are both Dravidian). (Telugu is not paid much attention in the literature on the Kupwar Sprachbund and so will not be discussed here.) In contrast to the situation in the Balkans, the languages spoken inside the Sprachbund are also spoken outside Kupwar. This enables a direct comparison to be made between the structure of each language in their Kupwar and non-Kupwar forms. There is evidence that Marathi and Kannada have been spoken in the village for at least six centuries and Urdu has been spoken there for three to four hundred years. Multilingualism has been maintained due to the fact that the language a person speaks natively is determined by the social group to which he or she belongs – and the dictates of the caste system mean that each major group of castes has its own neighbourhood within Kupwar. Almost all local men are bi- or multilingual but speech in the home, especially to women and children, is always done in the home language. However, the extensive interaction between these social groups in, for example, work situations, where Marathi is usually preferred, has led to a situation whereby all three main local varieties reveal an extensive degree of inter-translatability. This is illustrated in 2.5.a:

2.5.a The inter-translatability of the Urdu, Marathi and Kannada spoken in Kupwar

Kupwar Urdu	*pala*	*jəra*	*kat*	*ke*	*le*		*ke*	*a*	–	*ya*
Kupwar Marathi	*pala*	*jəra*	*kap*	*un*	*ghe*		*un*	*a*	*l*	*o*
Kupwar Kannada	*tapala*	*jəra*	*khod*	*i*	*təgond*	*i*		*bə*	–	*yn*
	greens	a little	having cut	having	taken		/I/			came
	'I cut some greens and brought them.'									

(Gumperz and Wilson 1971: 154)

Although the three sentences look very different from each other (*jəra* being the only word they have in common – this is a rare example of lexical borrowing), further analysis reveals that they are identical, both in terms of their grammatical categories and their constituent structures. For this to occur, all three Kupwar varieties have had to undergo some structural change.

Gender categorisations in the Kupwar Sprachbund have also been affected by interaction. In Urdu, all nouns are either masculine (which is the unmarked gender) or feminine. Marathi, however, has three gender categories – masculine, feminine and the unmarked neuter. In both these languages, gender is a grammatical category, but there is some correlation with sex if the referent is animate. In Kannada, by contrast, gender is semantically determined: all nouns denoting male humans are masculine, female humans are feminine and all other nouns are neuter. Analysis of the gender system operating in Kupwar makes it clear that the Kannada system has 'won out'. In Kupwar Marathi, only human males are masculine and only human females are feminine: all non-human nouns are neuter. In Kupwar Urdu, all non-human nouns have become masculine (which is the unmarked category) so that the only feminine nouns are those which denote human females. Kupwar Marathi has therefore become isomorphic with Kupwar Kannada and although Kupwar Urdu does not display the same degree of isomorphism with this system, it displays structural convergence with Kannada in so far as its attribution of gender is now only semantically determined (Gumperz and Wilson 1971: 155–6).

In another instance of Sprachbund-based change, Kupwar Kannada has acquired the use of the verb to be in sentences containing a predicate adjective under the influence of the syntactic structure of Kupwar Urdu and Kupwar Marathi (Gumperz and Wilson 1971: 159). Standard Kannada does not make use of this construction.

2.5.b 'Your house is big'

Urdu	tumhar-a	ghər	bər-a	hay
Kannada	nim	məne	doddu	
Kupwar Urdu	tumhara	ghər	bəda	hay
Kupwar Marathi	tumcə	ghər	mothə	hay
Kupwar Kannada	nimd	məni	dwədd	eti
	your	house	big	is

'Your house is big.'

Unlike the previous example, therefore, when Kupwar Kannada served as a model for the change, in this instance it is Kannada that has undergone the change.

In a final example of Sprachbund-induced change, Kupwar Urdu, unlike standard Urdu, now makes use of inclusive ('us and you') and exclusive ('us but not you') first-person plural pronouns: *apun* and *ham* respectively. This appears to be based on the patterns of both Kannada and Marathi (Gumperz and Wilson 1971: 160–1).

From the examples above we can see that unlike with the Balkans Sprachbund, in Kupwar it is possible to identify the model for the innovation in each case. However, it is also clear that no one language dominates in terms of being the main pattern supplier. The cases of the Balkans and Kupwar therefore provide two contrasting examples of convergence. We have seen that convergence can occur over both large and small geographical areas and that, according to its context, it can completely alter the structure of a language (as in the Balkans) or, alternatively, affect only one localised variety, leaving other varieties spoken outside the convergence area intact (as in Kupwar). Convergence areas are considerably rarer than instances of lexical borrowing. However, the following areas have all been proposed as Sprachbund, although the criteria on which the different claims are made vary quite widely: India (Emeneau 1956), south-east Asia (Henderson 1956), Black Sea and Caspian Sea area (Allen 1950), southern Africa (Guthrie 1967–71), Europe (Lewy 1964; Brosnahan 1961; Lakoff 1972).

It is noteworthy that some cases which, at first glance, look as though they might be due to convergence may, in fact, be attributable to other causes. For instance, Cremona (2002) demonstrates that the evolutionary processes of Arabic and Romance show certain shared tendencies such as a preference for analytical over synthetic structures, leading to the elimination of the case system, and elimination of redundant elements in morphology, leading to the disappearance of neuter gender in Latin and reduction in the number of exponents for the dual in Arabic. Although it is evident that these processes happened in quite early stages of their expansion, it is highly unlikely that Arabic and Latin could have undergone convergence as they developed in different parts of the world with hundreds of years between their respective spread and evolution.

Nonetheless, Cremona states that some of the above processes, which are clearly due to parallel development rather than to convergence, could also be used to explain certain features that are found in the Balkan Sprachbund, such as the use of analytic forms for the comparative of adjectives (cf. Romanian *mai bun* 'better', as opposed to French *meilleur*, Spanish *mejor*, etc.). He warns against being too eager to attribute all instances of structural similarity between languages to the presence of a Sprachbund, arguing, for instance, that the formation of the future tense with *volere*[3] 'to want' as the auxiliary (cf. Romanian *voi cînta*) as opposed to *habere* 'to have' could be seen as an internally motivated development – as *volere* is also used to form the future outside the Balkans in a number of northern Italian dialects and, sporadically, elsewhere in Italy. (Incidentally, Hock and Joseph (1996: 415) note that this feature is also found in Germanic.) Although Cremona (2002: 202) does not deny the existence of the Balkan Sprachbund, he claims that there is a need to 'sort out better those convergence phenomena that are clearly the result of the existence of a Sprachbund from those that have more diffuse, extra-linguistic motivations'.

In a similar vein, Britain and Sudbury (2002) examine the use of singular verb forms *to be* in existential clauses followed by a plural noun, as in *there's sheep and there's penguins* in New Zealand and in the Falkland Islands: two southern Hemisphere speech communities which are thousands of miles apart and which have witnessed very little contact with each other since settlement from Britain in the mid-nineteenth century. In both cases, the English varieties have changed towards near exclusive use of singular verb forms, and follow very similar patterns of grammatical constraints; and correlations between these findings and research done on Canadian, British and Australian varieties of English also hold. As the authors point out, these examples of parallel change following parallel linguistic constraints cannot possibly be seen as convergence and are, rather, better explained as a failure to diverge. In other words, Britain and Sudbury (2002) claim that similar linguistic changes have occurred in these communities, not as a result of contact but, simply, due to the fact that similar linguistic constraints are in operation there.

Overall, such studies show that, although it is therefore tempting to interpret structural similarity between different languages as examples of convergence, it is important to take the sociopolitical context into account when determining the overall picture.[4]

2.6 Code-switching

In communities where bilingualism is both widespread and stable, contact between languages can lead to a phenomenon known as *code-switching*, whereby bilinguals make alternating use of these languages within the same conversation. As seen in 2.6.a and 2.6.b, this may occur between different sentences (*inter-sentential code-switching*) or within the same sentence (*intra-sentential code-switching*, sometimes referred to as *code-mixing*).

2.6.a Inter-sentential code-switching (Swahili/English)
Haya mambo ya muva tuwache tu. Sisi hatuna uwezo. **We can do nothing.**
'Let's leave these matters of the rain. We don't have any power. We can do nothing.'

(Myers-Scotton 1993a: 4)

2.6.b Intra-sentential code-switching (Swahili/English)

Na kweli, hata mimi	*siko*		*sure*	*lakini*	*n-a-suspect*
	is-negative-be		sure	but	is-present-suspect
i-ta-Kuwa	**week**	*kesho*			
it will be	week	tomorrow			

'Well, even I am not sure, but I suspect it will be next week'

(Myers-Scotton 1993a: 5)

Drawing a distinction between code-switching and borrowing has not proved to be at all straightforward. As Poplack and Meechan (1998: 136) point out, scholars are sometimes sceptical about the possibility of defining such a difference. Indeed, even in cases where such a delimitation can be drawn, there can still be differences of opinion regarding the precise status of some contact forms. Thus, Myers-Scotton (1993b: 163) argues that all single-word contact forms are part of the same developmental continuum as code-switched forms whereas Poplack and Meechan (1998) consider most of these forms as borrowings on the grounds that they pattern in the same way as their indigenous base-language counterparts.

A detailed consideration of each set of theories that have been put forward as an attempt to distinguish code-switched forms and borrowings lies beyond the scope of the present discussion. We will, however, briefly outline three axioms which consistently emerge in this context:

(i) **Integration**. Borrowed words are felt to 'belong' to the recipient language. The clearest cases of borrowed forms therefore typically show more phonological, morphological and syntactic integration into the recipient language than do code-switched forms (see Poplack 1988).[5]

(ii) **Cultural loans vs. core loans**. Borrowed forms enter a language as either cultural loans or core loans. Cultural loans are seen as those that represent new objects or concepts which enter a language due to the presence of a lexical gap (such as *pizza*, see Section 2.2). Core loans, on the other hand, are seen to enter a language even though that language already has an indigenous term to refer to the object or concept in question (such as *soldat*, see Section 2.2). It is argued that core loans are more closely associated with code-switched forms, with most core borrowings entering the recipient language first as code-switched forms. On the other hand, the process by which cultural loans enter the recipient language has little relation to code-switching, as these tend to come abruptly into the recipient language in order to fill a lexical gap (Myers-Scotton 2002: 41; Pfaff 1979).

(iii) **Frequency**. Myers-Scotton (2002: 41) states that:

> While the status of borrowed forms vis-à-vis code-switching forms in any model designed to constrain the structure of code-switching is controversial, most researchers agree that borrowed forms and code-switching forms differ in regard to predictability. While one cannot predict when a borrowed form will reoccur, one can predict it definitely will reoccur because is has a status in the recipient language. [. . .] The code-switching form may or may not reoccur; it has no predictive value.

In other words, borrowings are considered to form part of the mental lexicon of the recipient language and are, to all intents and purposes, words of that language, whereas code-switches are not, and remain part of the donor language (see Myers-Scotton and Jake 2001: 92–3). As they are not part of the mental lexicon of the recipient language, code-switched forms for any given object/concept will appear less frequently than borrowed forms. Poplack (1988: 234) also advocates using frequency to distinguish between types of contact forms – albeit with the proviso that with studies of the spoken language, words may not necessarily reoccur even in large databases, which means that the status of some words must inevitably remain indeterminate. For Poplack therefore the frequency criterion can only isolate the most straightforward cases of borrowing (1988: 235). Although parallels may be drawn between code-switching and lexical borrowing, Myers-Scotton (1993b: 163) argues that they should be considered as distinct in that borrowed forms become part of the borrower language, whereas code-switched forms do not. Thus, a given borrowed word will occur far more frequently than a given code-switched form.[6]

Like lexical borrowing, code-switching does not imply that one of the languages will necessarily disappear. Indeed, its presence has been studied in many 'healthy' languages, such as Spanish and English in the USA (Timm 1975: 473–82; and Ma and Herasimchuk 1971: 347–464), where the phenomenon is considered as nothing more than speakers making full use of the resources offered by a bilingual situation, and is in no way stigmatised. However, when switching does occur in communities facing potential language death, the practice is often criticised. This, then, is an example of a set of changes which must be considered differently according to whether they occur in obsolescent or 'healthy' languages.

Another difference between code-switching in obsolescent and 'healthy' languages is that in the former code-switching is more likely to occur when modern topics, such as the world of business or politics, are discussed rather than traditional issues such as narrating stories from the past (Legère 1992: 110–11). The fact that a word might not exist in the obsolescent language for a technical term or concept incurs the necessity to borrow, which in turn may act as a trigger for the code-switch. However, it should also be pointed out that the situation is far from clear-cut and that code-switching will not necessarily be triggered by modern topics in all obsolescent languages. In East Sutherland Gaelic, for example, topic accounts for virtually no switches (Dorian 1981: 80).

2.7 Mixed languages

An extreme case of code-mixing is to be found in a language known as Media Lengua 'halfway language', which is spoken as the usual everyday language of Quechua-speaking Indians in South America and analysed in Muysken (1981). Eighty-seven per cent of the vocabulary of Media Lengua is Spanish, but the grammar is entirely Quechua. Appel and Muysken (1993: 131) cite the following example (2.7.a) of a Media Lengua sentence, with the corresponding Quechua and Spanish sentences:

2.7.a Media Lengua

Media Lengua	*miza*	*despwesitu*	*kaza-MU*	*i-*	NAKU-	*ndu-*	GA
Quechua	MIZA	*k'ipa*	*wasi-MU*	*ri-*	*naku-*	*pi-*	*ga*
	Mass	after	house to	go	**pl**	**sub**	**top**
Spanish	Yendo a la *casa después* de la *Misa*						

Media Lengua	*ahi-*	BI	*buda*	*da-*	NAKU-	N
Quechua	*chi-*	*bi*	BUDA	*ku-*	*naku-*	*n*
	that	**loc**	feast	give	**pl**	**3**
Spanish	*ahi da*n una *boda*					

'When you go home after Mass, they then give a feast there.'

Notes: **pl** 'plural', **sub** 'adverbial subordinator', **top** 'topic marker', **loc** 'locative marker', **3** 'third-person marker'.

Here, all the lexical roots are Spanish and most affixes (apart from Spanish *-ndo* > *-ndu* in Media Lengua) are Quechua.

Such mixed languages appear not to be as uncommon as one might expect (see, for example, Bakker and Mous 1994; Thomason 2001; Matras and Bakker 2003). Ma'a, spoken in Tanzania, is a Cushtic language whose basic vocabulary is Cushtic but whose phonology and grammar have mostly been borrowed from Bantu. Michif, spoken by communities of Indians in North Dakota, derives almost all its nouns and adjectives from French, but its pronouns, verbs and basic structure are Algonquian, which makes it likely that the language arose from communication between early French explorers and the native Algonquian-speaking people of the area.

Unlike the examples of code-switching described above, where the choice of when (or if) and how to switch lies in the hands of the speaker, such mixed languages represent the ordinary, everyday language of their speakers.

2.8 Discussion: internal and external change revisited

In contrast to Chapter 1, which focuses on internal change, this chapter has illustrated some of the ways in which a language can change as a result of contact (external change). As we have seen, sometimes this involves bilingualism and sometimes not. As mentioned in Chapter 1, it is now common practice to make a distinction between internal and external causation when describing language change.

However, linguists have often treated the internal/external division not merely as a descriptive tool for categorising different factors, but as a strict dichotomy requiring us to base our explanation of the change on *either* internal *or* external motivations, which potentially directs us to view them as mutually exclusive. As Nancy Dorian has stated (1993: 132):

> Dichotomies have the effect of nudging us in the direction of an either/or
> discrimination. The responsibility for this may lie with the user of the

dichotomy, but is certainly encouraged when the terms of the dichotomy are themselves antonyms, as is the case with *internal* and *external* in the phrases 'internally motivated change' and 'externally motivated change'.

The problem is that although some instances of language change are able to be attributed unequivocally to either internal or to external causation, examples abound where it is extremely difficult to separate out the motivation for change in such a neat way, as the following studies indicate.

2.9 Case study: Guernsey Norman French (Guernesiais)

Owing to increasing economic, political, legislative and commercial links with mainland Britain, English has replaced Guernsey Norman French (Guernesiais) as the dominant language of Guernsey. The Norman dialect is now obsolescent, with some 1,327 remaining fluent speakers.

In both mainland Norman and Guernesiais, unmarked qualificative adjectives, especially those of colour, often precede the noun, whereas other types of adjectives are generally post-posed (Université Populaire Normande du Coutançais 1995: 37; Tomlinson 1981: 47). Jones (2002: 154–5) found that in modern Guernesiais, 70 per cent of all adjectives were pre-posed with only 30 per cent post-posed, as would historically be found in the dialect. This tendency was so strong that even compound adjectives, which are usually longer and therefore more likely to follow the noun in mainland Norman (Université Populaire Normande du Coutançais 1995: 36), are being pre-posed, as illustrated in 2.9.a:

2.9.a Pre-posing of adjectives in modern Guernesiais
Ses anti-rouoyalistes principes
'His anti-royalist principles'
Ches prumière génératiaon Méthodistes
'Those first-generation Methodists'.

The fact that adjectives are pre-posed in English seems to provide an obvious contact-motivated explanation for this tendency in Guernesiais. However, on further analysis, the situation may in fact be more complex than it first appears. The data also conceivably admit an internal explanation in that this order already exists in the dialect, albeit in a restricted context (mainly with adjectives of colour). Many studies have demonstrated that where a variety expresses a particular function by means of two patterns, one of these is often generalised at the expense of the other through the process of simplification (Dorian 1981: 136; Mougeon and Beniak 1991: 91; Jones 1998: 250–1). It could be, therefore, that the simplificatory change from having two possible adjective positions to only one is an internal change in progress in Guernesiais and that the fact that pre-posing of adjectives is the strategy also used by English may be a factor favouring the 'winning out' of pre-posed over post-posed adjectives as part of this process (cf. Lass 1997: 200). In this case, we have two possible explanations for the change or, what is also likely, two mutually reinforcing processes. Despite the fact, then, that adjective placement in Guernesiais does seem to be moving towards the 'English' pattern (and in view of the current sociopolitical situation of the dialect, contact may indeed prove a likely explanation for the change) it is impossible to exclude either internal or external motivation here – and our explanation of the change should probably allow room for both.

2.10 Case study: Middle English

In Old English, there was no contrast between voiced and voiceless frica-tives. [v, ð, z] only appeared as allophones of the phonemes /f, θ, s/ in specific phonological environments (when the consonant was short, in medial pos-ition, and not followed by a voiceless consonant). Hence, /f/ is [f] in *faran* 'to go', *offrian* 'to offer' *wulf* 'wolf' but [v] in *ofer* 'over', and *wulfas* 'wolves' (Lass 1987: 124). During the ME period, however, these voiced allophones became independent phonemes of English – and have remained so up to the present day, contrasting in minimal pairs such as *vat* and *fat*, *vast* and *fast*.

Several explanations are possible for this change. The first is that the ME period saw the introduction of a large number of loanwords from French. Among these were words that had an initial [v] (such as *very*). Although this phone already existed in English and therefore did not represent a brand new sound it was, however, introduced into an environment from which it had hitherto been absent (word initially). In this environment there was therefore the potential for contrast (in words such as English *ferry* vs. French *very* (Lass 1987: 127)) which had been brought about by language contact.

However, this is not the only possible reason behind this development. ME also saw two internally motivated changes which probably contributed to the phonemicisation of the [f]/[v] distinction. The first of these was the loss of final unstressed vowels, which happened in the thirteenth and four-teenth centuries. This is illustrated in 2.10.a.

2.10.a The loss of unstressed vowels in Middle English

Old English	*lufu*	[luvu]	'love'
Early Middle English		[lo:və]	
Late Middle English		[lo:v]	

(Lass 1987: 128)

This sound change, therefore, had the effect of producing fully voiced word final fricatives – and established this as another new environment where [f]/[v] contrast was now possible (*lufe* [lo:v] vs. *luff* [lo:f]).

The second internal change involved the degemination of medial clusters to the corresponding simple consonant, which happened in the fourteenth century. This removed the constraint on medial contrast in all environments.

It will therefore be seen that in both adjective placement in Guernesiais and in the phonemicisation of the English [f]/[v] contrast, a role has been played by both internal and external factors. To concentrate exclusively on one type of change in this context would therefore be to lose sight of the whole picture. Mougeon and Beniak (1991: 218) define as ambiguous change such 'innovations which admit both an internal and an external explanation, and for which it is not possible to favour internal simplification over interference from the majority language, or vice versa'. Another term used for this phenomenon is 'multiple causation' (Thomason and Kaufman 1988: 57).

In these first two chapters, we have seen that language change comes in many shapes and forms. By turning to consider language birth and language death, we will now examine how related processes of change can, over time, have far-reaching effects on a linguistic system.

3   Language birth

3.1 Introduction

As we saw in Chapter 1, linguistics has long made use of biological and evolutionary metaphors to describe both languages and the changes they undergo: change has been referred to, for instance, as *development*, *progress* or indeed, *evolution*; obsolescent languages as *dying* and creole languages as *young*. It is therefore no surprise that such life-cycle metaphors have also included *birth* as a generic label for the emergence of new languages through processes of language change. Like its antonym *(language) death*, *(language) birth* has however proved to be a convenient but ultimately imperfect metaphor in its application to this kind of linguistic phenomena; imperfect largely because its inescapable biological connotations impose a misleading, or at the very least inaccurate, perspective on the nature of language systems and of linguistic change. For instance, birth carries connotations of 'parent' organisms, goal-oriented processes of formation and even of specific dates of emergence or 'birthdays'. It is of course arguable that certain processes in specific cases of language birth can be allegorised through the use of such concepts: pidgins and creoles, for instance, may be said to arise through contact between 'parent' super- and sub-stratal languages, and invented a posteriori systems (such as Esperanto) are also derived from a variety of natural languages, are often teleological in purpose and 'born' or launched at a specific time (see Chapter 7).

As the specificity of such examples imply, linguistic 'parents' and 'birthdays' are by no means ubiquitous to all situations of language birth. Indeed, putting aside for the moment cases that specifically emerge from contact situations, many instances of 'natural language birth' (that is, the birth of natural, as opposed to invented, languages) are at the very least partly attributable to factors such as population migration, change through intergenerational transmission and sociopolitical considerations. A particularly good example of this can be seen in the changes undergone by Latin when it was taken beyond its original Rome-based speech community to become the primary language of an extensive and geographically diverse empire. With significant numbers of new speakers across southern and western Europe and the Balkans, new dialects of vulgar or common Latin began to emerge, diverging not only from those spoken in Rome, but also from each other. The collapse of the Empire in the fifth century concomitantly destroyed any centralising political, cultural and linguistic authority that Rome may once have exerted and by the eighth century, the 'Latin of the Roman Empire [had] gradually dissolved into a vast dialect continuum' (Trask 1996: 178), so that

> a traveller crossing the former Empire in the 7th or 8th century would have found the language changing only very gradually in any direction. Any speaker could communicate easily with people within a few dozen kilometres, with some difficulty with people 200 or 300 kilometres away, and not at all with people farther away than that.
>
> (Trask 1996: 178)

By about the ninth century, these one-time dialects of Latin had diverged so substantially and become so entrenched as the native, indigenous tongues of different areas that they were being referred to not as Latin, but as Tuscan, Provençal, Castilian or Leonese, to name but a few. This sense of linguistic distinctiveness and discreteness would also have been strengthened by factors such as literary production in these tongues, as well as the cultivation and maintenance of individual national identities. Thus Castilian, which enjoyed both prestige and popularity as a literary medium in the twelfth century, eventually became known as Spanish, and not Castilian Latin. As Trask (1996: 178–9) notes, such labelling strategies have always ultimately been a matter of choice: 'we might', he states, 'if we chose, give . . . modern descendants of Latin names like *Parisian Latin*, and *Madrid Latin*, but no one has seen any point in this, and we speak instead of *French*, *Spanish*, *Italian* and so on'. And in this possibility of choice lies one of the fundamental characteristics of language birth, namely that it is not only a linguistic but also a psychological phenomenon; indeed, one that is arguably more heavily dependent on the birth of the *concept* of a new language than on the emergence of a system that is structurally entirely 'new'.

We will revisit this notion in this chapter's case studies of natural language birth, which highlight particular factors – such as population movement and linguistic divergence, contact and ideological issues – that seem to be important in the unfolding of this phenomenon. Our first case study (Section 3.2) outlines, in the context of migration and divergence, the hypothesised, pre-historic emergence of Proto-Germanic from Proto-Indo-European, and the later birth of (Old) English (OE) – a relatively well-documented language in its time-frame – from Proto-Germanic. Since features and patterns of Proto-Indo-European and of Proto-Germanic are not textually attested, we will confine later discussion of this case study to English. Section 3.3 looks at Tok Pisin, an instance of birth through contact, while Section 3.4 outlines the historical separation of Scots from English in the context of relevant ideological and sociopolitical perspectives. While each case study has been chosen to emphasise particular factors that can be important in language birth, it should be noted that they are by no means mutually exclusive, and their separation in this chapter is an artificial device adopted primarily for the sake of explanation.

3.2 Case study: Proto-Indo-European, Proto-Germanic and (Old) English

In the eighteenth and nineteenth centuries, the work of European philologists and scholars such as Sir William Jones, Rasmus Rask, Franz Bopp and Jacob Grimm formally established two of the fundamental cornerstones of historical linguistic work – the concept of linguistic relatedness, and the assumption of systematic diachronic change (at the very least in relation to phonology). Models such as August Schleicher's family tree for Indo-European languages (see Figure 3.2) not only captured the fact that individual languages over time engender new ones but also, importantly, reflected the belief that the processes which would give rise to such change were internally motivated: as Figure 3.2 shows, only one linguistic ancestor exists per node.

In addition, the contemporary distribution of languages within such a family clearly demonstrated that social processes such as migration must have played a significant role in catalysing change. Unsurprisingly, what we might term traditional historical linguistics therefore came to consider internally motivated change through intergenerational transmission – and in many cases, population dispersal into new environments – integral mechanisms of language birth (notions, incidentally, which would later be incorporated into Sapir's conceptualisation of social and linguistic drift; see Chapter 1).

It is noteworthy that this perspective has, over the course of the twentieth century, been expanded to acknowledge the significant role that factors such as contact may play in processes of language change. However, in cases of change and birth where records and textual data are limited or non-existent, explanations that emphasise what is *known* to occur in speech communities – namely, internally motivated, intergenerational change – have remained plausible and therefore established. Thus accounts of (pre-)historic birth have tended to emphasise factors such as geographical spread and concomitant linguistic divergence rather than contact, which may have occurred but remains unattested. The account of the emergence of modern Romance languages from Latin in Section 3.1 is one such example;[1] and we turn now to another in the dominant narrative of the (unattested) births of Proto-Germanic and of (Old) English.

Many students of historical linguistics are doubtless acquainted with Sir William Jones's 'The Third Anniversary Discourse' to the Asiatic Society in Calcutta (1786), in which he posited a 'strong affinity' between languages

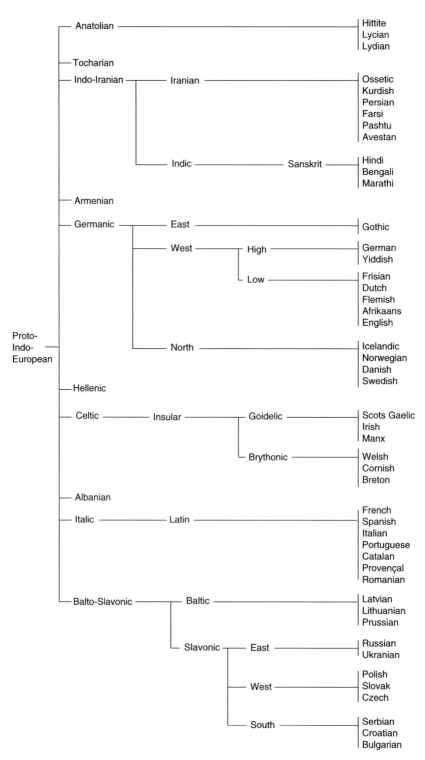

Figure 3.2 The Indo-European family
Source: Singh 2005: 51.

such as Sanskrit, Latin and Greek, 'so strong that no philologer could examine all the three without believing them to have sprung from some common
source which, perhaps, no longer exists.' That 'common source', or Proto-
Indo-European (PIE) as it came to be known, is thought to have been the
language of an ancestral Indo-European community whose life, given the
lack of historical record, has been the subject of much conjecture and
debate. V. Gordon Childe (1926) and Marija Gimbutas (1970), for example,
posited a homeland for the Indo-Europeans situated in the South Russian
steppes, and Gimbutas equated this ancestral community with a seemingly
warlike and nomadic Kurgan culture that appeared in the area in the fifth
and early fourth millennia BC. On the other hand, Colin Renfrew (1987),
Thomas V. Gamkrelidze and V.V. Ivanov (1990) have argued for a homeland
in Anatolia, which Renfrew has suggested was settled by Indo-Europeans as
early as the seventh millennium BC and made home to a peaceful, pastoral
community.

Debates over such issues are not easily resolved and, given the enormous
time-depth and lack of historical record, are unlikely to be definitively
settled soon, if ever. What does seem beyond question however, is the fact
that at some point in the BC era, members of this Indo-European community
began to move out of their original homeland and into other areas of Europe
and Asia. While explanations of the catalysts for such migration have
also differed,[2] what seems certain is that this 'social drift' (see Sapir 1921
[2000]) began a process of linguistic divergence not unlike that which
would be experienced much later by its descendant Latin as it dispersed
over the Empire. Thus, as PIE speakers became 'sufficiently disconnected to
drift apart' (Sapir 1921 [2000]: 1; see Chapter 1) into new and diverse areas,
dialectal divergence – both from each other and from the 'mother' speech
community – would necessarily have followed, eventually resulting in the
birth of new and distinct languages.

It is very likely that vast areas of Europe and Asia were unpopulated at the
time of these early migrations, so it seems plausible to assume that some
groups of PIE settlers did not, at least initially, experience contact with other,
non-Indo-European communities. It is possible, however, that others did:
evidence of contemporary non-Indo-European peoples remains, most
notably in the linguistic isolate Basque, which appears to have no known
relation to any existing language family, and also in place names such as
Athens, Corinth and the *Scandi-* in *Scandinavia*, which are not PIE in
origin.[3]

Contact, however, does not seem to have had significant effects on the
fundamental, Indo-European structure of PIE's descendants, which display
striking similarities in cognate vocabulary and grammatical patterns, as well
as systematic phonological correspondences. Such data has allowed not only
for the plausible reconstruction of posited ancestral languages for which
no linguistic record exists – such as Proto-Celtic, Proto-Italic and ultimately,
of course, Proto-Indo-European – but also for a reasoned approach to

understanding the changes that are likely to have taken place in these languages over the centuries.

We take, as our example, one of PIE's posited daughter languages, Proto-Germanic. Available evidence suggests that a community of Indo-European descendants, whom the Romans at the beginning of the Christian era would call the *Germani*, had come to settle in the north of Europe, possibly in a small area of southern Scandinavia. They appear to have been a culturally homogenous group who spoke what has come to be known as Proto-Germanic, one of the early daughters of PIE. Reconstructions of PIE (on the basis of data from various daughter languages) and of Proto-Germanic (on the basis of data from Germanic languages such as English, Dutch, Yiddish and Flemish) suggest that the centuries of separation between mother and daughter cultures had engendered a measure of linguistic divergence. For instance, PIE appears to have been a synthetic language, making substantial use of a range of inflectional markers across syntactic classes. While Proto-Germanic is thought to have retained much of this synthetic character, it seems likely that it did so in a reduced version of PIE systems. For example, it is hypothesised that PIE made use of at least eight cases, of which Proto-Germanic essentially retained five: the nominative, accusative, dative, genitive and instrumental (Barber (1993: 89) notes that only traces of the vocative and locative remained in Proto-Germanic). In terms of number, PIE speakers are thought to have distinguished between singular, plural and dual; the latter of which is only vestigially preserved in Proto-Germanic. Similarly, in terms of verbs, Proto-Germanic appears to have maintained only present and past tense inflections from a much more extensive PIE system.

In another characteristic trait of divergence, Proto-Germanic also innovated features not shared by its PIE ancestor. For instance, PIE nouns and modifiers appear to have carried inflectional agreement in terms of case, gender and number, and adjectives carried the same inflections as the nouns they qualified. However, Proto-Germanic speakers also made use of *strong* and *weak* adjectival declensions, a distinction which survived into daughter languages such as OE. In the latter, weak forms were used when preceded by a determiner (as in *se gōda cyning* 'the good king'), and strong forms when not (as in *gōd cyning* 'good king'). Another Proto-Germanic innovation was the creation of *weak verbs*, or verbs whose past tenses and past participles are formed through the addition of an alveolar suffix (as in modern *walk ~ walked ~ (had) walked*). These appear to have existed alongside *strong verbs* – or verbs which yielded past tense and past participle forms through *ablaut*, or vowel change (as in modern *sing > sang > (have) sung*) – inherited from PIE.

It is, however, in the realms of phonology that we see some of the clearest indications of Proto-Germanic's divergence, not only from its PIE ancestor but from its sister languages as well. One of the best-known pieces of evidence for this lies in the set of consonantal changes known collectively as the First Germanic Consonant Shift. Formalised by the philologist Jacob

Grimm, and hence sometimes known as Grimm's Law, the Shift (a simplified version of which is provided in 3.2.a) entailed changes to PIE aspirated voiced plosives, and unaspirated voiced and voiceless plosives, in Proto-Germanic. These changes proved to be remarkably consistent, as is evident in cognate data comparisons between descendants of Proto-Germanic, such as Old Norse (ON) and OE, and non-Germanic languages such as Latin and Sanskrit, which are thought to have instead largely preserved the original PIE consonantal values.

3.2.a First Germanic Consonant Shift

PIE unaspirated voiceless plosives	*> Proto-Germanic voiceless fricatives*	
*p (Sanskrit *purna-*)	> f (OE *full*, ON *fullr*)	full
*t (Latin *tonare*)	> θ (OE *þunor*, ON *þorr*)	thunder
*k (Latin *canis*)	> h (OE *hund*, ON *hund*)	hound

PIE unaspirated voiced plosives	*> Proto-Germanic voiceless plosives*	
*b (Latin *cannabis*)	> p (OE *hænep*, ON *hampr*)	hemp
*d (Sanskrit *dant-*)	> t (OE *tōþ*, ON *tönn*)	tooth
*g (Latin *grānum*)	> k (OE *corn*, ON *korn*)	corn

PIE aspirated voiced plosives	*> Proto-Germanic voiced plosives*	
*bh (Sanskrit *bhrātar*)	> b (OE *brōþor*, ON *bróðir*)	brother
*dh (Sanskrit *dhwar*)	> d (OE *duru*, ON *dyrr*)	door
*gh (Sanskrit *ghost-*)	> g (OE *giest*, ON *gest-r*)	guest

(an asterisk indicates a reconstructed form)

Another important phonological change from PIE to Proto-Germanic, and one which would have repercussions for Grimm's Law, involved change in *accent*. In a syllable, accent depends partly on stress as well as on intonation, although in some languages, speakers rely more on one than the other. It is thought that PIE speakers made more use of intonation than stress, and also utilised what is known as *free accent*, or the placing of accent on any syllable of a word regardless of whether it comprised the stem, an affix or an inflection. In Proto-Germanic however, speakers appear to have confined accent mainly to the first syllable of a word, and also to have depended more on stress than intonation. This change eventually had significant consequences in daughter languages such as English, where the continuing tendency to 'de-stress' final syllables would lead to the loss of certain inflections. For instance, OE nouns in the dative plural ended in an inflectional *-um* (as in *hundum* 'dogs', *dēorum* 'animals'). This appears to have undergone, in the ME period (1300–1500), change to *-en* and eventually to unstressed *schwa*, spelt *-e* (as in *hunde*, *dēore*).

In relation to Grimm's Law, this change in accent obscured one of the conditions which governed the production of apparent exceptions to the Shift. For instance, the Germanic languages sometimes have [d] or [ð] where Grimm's Law predicts [θ], as can be seen in cognates such as OE *fæder*,

ON *faðir*, and Gothic *fadar*. Initially classed as irregularities, such seeming anomalies were plausibly explained by a modification to Grimm's Law – Verner's Law – which postulated that the predicted *PIE voiceless plosives* > *Proto-Germanic voiceless fricatives* shift had indeed taken place, but that a subsequent voicing change had applied when the fricatives occurred between voiced sounds, and when the preceding syllable had been unstressed. Such conditions had been salient for words such as *father*, in which the consonant occurred medially between voiced vowels and where historically, the first syllable had been unstressed. The later change in Proto-Germanic accent described above had however, obliterated any trace of this latter conditioning factor.

In about 300 BC, the Proto-Germanic community began another wave of migrations, possibly because of overpopulation. According to Barber (1993: 83), 'over the course of a few centuries they pushed northwards up the Scandinavian peninsula into territory occupied by the Finns . . . westwards beyond the Elbe, into North-West Germany and the Netherlands . . . eastwards round the shores of the Baltic Sea . . . [and] southwards into Bohemia and later into South-West Germany'. As a result, Proto-Germanic itself began to undergo a process of divergence, eventually splitting into North Germanic, West Germanic and East Germanic (see Figure 3.2).

Sometime in the fifth century (the seventh-century monk Bede gives the date AD 449) dialects of West Germanic, spoken by Angles, Saxons, Jutes and Frisians, travelled to an abandoned outpost of the Roman Empire which was at the time home to (now) distant relatives in the Indo-European family, the Celts. The Germanic migrants, who have become known to posterity generically but somewhat misleadingly as the Anglo-Saxons, became the dominant settlers on what would eventually be called English soil, and in this new environment their dialects inevitably continued to change and diverge from their continental Germanic sisters. Interestingly, these processes of change appear to have not been significantly influenced by the Celtic tongues, and it seems that interaction between these distant cousins was characterised more by hostility than camaraderie. Indeed, the Anglo-Saxons tellingly called the Celts 'foreigners' or *wealas*, the word from which modern *Wales* is derived.

Thus, it seems plausible to assume that between the fifth and eighth centuries – essentially, the time span between the first Germanic landings and the extensive Scandinavian settlements that would begin in England after 878 – what would become known as *Englisc* (and which we will refer to here as OE for convenience) underwent processes of intergenerational change which moved it further away from its Proto-Germanic ancestor. Indeed, reconstructions of this early stage of OE (based on available data, which dates mainly from the tenth and eleventh centuries) suggest the similar patterns of retention, reduction and innovation observed earlier in relation to PIE and Proto-Germanic. For instance, the five cases of Proto-Germanic were largely reduced to four in OE, which did not make extensive use of the instrumental; and dual number was retained only in the pronoun system: OE made use of forms such as *wit* ('we both'), *unc* ('us both'), *git* ('you both') and *inc* ('you both'). The various noun declensions which Proto-Germanic had inherited from PIE, in which nouns conformed to different inflectional patterns marking case, gender and number, were reduced in OE. In addition, the inflectional endings of OE noun declensions had themselves undergone reduction, falling together into identical forms both across and within paradigms. This syncretism also affected adjectival inflections for agreement, and was additionally evident in forms of the determiner *the* which, as in its Proto-Germanic and PIE ancestors, agreed with the case, gender and number of the nouns they modified. The data in 3.2.b, which illustrates plural noun and modifier use (here, determiner plus adjective), exemplifies the reduction of distinctive inflected forms in OE.

3.2.b OE plural nouns and modifiers (determiner + adjective)

	'the good men' (masculine gender)	'the good women' (feminine gender)	'the good children' (neuter gender)
Plural nominative and accusative	þā gōdan guman	þā gōdan idesa	þā gōdan cildru
Plural dative	þǣm gōdum gumum	þǣm gōdum idesum	þǣm gōdum cildrum
Plural genitive	þāra gōdra/gōdena gumena	þāra gōdra/gōdena idesa	þāra gōdra/gōdena cildra

In terms of verbs, OE retained the Proto-Germanic distinction between weak and strong, but OE speakers appear to have made the majority of verbs conform to the weak verb paradigm (which, indeed, has become the only productive paradigm for English). OE also retained the Proto-Germanic two-tense system but not the latter's passive inflections, which remained evident in Germanic languages such as Gothic (descended from East Germanic), as in *haita* 'I call' ~ *haitada* 'I am called' (Barber 1993: 91).

Phonological changes also marked the transition from Proto-Germanic to OE and, indeed, many of these changes were not shared by the latter's Germanic cousins. Thus, it appears that Proto-Germanic *ai* and *au*, for instance, which were retained in languages such as Gothic, respectively became OE *ā* and *ēa* (as in Gothic *stains* 'stone' ~ OE *stān*; Gothic *ausō* 'ear' ~ OE *ēare*). Finally, certain words underwent a process known as *front mutation* (or *i-mutation, umlaut*) in OE, which was not necessarily paralleled in the other Germanic languages. This process of assimilation could occur when a syllable preceded another containing a conditioning front vowel such as [i]. Eventually, the conditioning sound became lost, leaving an altered vowel in the stem. For instance, *mūs* ('mouse') once had a plural form **mūsiz*. Assimilation to the vowel in the second syllable changed the initial vowel to *y*, and subsequent sound changes resulted in the loss of conditioning [i] in *-iz*, leaving *mys*. Much later sound changes in English, such as those involved in the Great Vowel Shift, would yield the modern [aɪ] pronunciation of *mice*. Front mutation also produced singular/plural pairs such as *foot ~ feet* (*fōt ~ *fōti*), *goose ~ geese* (*gōs ~ *gōsi*), and semantically related pairs such as *full* and *fill* (the latter from earlier **fulljan*).

A sample of OE is given in 3.2.c:

3.2.c Excerpt from *Deor*
Wē þæt Mǣðhilde   mōne gefrugnon
wurdon grundlēase   Gēates frīge,
þæt hī sēo sorglufu   slǣp ealle binōm.
þæs oferēode,   þisses swā mæg.

We know that Meathhild the sad wife of Geat
Had endless cause for tears and lamentation.
Unhappy love deprived her of all sleep.
That passed away, and so may this from me.

(Hamer 1970: 90–1)

Overall, the prehistoric 'splitting' of PIE into daughter languages (such as Proto-Germanic) and their subsequent (early) divergences, as in the chain of change from Proto-Germanic to early OE, have been considered classic situations of language birth in the historical linguistic tradition, dependent primarily on intergenerational, internally motivated change. It is noteworthy too that the generally accepted history of a language such as English – at least up until its Early Modern period – has also traditionally stressed the importance of such change over that catalysed by contact: a perspective that has in recent years engendered debate and, consequently, alternative historical narratives. We will not pursue this extensive range of research here[4] but turn now to a case in which contact has played a primary role in the emergence of a new system: Tok Pisin in Papua New Guinea.

3.3 Case study: Tok Pisin

In the field of pidgin and creole studies, Tok Pisin, or New Guinea Pidgin, is perhaps one of the best-known and most extensively researched languages. Considered one of the offshoots of Melanesian Pidgin English (MPE) (others are Bislama in Vanuatu and Pijin in the Solomon Islands), it has come to serve as both native language and lingua franca in an area of vast linguistic diversity – Papua New Guinea is estimated to have some 750 languages, and Melanesia as a whole is thought to be home to over 900. In addition, Tok Pisin has been granted official recognition as one of the national languages of Papua New Guinea (alongside English and Hiri Motu), despite which perceptions of its inferior status vis-à-vis English still persist. This is not, however, an unusual attitude towards pidgins and creoles which, as the linguistic results of trading and colonial contact, have long been dismissed as

the 'broken' and 'bastardised' versions of the languages of the more powerful trading/colonising partner. Indeed, such attitudes have only begun to be
addressed and deconstructed in the twentieth century as the study of pidgins
and creoles as adequate systems born of contact has progressed. We will
return to the question of attitudes later in this section after a brief consideration of pidgins and of the specific history of Tok Pisin.[5]

In linguistics, pidgins and creoles have traditionally been linked in what
has come to be known as a *pidgin > creole life cycle*, in which pidgins
constitute an early, rudimentary, auxiliary system created and used in
contact between adult groups natively speaking mutually unintelligible
languages; and creoles, the later result of a pidgin's *nativisation* as a mother
tongue for new generations born into the pidgin-using context (see Singh
2000). We note that this perspective has not gone unquestioned, and many
creolists acknowledge that an early pidgin stage is not integral to the birth
of a creole (see in particular Bickerton 1981). Recently, creolists such as
Mufwene (2001: 8–9) have argued that the contact environments which
gave rise to pidgins were in fact socio-economically and consequently, sociolinguistically distinct from those which produced creoles, and that assumptions of a *pidgin > creole* line of change, as well as of the role of nativisation
in creolisation, therefore have to be treated with caution. Mufwene (2001:
8–9) instead suggests, on the basis of available evidence, that creoles tended
to be born in settlement colonies where contact was initially 'regular and
intimate' between the colonised (usually slaves in this context) and the
colonisers; whereas pidgins typically emerged as basic communication systems in contact situations defined in the first instance by trade. If, following
initial contact, primarily 'commercial' colonies emerged, pidgins very likely
continued to be used, undergoing stabilisation and expansion.

The postulated emergence of MPE certainly fits this particular template.
It appears to have had its beginnings in various (trading) contact situations
between English speakers and Melanesians during the nineteenth century.
In the 1820s, English, American and Australian interests lay in whaling near
the Melanesian islands, and later extended to the region's trade in sandalwood and an edible, allegedly aphrodisiac sea-slug known as beach-la-mar
(from Portuguese *bicho de mar* 'creature of the sea'; the name survives in
Vanuatu's Bislama). Trade in the latter two commodities (in particular of
beach-la-mar, which had to be cleaned, boiled and smoked prior to ship-
ment) necessitated close contact between English speakers and the islanders;
and the result was a trade language known as Beach-la-mar, or Sandalwood
English (Holm 1989: 527).

Beach-la-mar was an 'unstable pre-pidgin with considerable fluctuation
from place to place and speaker to speaker' (Holm 1989: 527) which would
lay the foundations for the emergence of Melanesian Pidgin. In the 1860s,
the British set up cotton and sugar plantations in Queensland, Australia and
began importation of indentured labour from Melanesia. Over the following
forty-five years, approximately 60,000 Melanesian indentured labourers

travelled to these plantations, and a number of others to smaller German-run copra plantations in Samoa. Initially, the majority of labourers on the Queensland plantations came from the Solomon islands and the New Hebrides, while those who went to Samoa largely came from New Guinea. In the late 1870s, workers from other areas (many of whom had already worked in Queensland) began indentureship in Samoa, and between 1883 and 1884, inhabitants of New Guinea travelled to the Queensland plantations.

Although, as just indicated, significant numbers of plantation workers ultimately came from the same geographical region, they did not necessarily share the same language. This must have been particularly problematic on the Queensland plantations, which employed large numbers of workers. It is likely though that a significant proportion of these islanders knew – and therefore began to use – Beach-la-mar as a lingua franca; usage that would have been concomitant with linguistic stabilisation and functional expansion. If this was indeed the case, then the Queensland plantations were very likely the 'cradle' of Melanesian Pidgin English (Wurm 1966).[6] We should note however that, in the case of the genesis of Tok Pisin, the use of MPE in other plantation settings proved to be important: the late nineteenth-century movement of ex-Queensland workers to Samoan plantations took MPE into a new environment, as well as to the New Guinean labourers who were in the majority there (see above). In Samoa, it therefore began to diverge and stabilise into a variety somewhat different from that in Queensland (Mühlhäusler 1976).

When indentureship contracts ended, labourers returning to their native islands took the pidgin with them, where it continued to serve as a useful lingua franca and inevitably, to change under the influence of the local indigenous languages as well as those spoken by the relevant colonising powers. In New Guinea, the latter languages were English and German: in 1884, south-eastern New Guinea was made a protectorate of Britain and north-eastern New Guinea (renamed Kaiser Wilhelmsland), of Germany. 'Samoan MPE' appears to have continued in use initially on plantations established in New Guinea, where it proved an indispensable communication tool, not only among the workforce (including new recruits) but also between labourers and colonisers as well. This was particularly the case in German New Guinea, where despite some reluctance about using a communication system based on the language of their British rivals, 'the early establishment of the pidgin solved their [the Germans'] most pressing problems in communicating with the inhabitants of the Bismarck Archipelago, where their first plantations and trading centers were located' (Holm 1989: 530; our insertion).

The pidgin that would eventually produce Tok Pisin therefore continued to stabilise in late nineteenth-century New Guinea and ultimately began to be used as a lingua franca outside of the plantation setting.[7] The expansion of its use into new domains was concomitant (as is the case for all languages) with structural expansion: in other words, the linguistic resources of Tok

Pisin increased as its use for different purposes grew. This functional and structural expansion has continued: today, Tok Pisin is used in radio and television broadcasts, newspapers (including the Tok Pisin-medium paper *Wantok*), government publications and biblical translation.

Tok Pisin therefore functions like other systems whose status as languages is established (such as English, German, Ewe, Chinese and so on) apart from one significant fact: the majority of people who use it are native speakers of other languages. In pidgin and creole studies, this has meant that Tok Pisin has long been categorised as an *expanded pidgin*, since an accepted trait of pidgins is a lack of native speakers. However, the second half of the twentieth century has seen increasing use of Tok Pisin in domestic settings, especially in urban areas where members of different language groups – but with Tok Pisin in common – have set up home together. Children born into these environments have therefore acquired Tok Pisin as a native language, making it, in the established *pidgin > creole* framework, a creole. Its status as pidgin or creole is, however, by no means settled: Siegel (undated) points out that each classification has its supporters and detractors. The issue is further problematised by approaches such as Mufwene's (cited earlier) which do not see the acquisition of native speakers as a prerequisite for the emergence of a creole. This debate notwithstanding, Tok Pisin remains, for our purposes, a system born of contact and we end this section with a brief outline of some of its linguistic features.

As indicated earlier, MPE diverged into different daughters in individual environments, and under the influence of continuing contact with both indigenous and colonisers' languages. In the case of Tok Pisin, features and processes have therefore been drawn in part from Austronesian languages such as Tolai, as well as from German and English, the latter of which has also served as the primary lexifier. Thus, the majority of Tok Pisin vocabulary is derived from English, but also incorporates items from German (such as *gumi* 'rubber', *beten* 'to pray', *bros* 'chest') and Tolai (as in *lapun* 'old', *kiau* 'egg' and *palai* 'lizard'). The sound system also shows influence from these various 'parents': as Holm (1989: 533) states for instance, 'the phonetic qualities of the consonant allophones are largely unlike English and are reminiscent of those of local languages . . . e.g. /r/ can be realised as an alveolar or retroflex flap . . .; some stops have fricative allophones and labial fricatives are mostly bilabial rather than labio-dental'. In addition, Tok Pisin also has pre-nasalised stops, as in *ndai* 'die'. Tok Pisin also makes use of [s] and [p] where English has [ʃ] and [f] respectively (English *shell*, *fish* and *fellow* are therefore Tok Pisin *sel*, *pis* and *pela*) and like German, has word-final devoicing of consonants, as in *rot* 'road' and *pik* 'pig'.

While certain Tok Pisin features and processes appear to have clear parallels in one or more of the source languages, there are many others that, importantly, may be classed as Tok Pisin innovations. For instance, many Tok Pisin words have remained similar in form to their sources but have diverged semantically. Thus, Tok Pisin *baksait* refers literally to someone's back and not to the posterior region, *kilim* (< *kill him*) can mean 'hit' or 'beat', *pisin* (< *pigeon*) 'bird' and *gras*, 'grass', 'hair', 'fur' and 'feathers'. Tok Pisin pronouns are also, in terms of form, derived from English pronouns but signal distinctions common to the Austronesian languages. For instance, pronouns express singular (*yu* 'you'), dual (*yutupela* 'you two'), trial (*yutripela* 'you three') and plural (*yupela* 'you all'). In addition, Tok Pisin makes a distinction between 'inclusive' and 'exclusive' in 'we' pronouns. Thus, forms of 'we' such as *yumi*, *yumitupela* and *yumitripela* include the person being spoken to, but *mitupela* ('we two'), *mitripela* ('we three') and *mipela* ('we all') do not.

Pela is not only used in Tok Pisin pronouns, but is also suffixed to certain categories of adjectives and numerals (as in *tripela/wanpela pik* 'three/one pig(s)', *bikpela haus* 'big house'). *Ol* is typically used as a plural marker, and is inserted before the relevant noun, as in *mi lukim dok* ~ *mi lukim ol dok* ('I saw the dog' ~ 'I saw the dogs'). In terms of verbs, Tok Pisin makes use of a predicate marker *i* in sentences where the subject is a noun as opposed to a pronoun (apart from *em* 'he/she/it'), as in *mi wok* 'I worked' but *Tom i wok* 'Tom worked'. Verbs can also carry a transitive suffix *-im*, which is used when preceding a direct object, as in *em i rit* 'he is reading' but *em i ritim buk* 'he is reading a book'. Finally, Tok Pisin makes use of a range of tense and aspect markers. *Bin*, for instance, is an optional tense marker which precedes the main verb, as in *Tom i bin wok asde* 'Tom worked yesterday', but the future marker *bai* can precede or follow the subject, as in *Tom bai i wok tumora* 'Tom will work tomorrow' or *bai ol i wokim house* 'sometime in the future, they will build a house' (Wurm 1977: 524). *Save* is used as a pre-verbal habitual marker *Tom i save wok long Sarere* 'Tom works on Saturday', and post-verbal *i stap* is used to indicate an action in progress, as in *Tom i wok i stap* 'Tom is working'. *Pinis* is used post-verbally to indicated completed action, as in *Tom i wok pinis* 'Tom is finished working'.

A sample of Tok Pisin, excerpted from the *Universal Declaration of Human Rights*, is given in 3.3.a:

3.3.a Universal Declaration of Human Rights
Tok Pisin

Long luksave olsem olgeta manmeri mas igat respek, na olgeta manmeri long dispela graun igat wankain raits long bihainim laik bilong ol, long gat lo na oda na gat gutpela sindaun.

Long ol hap nambaut taim manmeri i no luksave long raits bilong ol narapela manmeri, dispela tingting we ol manmeri mas gat fridom long toktok, gat fridom blong igat bilip, fridom long noken poret na fridom long laikim ol kainkain samting. Dispela em i bikpela samting bilong olgeta manmeri.

English
Whereas recognition of the inherent dignity and of the equal and inalienable rights of all members of the human family is the foundation of freedom, justice and peace in the world,

Whereas disregard and contempt for human rights have resulted in barbarous acts which have outraged the conscience of mankind, and the advent of a world in which human beings shall enjoy freedom of speech and belief and freedom from fear and want has been proclaimed as the highest aspiration of the common people, . . .

Tok Pisin, therefore, is clearly a system born of contact and like the languages in Section 3.2, displays both a measure of continuity with 'ancestral' forms as well as structural distinctiveness, the latter of which may play some part in determining whether a system is classed as 'new'. Another important consideration in language birth which we have not emphasised in these two case studies however, is the ideological: a dimension we will explore in our third and final case study, Scots.

3.4 Case study: Scots

With the modern, increasing focus on the global spread of English and its frequent association with indigenous linguistic and cultural loss, many today are aware of Scotland as being one of the last repositories in Britain – along with Ireland and Wales – of the nation's once thriving Celtic past, now partly embodied in endangered languages such as Scots Gaelic, Irish Gaelic and Welsh. Less well known however, is the fact that another tongue, also considered to be endangered and equally worthy of preservation, exists alongside Gaelic in Scotland, namely Scots. As in other cases of language endangerment, Scots has suffered the lack of social prestige and associations with social advancement that a language such as English has long possessed. This, however, has been complicated by the fact that Scots has oftentimes been characterised as a dialect of English (and indeed, denigrated as 'bad English'), making attempts at official recognition and promotion difficult. We will return to this point later, but begin with a brief discussion of the linguistic lineage of Scots.

The roots of Scots partly lie in the Old English spoken in what are now considered the Lowlands of Scotland, but which were once part of the Anglo-Saxon kingdom of Northumbria (whose northern border ran as far as Edinburgh). The more northern territories of modern Scotland had been home to Pictish communities (about whom little is known), and were invaded by Celtic tribes from Ireland known as the Gaelic Del Riata (whom the Romans called *Scoti*), possibly from about 750 BC. Two kingdoms, Pictish and Del Riata, came to coexist (often in hostility) until the ninth century, when they united under the Pictish king Constantine (AD 811–820) possibly as a consequence of the Viking raids which were beginning to severely threaten the economic and social well-being of the land. In 847, both kingdoms merged as Alba under Kenneth MacAlpin (originally King of the Del Riata). Such merger also appears to have had linguistic consequences: eventually the Picts assimilated to the Gaelic of their neighbours.

Alba was bordered in the south by the kingdom of Strathclyde (home to Celtic Britons) and the Anglo-Saxon (but predominantly Angle) settlement of Lothian, areas which eventually merged with Alba in the eleventh century as a result of the territorial campaigns of its king Malcolm II (1005–34). The extension of Alba's borders to include Lothian in particular brought Anglo-Saxon speakers into the predominantly Gaelic-using kingdom and began the process through which Scots would eventually emerge.

Malcolm III (1057–93) and his son David I (1124–53) attempted to reshape the Scottish monarchy along English lines, and subsumed in this was the preference of both monarchs for (Old) English (specifically, the Old Northumbrian dialect) over Gaelic. This royal bias was furthered in the thirteenth century when, as a result of the dearth of the Celtic royal line, the throne of Alba passed to Lowland families such as Balliol, Bruce and Stewart. Indeed, the seat of royal power also physically moved southwards from Perth to Edinburgh, the latter of which had once been part of (Old) English-speaking territory. Inevitably, this almost continuous process of Anglicisation of, and by, the monarchy served not only to create psychological and cultural distance from the Gaelic-speaking Highlands, but also to cement an association between English and 'modernity ... trade and commercial opportunity, enterprise and prosperity' (Fennell 2001: 192).

Lowland English therefore came to be increasingly used (alongside Latin) in court and government administration, and from the late fourteenth century, a national literature – typically dated from Barbour's *Brus* (1375) and including the late fifteenth- to sixteenth-century poetry of Gavin Douglas and William Dunbar – emerged in this local vernacular. The production of prose-writing grew steadily throughout the sixteenth century, and included translations, biblical adaptations, religious works as well as legal and medical treatises (Görlach 1991: 18).

The fifteenth century also saw the emergence of a new 'language consciousness' when the Lowland vernacular, typically called *Ynglis*, began instead to be labelled *Scottis*. As is often the case, a new political perspective entailed new language: *Scots/Scottis* had originally labelled the (Goidelic) Celtic of the Del Riata settlers and, by the late fourteenth century, referred generally to the 'vernacular of the entire area north of the dividing line between the estuaries of the Forth and Clyde' (Ward et al. 2000: 2); in essence, the boundaries of the old Alban kingdom. *Scots* had therefore denoted the 'national' (Gaelic) language of Alba before its boundaries had been extended southwards. With the latter expansion, and the subsequent Anglicisation policies of monarchs such as Malcolm III and his successors, the ideological as well as political map had changed: as this 'wider political idea of a *Scotland*' emerged, '*Ynglis* [became] the name of the speech of the "Scottish" court . . . and *Scots* that of the speech of the northern and western provinces' (Ward et al. 2000: 3). Ward et al. (2000: 3) also note that in this context, Scots was sometimes used as a pejorative term of reference for the language of 'savages' and 'brokin men'. However, by the fifteenth century, a growing sense of distinctive national identity, no doubt fuelled by political tensions with England, rendered *Ynglis* problematic: as the language of the 'auld enemy', it 'no longer commended itself to northern patriotism' (Ward et al. 2000: 4). The term *Scots* was therefore appropriated to refer to the politically dominant language of the new Scotland.

It is important to note however, that the separation of Scots and English was not just ideologically but linguistically based. Middle Scots (as it has come to be known) made use of, for instance, distinctive orthographic conventions such as *quh/qhu* (pronounced [hw]) and *ch* (pronounced [x] medially) where English used *wh* and *gh* respectively, as in *qhwair* 'where', *quhat* 'what', *nicht* 'night' and *bricht* 'bright'. The letter *i* was also inserted after stem vowels in certain words to indicate length, as in *rois* [ro:z] 'rose' and *haim* [ha:m] 'home'.

In terms of pronunciation, OE long ō became rounded [y:] in northern English-speaking areas (remaining [o:] in the south) and was signalled in spelling by *u/ui*, as in Middle Scots *guid* 'good', *fud/fuid* 'food'. In addition, OE long ā had rounded to [ɔ] south of the Humber (as indicated in southern Middle English *bon* and *stoon* (OE *bān* 'bone' and *stān* 'stone') but had remained [a:] in the north (as in Scots *haim*; above). This eventually changed in Scots to [e:], as can be seen in spellings such as *hame* 'home' and *stane* 'stone'. From about the late sixteenth century, all vowels in Scots, apart from /ɪ/, /ʌ/ and /ɛ/ underwent lengthening before voiced fricatives, /r/ (Middle Scots appears to have been rhotic) and word or morpheme boundaries: a conditioned change known as the Scottish Vowel Length Rule and still observable in Scots pronunciations such as *bee* [bi:] (versus *bean* [bin]), *tied* [ta:ɪd] (versus *tide* [tʌɪd]) and *peer* [pi:r] (versus *peel* [pil]). It is noteworthy that modern Scots has retained many of these features: it is, for instance, still rhotic and *ui* ([y:]) is still used, as is medial *ch* ([x]). Middle Scots *quh/qhu* has been replaced by *wh* in modern written Scots, but the pronunciation of this sequence remains [hw].

Scots also made use of inflectional morphology distinct in form from that of southern English such as, for instance, present participle *-and* (as in *simuland* 'feigning') and plural *-is* (as in *wayis* 'ways'). Inflectional *-is* also served as a possessive suffix (*moderis breast* 'mother's breast') and as the third-person singular inflection (as in *he takis* 'he takes'). Verbs used in the present tense with second-person pronouns would also take *-es*, as in *thee takes* 'you take'. Again, it is worth noting that many such features have been retained in modern Scots and, indeed, were consciously and deliberately incorporated into literary Scots in later centuries.

Yet, as a result of political, economic and cultural factors, Scots did not gain the same kind of 'affirmation' as a national language that others such as English, French and German did from the Renaissance period onwards. Indeed, it is arguable that the authority gained by English as *the* language of the modern nation-state through media such as increased literary production (significantly facilitated by both printing and a growing literate audience) and biblical translation cast Scots in the shadows. Thus, the emulation of English authors such as Chaucer in the work of Scottish court poets (or *makars*) – notably William Dunbar and Gavin Douglas – reinforced not only the prestige of English as a literary medium but also, in their extensive incorporation of (southern) English vocabulary and phraseology into Scots, the perception of the latter as a *dialect* of English. In terms of printing, the range and quantity of Scots publications produced in Edinburgh never surpassed the output of London. Indeed, by the start of the seventeenth century, the production of English titles in Edinburgh had increased significantly while Scots had effectively 'ceased to be a book language except for antiquarian purposes' (Görlach 1991: 19).

English was also promoted at the expense of Scots through the work of Protestant religious reformers such as John Knox, who wrote almost exclusively in English. In addition, although adaptations of the Bible into Scots were made in the sixteenth century, a Scots Bible was never printed, a 'failing' which essentially reinforced the autonomy of the English Bible in Scotland and, simultaneously, the authority of English vis-à-vis Scots. Finally but importantly, the explicit royal preference for English (and English culture) over Scots – as exemplified by James VI of Scotland's (later James I of England's) literary output, which unequivocally demonstrates an increasing use of English (see Görlach 1991: 20, 350–3) – doubtless aided in cementing the prestige of the 'southern language'. As Görlach (1991: 20) notes, 'In view of such tendencies, and the flow of English books onto the Scottish market, it is not surprising that neither writers nor printers used pure Scots between 1575 and 1603, and that their texts are marked by deliberate or unconscious interference from English.' Thus, by the time of the 1603 Union of Crowns, which effectively shifted the seat of Scotland's political power to London, the Anglicisation of Scots and Scottish culture had already been well underway for at least half a century.

The de facto status of English as the sociopolitically dominant language of Scotland was furthered by the 1707 Act of Union while Scots, now disparagingly referred to as *Doric*, became increasingly associated with rural, 'non-progressive' society. Such perspectives were doubtless reinforced in the nineteenth century, when English usurped Scots as the language of the classroom, a change that was formalised in the 1872 Act of Education.

We should note, however, that Scots did remain a thriving home language and continued to be used as a literary medium during the seventeenth and eighteenth centuries. Indeed, the latter century is typically associated with a revival of literary Scots in the work of *scrievnars* such as Robert Fergusson

(1750–74), Robert Burns (1759–96) and Walter Scott (1771–1832). This literary movement has continued, with occasional periods of significant public awareness and interest, such as with Hugh MacDiarmid's work in the 1920s and Irvine Welsh's *Trainspotting* in 1996. However, as Barber (1993: 174) points out, writing of this kind is still perceived as constituting a *dialect-*, rather than *national-*, *literature*, largely because English remains dominant in practically every literary genre, as well as in non-literary texts.

Nonetheless, the twentieth century has seen the formation of various organisations dedicated to increasing the use, and improving the status, of both written and spoken Scots: the Scottish National Dictionary Association was formed in the 1920s, and the Scots Leid Associe (Scots Language Society), from which extract 3.4.a is taken, in 1972.

3.4.a From the Scots Leid Associe homepage
Scots
The Scots Leid Associe wis foondit in 1972 an aye ettles ti pit forrit a feckfu case for the Scots language in leiterature, drama, the media, education an ilka day uiss. Sen Scots wis aince the state language o Scotland, an is aye a grace til oor national leiterature, it lies at the hert o Scotland's heirskep. The Associe threips on the view that Scots maun staun its ben as ane o three leids o the kintra, alang wi Gaelic an Inglis.

English
The Scots Language Society was founded in 1972 and constantly endeavours to make a strong case for the Scots language in literature, drama, the media, education and every day use. Since Scots was once the state language of Scotland, and continues to be a vital force in our national litera-ture, it lies at the very heart of Scotland's heritage. The Society's belief is that Scots must maintain its status as one of the three languages of the country, along with Gaelic and English.

Reference books, dictionaries and grammars of Scots have also been pro-duced in abundance, and courses on the language, its history and change over the centuries are offered at the universities of Edinburgh, Glasgow and Aberdeen. Educational and general governmental policy has also come to officially acknowledge Scots: in the 1990s, the ban on the use of Scots in the classroom was revoked (although no official policy on its use exists), and the language is now recognised and protected under Part Two of the European Charter for Regional and Minority Languages, which came into force in July 2001 and which stipulates that the United Kingdom government is required to promote Scots. In addition, the Scottish Nationalist Party aims to intro-duce a coherent and explicit pro-Scots policy in schools if it gains a majority in the Scottish parliament (an independent parliament was (re-)established in Edinburgh in 1999). Overall, then, Scots appears to have significant official backing for its status as an independent language. In the following section, we will consider how effective such support is in practice.

3.5 Discussion: what makes a new language?

Our three case studies have outlined instances in which various processes of language change have produced what are agreed (albeit not unanimously) to be new languages. We should not however, assume a direct relationship of cause and effect: population migration, cultural and linguistic contact and political tensions do not inevitably lead to the emergence of new languages. Thus, centuries of separate change including contact with various cultures and political independence have not resulted, for instance, in the emergence of a new Hispanic language in Latin America: the region still makes use of varieties of *Spanish*. Given then that language birth is not predictable or inevitable, the question of criteria for *new-language* status inevitably arises: on what basis can the claim for the emergence of a new language be made?

Of course, this is in itself predicated on the fundamental issue of what constitutes a *language*, a question to which no unequivocal answer yet exists. A heuristic approach has produced certain generally agreed criteria by which *language* – and, by extension, *new-language* – status may be judged, but they are by no means absolute and unproblematic. Many students of linguistics learn, for instance, that a basic distinction may be drawn between *dialect* and *language* on the basis of mutual intelligibility: *dialects* of a language have reciprocal intelligibility while *languages* do not. This assumption about language is often cited in conjunction with a second defining criterion, namely that languages are concomitant with political boundaries, leading to the generalisation that distinct political entities have distinct (mutually unintelligible) languages. Linguistic research has however, thrown up numerous evidence to the contrary. China, for instance, maintains that its populace speaks at least seven dialects of one single language, yet these seven are mutually unintelligible. Conversely, northern German and Dutch are very close structurally, but their association with distinct political entities has determined their status as distinct languages. In relation to our case studies, the political boundary between northern England and Lowland Scotland does not reflect a language division: the speech of communities on both sides of the border is mutually intelligible. Indeed, scholars such as Görlach (1991: 18–23) argue for a much wider intelligibility between Scots and English (the result of both their common origin and convergence from the fifteenth century onwards), stating that the main areas of difference lie in certain phonological and lexical features, but not in aspects of morphology and syntax. In this perspective, Scots is considered a subsystem of English, regardless of ideological arguments for its status as a distinct national language of Scotland.[8]

In a similar vein, contact languages such as Tok Pisin have not historically, and unanimously, been granted the status of *(new) language*: as indicated in

Section 3.3, an established perspective of pidgins and creoles has been that they are 'broken' or 'degenerate' versions of their lexifier languages (see Holm 1989; Sebba 1997; Singh 2000). Indeed, Holm (1989: 530) implies that the English generally did not consider Tok Pisin a separate language despite the fact that reciprocal intelligibility may have been limited.

Other proposed criteria for distinct language status include the existence of a standard written form and a literary tradition. English has been undergoing written standardisation since the fifteenth century, when the normalising procedures of printers and scriptoria first began to take effect (see Milroy and Milroy 1999; Fennell 2001; Singh 2005), and the processes have continued across the globe in areas where English has become an official language (linguists recognise for instance, standard American English, standard Australian English, standard Indian English, and so on). An orthographic system has been devised and is largely maintained for written Tok Pisin, but grammatical and lexical standardisation has not yet officially begun in earnest. However, Tok Pisin is regularly used in writing: the newspaper *Wantok* is a Tok Pisin-medium publication, government and public service documents are required to appear in the language and a Tok Pisin translation of the Bible is also in use. In addition, Tok Pisin is now widely used in elementary-level education. It is therefore highly likely that written norms have emerged from such usage. In relation to Scots, the dominance of English in print and its prestige as a written language historically hindered the emergence of a Scots standard and today, standard Scottish English is virtually identical (apart from phonologically and a few aspects of lexicon) to that of British English. However, Scots dictionaries and grammars (which are partly based in conventions observable in the historical corpus) provide examples of written usage which arguably establish a norm for the use of Scots in this particular medium. In addition, the Scots Leid Associe publishes orthographic and grammatical conventions for written Scots, and expects their observance in submissions to the association's magazine *Lallans*. In terms of literary tradition, that of English extends back to the tenth century (and possibly predates this), while that of Scots is typically taken to date from the fifteenth century. Writing in Tok Pisin has been a much more recent undertaking, and has mostly been confined to religious, political and governmental domains. Recently, however, the Masalai Press have published a collection of folk tales in Tok Pisin which were originally sent in to *Wantok* by readers (*A Thousand One Papua New Guinean Nights: Folktales from Wantok Newspaper* (2001)), and it is likely that more such local publications will follow.

It is unarguable that use in the written medium bestows a significant degree of validity to a system. More specifically, a literary tradition and the presence of written norms are typically taken to reflect a language's pedigree (and as an indicator of its community's level of 'civilisation'), and standardisation can generate the media (such as spelling guides, dictionaries and prescriptive grammars) through which the distinctiveness of a system is expressed and again, validated. It seems misleading to us, however, to treat standardisation and the existence of a written literature as a criterion for language status, since it is patently not cross-linguistically applicable. It is uniformly accepted that natural languages begin their existence as oral systems and that a significant number continue as such: speech communities are under no linguistic obligation to develop written norms and a written literature. Thus, although these are evident to varying degrees for English, Scots and Tok Pisin, standardisation and literary writing constitute, in our opinion, not criteria for independent language status but instead, developments that reflect a speech community's awareness of, and confidence in, a distinctive linguistic identity. It is no coincidence that concerns about written norms, expression and usage become most explicit when sociopolitical identity is an issue. Thus, the standardisation of English began in earnest, and literary production in the language increased, in the Early Modern period (1500–1700), an era which signalled the rise of England as a nation-state. The delimitation of Scots as a language distinct from English, and its deliberate use in not only Scottish literature but also in more prosaic writing (such as governmental, legal and administrative documents) first occurred in the fifteenth century, a time when Scotland's political relationship with England was extremely strained. More recently, arguments for the promotion of Scots as a separate language continue to be predicated on the fact that Scotland is a distinct political and cultural entity from England. Similarly, issues of standardisation and of literary production in Tok Pisin have only been addressed since Papua New Guinea gained independence in 1975.

It is highly likely, therefore, that one of the most important criteria for language status is acceptance of a system as such by a speech community. Such awareness and acceptance is at least partly influenced by institutional positions but, it should be noted, the latter are by no means definitive. Thus, it is very likely that awareness of English as the distinct language of England was concomitant with an emerging sociopolitical sense of 'Englishness' under Alfred the Great (AD 871–99), whose use of the language for translation as well as original work must have reinforced this perspective. Similarly, the official recognition of Tok Pisin has meant public awareness of its status is high: as a national language, it must, for instance, be considered in educational policy, and public and government documents must be produced in it. As in the case of (Old) English, the fact that Tok Pisin can be used in written as well as public and formal domains, and also has proactive governmental support, very likely underlines its language status for members of its speech community. The work of organisations such as the Scots Leid Associe and of political bodies such as the Scottish National Party in championing Scots has doubtless contributed to heightened awareness of it as a national language of Scotland; and its inclusion in the European Charter for Minority Languages has meant, in theory, that governmental support can be given to such promotional endeavours (although complaints have been made that this has not been forthcoming).[9]

At the same time however, official recognition as well as use in public, written and formal domains has not obliterated perceptions of Tok Pisin as 'bad English', or of Scots as an English dialect (although we should note that such perspectives have not caused speakers to abandon them either). It is arguable that while English remains a language associated with social advantage, as well as one that is perceived to have global value, it will also provide a standard by which others that have primarily local currency and, in some cases, a long history of stigmatisation, are judged adversely. In other words, until Scots and Tok Pisin are associated with a positive and confident national identity (which is dependent in large part on socio-economic prosperity), it is unlikely that they will be uniformly accepted consciously as languages and, indeed, as languages equal to others such as English.

It seems therefore that no unequivocal, (socio)linguistic criteria for defining a language exist which, in the context of our discussion, means that it is difficult, if not impossible, to predict exactly when, through processes of internally and externally motivated change, such a system is *born*. The birth of *language consciousness* however, appears to be a much more explicit process, one that is concomitant with sociopolitical change and ideological shifts and, indeed, that is reflected in many of the developments which have been accepted heuristically as criteria for the definition of language status, such as standardisation, the fostering of a literary tradition, acceptance and service as a national language. It would seem therefore that languages are not truly 'born' until their speakers consider them as such. And since it is speakers who decide on *language birth*, it is no surprise that they also determine the other end of the 'life cycle', *language death*. We explore the latter phenomenon in Chapter 4.

4 Language death[1]

4.1 Introduction

The study of *language death* represents a relatively new field of enquiry within historical linguistics. However, the phenomenon itself is neither recent nor uncommon. Hittite (spoken in Asia Minor) ceased to be spoken several thousand years ago and Etruscan (spoken in central Italy) has been dead for over 1,500 years, and neither of these languages have left much trace. During the twentieth century, dying languages were attested and documented all over the world. Swadesh (1948) and Coteanu (1957) were two early commentators in this area, but it is only since the early 1970s that the field has become established as a separate subdiscipline of linguistic study. Indeed, Dorian's (1981) work on East Sutherland Gaelic, less than a quarter of a century ago, probably represents one of the earliest major case studies.

According to current estimates, some 6,000 different vernaculars are now spoken in the world and, of these, about half will probably die out during the next 100 years (Krauss 1992). As Crystal (1999) points out, this means that, on average, the world loses one speech variety every fortnight. Given these figures, it may seem surprising that linguists have only been studying language death for a comparatively short time. This is partly because until relatively recently, linguists tended to think that dying languages, displaying evidence of grammatical change and heavy structural and lexical interference from another variety, did not in themselves represent worthwhile objects of study. Indeed, if any investigation was made of such varieties, it was of their 'better' speakers, in an attempt to document a particular speech variety before its ultimate extinction. Those speakers showing less competence in the dying variety were more often than not neglected as 'imperfect' or 'aberrant' speakers:

> Voegelin was told in the early thirties almost all names of South Fork Indians who spoke Tübatulabal and how old, approximately, each speaker was; but he worked only with middle-aged and old speakers. Like other anthropological linguists, he was interested in recording the

'best' variety of the language he was studying, rather than in recording most varieties. (So also in our ongoing study of Hopi, we used to refrain from recording the speech of young Hopi, described by their elders as 'broken-down Hopi'.)

(Voegelin and Voegelin 1977: 336)

However, it has subsequently been realised that the study of dying languages can provide us with information about both the way in which the brain deals with language and the structure of language itself. By comparing ways in which different languages are lost, it may be possible to collect evidence about possible universals of language death through the observance of general patterns. Moreover, as dying languages often exhibit evidence of large amounts of linguistic change, we are also afforded an opportunity to further our investigation of this field. As Schmidt stated 'Can grammatical change in the final stages of a language facing extinction be shown to proceed in the same orderly way as grammatical changes in less drastic phases of linguistic evolution?' (1985: 5). Put another way, does language change proceed differently in 'healthy' and 'dying' languages?

As we saw in Chapter 1, in linguistics the term *language death* is used exclusively to refer to the study of varieties that are typically undergoing both reduction in terms of their speaker numbers and territorial contraction. It may be defined as the end-point of *language obsolescence*, a process whereby a language is ousted from its territory by another variety. The rapidity of this process may vary greatly: some indigenous languages spoken in Australia (such as Marithiel) are dying fairly quickly (two to three generations) but Scots Gaelic has taken hundreds of years.[2]

The language in question does not necessarily have to be located within what are considered to be the geographical frontiers of the territory occupied by its original native speakers. For example, a variety of German is spoken by certain religious communities in Pennsylvania (see Section 4.4) and Greek is heard in several parts of Canada. Both these languages are currently undergoing a dramatic reduction in their number of speakers, who are looking increasingly to English. As their language is gradually submerged, it may undergo structural or phonological modification, with the result that it may diverge greatly from its original territorial vernacular, but, nevertheless, it remains an identifiable form of that variety. Thus, if the extraterritorial variety is lost, the language as a whole will not die – Pennsylvania German may, one day, cease to exist but German will live on, or if it does not, this will have nothing to do with the fate of the Pennsylvanian variety.

As we will see, the death of a language within its native speech community is an extremely complex process, involving the intertwining of both linguistic and non-linguistic factors, so that no two case studies ever present an identical picture. This has meant that most comparative work on threatened languages tends to focus on points they have in common rather than on the characteristics that separate them.

The most frequently cited classification of language death situations is that proposed by Campbell and Muntzel (1989: 182–6), who describe four possible scenarios:

a) **Sudden death**, where there is language loss due to the sudden death, or massacre, of most of a variety's speakers, such as in the case of Tasmanian.

b) **Radical death**, where loss is similarly rapid and is usually due to severe political repression, often with genocide, with the result that speakers stop using the language out of self-defence, as was seen in El Salvador in the early 1980s when many people stopped speaking their native languages in order to avoid being identified as Native Americans and killed.

c) **Gradual death**, where a language is lost in a contact situation, with the dominant language gradually ousting the subordinate – often minority – variety in a scenario that typically involves intermediate stages of bilingualism, an age-governed proficiency continuum, where young speakers tend to be least proficient in the dying language and older speakers most proficient, and the existence of one or more generations of imperfect speakers (see Section 4.2).

d) **Bottom-to-top death**, where a language is lost in intimate contexts and remains exclusively in ceremonial usage. This category is rarer and is illustrated by Campbell's own fieldwork in South America, where he found four men who were able to recite several prayers in south-eastern Tzeltal which speakers of other Tzeltal dialects were unable to translate as they no longer used this form of ritual language.

In fact, most existing studies of language death relate to category (c) above, where the language in question is not actually dead but, rather, seems to be embarking on the path that may ultimately lead to its extinction. Another important misassumption that needs to be cleared up, then, is that the field of language death is concerned with dead languages. Languages only die with the disappearance of their last native speaker and, at this point, are little more than curiosities – they cannot develop and, in most cases, have no function.

It also should be stressed that the term *obsolescence* carries the meaning 'gradually disappearing' and has none of the prescriptivist connotations of 'becoming replaced by a better model', which are often associated with its contemporary usage – despite the fact that, in the speakers' minds at least, this is precisely what may be taking place. Language obsolescence, then, is a process occurring in a specific group of languages, currently undergoing a progressive decline in the number of their speakers, during which gradual reduction in use, due to domain restriction, may result in the emergence of historically inappropriate morphological or phonological forms together with extensive lexical borrowing. These structural changes may or may not be directly attributable to the influence of an encroaching language. Finally, it should not be assumed that obsolescence will necessarily end in the extinction of a language. As we will see in Chapter 5, the process may be halted and *revitalisation* may occur.

The loss of a speech variety can have emotive connotations for its speakers, and the field of language death has given rise to its fair share of emotive terms, two of the most widely found being *language suicide* and *language murder*. These are distinguished by Aitchison (1991: 198–208), who uses the former to describe the death of a variety which is being ousted from its historical territory by a variety to which it is 'fairly similar', and the latter when two languages in contact are 'dissimilar' (Aitchison 1991: 208).[3] Although the terms may still be found regularly in the literature, much current work on language obsolescence now tends to avoid them. Aitchison's definitions are not easy to apply and raise the perennial problem of defining what are and what are not 'similar' or 'dissimilar' varieties. (For example, it could be argued that two languages such as Scots Gaelic and Irish are far more similar than, say, French and Spanish, and that the latter two are more similar than Latin and Greek.) Moreover, there has been a certain amount of variation in the way certain terms have been used within the field (for example, Denison (1977) uses the term 'language suicide' in a very different way). But more significant than this is the feeling among linguists that such anthropomorphic, biological terms do not fit language well, and that the use of 'loaded' words such as these is best avoided.

4.2 Setting and structure: the two aspects of obsolescence

Studies of language death have to date highlighted two different areas of enquiry, namely the sociopolitical background that precipitates obsolescence and the linguistic changes that arise in the obsolescent language. Individual case studies have usually focused on one area or the other, although there has been some attempt to correlate the two (Dorian 1981; Jones 1998). The reason for this 'double focus' is that the decline of a language does not take place in a vacuum, and the sociopolitical setting is often instrumental in precipitating linguistic change. As we will see, language obsolescence may therefore be seen as the occurrence of language change, typically in large amounts and at an accelerated rate, within a particular sociopolitical situation. We turn now to an examination of both the sociopolitical and linguistic aspects of obsolescence.

4.2.1 The sociopolitical setting

It is important to emphasise from the start that language obsolescence has nothing to do with the linguistic structure of a speech variety. As Swadesh commented (1948: 234), 'There are no such things as inherently weak languages that are by nature incapable of surviving changed social conditions ... As for different kinds of linguistic structure, none has ever prevented the adaptation of a language to a new cultural context.'

Language obsolescence, therefore, does not occur due to the existence of either 'weak' or 'overly complicated' languages but instead often because of the introduction of a second language into a speech community due to a period of sociopolitical change. Such periods may follow invasion or colonisation, and, importantly, the question of whether the language of the conquerors or of the conquered people prevails is largely determined by sociopolitical rather than linguistic factors. For example, although English has emerged as dominant over the indigenous languages of Australia, Anglo-Norman failed to supplant English in England in the period following the Norman Conquest of 1066.

Industrialisation, with its common corollary of urbanisation, is also frequently responsible for major social upheaval as people leave their homes in search of employment. When this entails an influx or exodus of people who do not speak the language variety of their adoptive community there are immediate linguistic repercussions, the nature of which again depend totally on the sociopolitical situations of the languages in question. For example, in the case of Nubian the male speakers who travelled to Cairo and Alexandria in search of work were obliged to learn Arabic which, on their return, they brought back with them to their homelands (Rouchdy 1989a: 93). In Wales, on the other hand, the English-speaking immigrants who came to work in the coal mines had the effect of Anglicising the community since they brought their language with them.

Arabic and English dominate Nubian and Welsh respectively both in terms of number of speakers and geographical expansion. Nubia is merely a small part of the larger Egyptian whole and the 3 million Welsh have been officially united with the 45 million or so English since 1536. Arabic and English are both languages of government and legislation, schools and religion. Nubian fulfils none of these functions (Rouchdy 1989a: 101) and despite having some for many years, Welsh only acceded to others as recently as 1967, with the passing of the first Welsh Language Act. In all cases, it is economic might and political status which count in securing language maintenance.

Of course, there exist many factors responsible for the introduction of a second language into a community. The easing of communication due to better roads and an increase in tourism have led to Ugong and the Gressoney dialect of the Val d'Aosta having to tolerate competition from Thai and Italian respectively (Bradley 1989: 33; Giacalone Ramat 1979: 143). However, once introduced into a speech community, the newcomer language will take root and, if backed by a favourable sociopolitical situation, will be learnt by an increasing percentage of the indigenous population. If the newcomer language happens to stem from a nearby territory, with a certain amount of political influence over that of the indigenous language, then it is not uncommon for it to be forcibly introduced via the public institutions that lie within the latter's linguistic territory. The most common of these is the education system.

Examples abound of obsolescent languages which have, at some stage, been outlawed in the classroom. In Brittany, compulsory French-medium education was introduced in 1886 and speaking Breton at school was a crime that was severely chastised by use of the *symbole* – usually a piece of wood hung around the neck of a pupil caught speaking Breton on school premises. It could only be passed on to another pupil if the wearer caught a classmate transgressing in a similar way and the person wearing it at the end of the day was punished. An identical strategy was used as recently as the first half of the twentieth century in Wales, where the object was known as the 'Welsh Not'. In Greece, Arvanitika (a variety of Albanian) has never been the language of instruction (Trudgill 1983b: 128), and, similarly, for a long time the Inupiat Eskimos 'were not allowed to use our native language in . . . school . . . and . . . got reprimanded for using our native language in the schoolground' (Blackman 1989: 66). Moreover, parents were instructed not to speak the minority language to their offspring lest they be backward at school. Kuter (1989a: 80) states that in Brittany, due to the fact that in the late nineteenth and early twentieth centuries:

> the civilizing influence of schools was limited in Breton-speaking rural communities since children needed on farms left school by the time they were 14 years old . . . [a] solid knowledge of French was not transmitted to children, but the idea that being a Breton peasant is a negative identity *was* effectively transmitted. The Breton language was viewed by rural Bretons as an old tool, no longer useful in a world where power depends on a knowledge of French.

This is similar to the case of Nahuatl (Hill and Hill 1977: 59), whose speakers are beginning to view it as a 'village thing' which a forward-looking, ambitious person would do well to abandon. Such a decision to cease language transmission to one's descendants is an important precipitator of the shift from one's primary language and is often linked to the development of a negative language attitude resulting in collective doubts about the usefulness of language loyalty.

As part of this blatant stigmatisation, common in situations of language obsolescence, speakers are made to feel that their language is unimportant or even inadequate and that by speaking it, they are associated with a backward, inferior social group: 'We were no class' (Dorian 1981: 61 on East Sutherland Gaelic); 'It makes you feel embarrassed' (Trudgill 1983b: 130 on Arvanitika); 'Nubian is not an important language' (Rouchdy 1989a: 101); 'It's a general burden on the kids' (MacKinnon 1982: 53 on Scots Gaelic). Speakers also associate their language with economic hardship: 'Irish will butter no bread' (Hindley 1990: 179) and consequently try to disassociate themselves from it and the implicit unsophisticated and poverty-stricken identity it brings. On the other hand, the dominant language is often associated with economic prosperity, upward mobility and progressive modernisation. The situation may be encapsulated in the words of an elder of the Yaaku tribe in East Africa who blamed the loss of his language on the younger generation who, he said, were 'no longer interested in their own culture, they only like cattle [an item of value in the prestige culture] and strive to be Maasai [the socially dominant and prestigious group]' (Brenzinger 1992: 225; our insertions). A crucial stage in the fate of the language was undoubtedly reached when someone with no command of the Yaaku language could still be considered as a member of the Yaaku community. Such a scenario may be observed as close to home as Brittany, Ireland and Wales where, for the majority of inhabitants, the language is no longer the central, unifying force in the community or the hallmark of membership of that community, hence the loss of an important motivation for language maintenance.

As the native speakers of the minority language gradually turn their back on their indigenous variety and strive to acquire the dominant variety, the community becomes bilingual and, more often than not, diglossic. The term *diglossia* was first used by Charles Ferguson to describe a situation 'where two varieties of a language exist side-by-side throughout the community with each having a definite role to play' (1959: 325–40). Joshua Fishman introduced an important modification to this concept, stating that 'diglossia exists not only in multilingual societies which officially recognise several languages and not only in societies that utilise vernacular and classical varieties, but also in societies which employ separate dialects, registers or functionally differentiated varieties of any kind' (1972: 92). According to this definition, then, diglossia involves two or more varieties being spoken in the same speech community, but it differs from bilingualism in that the varieties are mutually exclusive in function. One variety, termed 'high' (H) is used at the 'official' level – for example, government, education, literature and so forth, and the 'low' variety (L) is reserved for more familiar discourse – for example, with family, friends and so forth. Diglossia therefore can represent a stable situation in which two varieties can coexist without impacting upon each other to any significant degree.

However, diglossia may 'leak'. This happens when one variety starts being used for the functions normally reserved for the other. The result of this will be bilingualism without diglossia, which will often subsequently result in the replacement of one variety by the other. This is the situation which normally prevails in language obsolescence where, as it grows in prestige, H usually succeeds in gradually eliminating L from all its former domains. Mahapatra (1991: 185) notes the beginnings of this situation in India, where the Bihari and Pahari groups of languages are losing more and more of their domains of usage to Hindi.

Ousted from these domains, the obsolescent language is no longer considered to be a 'full' language. As a result of its restricted social usage it may undergo loss of registers (although, as Dorian (1994b) points out, this reduction of stylistic options does not necessarily imply that all such varieties become monostylistic). In the modern world, with its constantly increasing need for more styles and registers for discussion of an abundance of new concepts and ideas, an inability to communicate satisfactorily through lack of linguistic resources will inevitably lead to speakers resorting to another language. The obsolescent language may become ridiculed – used as a language suitable for joke telling or being funny or merely as a way of communicating with older people – and often comes to be used as a 'secret' language used for exclusionary speaking. Wurm (1991: 15) mentions this latter use as an important factor in keeping alive 'apparently doomed' languages.

Schlieben-Lange (1977: 102) states that 'We may assume that every time a language no longer performs a function, it will be abandoned, and if this abandonment extends to the whole geographic area where the language is spoken it will die'. As will be seen in Chapter 5, efforts are often made to revitalise obsolescent languages. These usually involve extensive language planning, including teaching the obsolescent language in school, furnishing it with a standard, codified form if one does not already exist and seeking its inclusion in some form of media. Such efforts may often be precipitated by pressure groups such as Sav Breizh (Brittany), the Section de la Langue of the Société Jersiaise (Jersey) (see Chapter 5) or Cymdeithas Yr Iaith Gymraeg (Wales), whose aims are to call attention to the plight of their language and demand that more be done to ensure its survival.

It has been seen that language is often intrinsically linked to the identity of a community. This is why, according to Dixon (1991: 248), the fact that many of the languages spoken in the Pacific Islands are the official languages of independent nations means that they all have a good chance of indefinite survival. However, this link with the identity of a community makes a language vulnerable when members of the said community no longer wish to be identified with it or rather, wish to be associated with a different social group and begin to abandon their own customs and beliefs for those of the new group. Language loyalty is therefore an important element of language maintenance. For example, Wurm (1991: 16) mentions how, in the 1970s and 1980s, the Papua Independence movement, with Police Motu as its rallying point, resisted the onslaught of Tok Pisin, despite the fact that the latter had far more speakers. In some contexts of language obsolescence, the link between the dying language and a negative identity is so strong that even personal names in the obsolescent language are replaced by ones associated with the dominant variety. Post-Second World War Wales was submerged in a flood of Raymonds, Cecils and Elizabeths and it is only relatively recently that the Rhodris and Sioneds have staged a comeback! Thus language planning is also starting to encompass an element of what Pool (1979: 5) terms 'identity planning'.

As mentioned earlier, situations of language obsolescence often give rise to the existence of 'imperfect speakers', of which there are two types. First, there are the *rusty speakers* (Sasse 1992: 61), people who despite having a reasonable knowledge of the grammatical system of a language usually have certain gaps in this area and in their vocabulary. These are individuals who were born before transmission of the language had been significantly interrupted but who have not attained fluency due to a lack of regular communication in the language. The second category of imperfect speakers found in such situations are the *semi-speakers*, a termed coined by Dorian during the course of her work on East Sutherland Gaelic. These are people who, despite having a reasonable passive ability, have insufficient active control over the language to be able to engage in fluent conversation and whose speech is characterised by historically inappropriate forms. These are people who have not learned the language by way of a normal language acquisition process due to the interruption of language transmission. It goes without saying that such imperfect speakers will form a continuum in the speech community, with the rusty speakers at the top, followed by the semi-speakers who typically range from competent to *rememberers*. Sasse (1992: 70–2) lists the following as the main characteristics of the speech of remembers:

(i)   loss of subordinative mechanisms
(ii) loss of systematic integration, for example in the lexicon
(iii) breakdown of grammatical categories, such as tense, mood and aspect
(iv) agrammatism, for example some syntactic rules may not be observed
(v)   word retrieval problems
(vi) extreme phonological variations and distortion
(vii) phonological hypercorrection.

In addition, when addressed in the obsolescent language imperfect speakers will often reply in the dominant language. It is not uncommon for whole conversations to take place where both speakers are using a different language to address one another, yet there is at no question of comprehension difficulties on either side. Both Gal (1979: 110) and Schmidt (1985: 37) note that it is often older adults who adhere to the obsolescent language and children who use the dominant one.

It is also worth noting that there is a low degree of literacy in the obsolescent language. Indeed, the obsolescent language may even lack a widely used written form. This makes it especially open to influence from languages which do have a writing system. This happened, for example, in the case of the Siberian peoples and the Russian language (Wurm 1991: 10).

It is clear, therefore, that many varieties in the throes of obsolescence may display a similar sociolinguistic profile. However, although such generalisations are possible in the abstract, the complexity of issues involved in language death means that it is impossible to foretell the fate of any variety with great accuracy. Although language contact evidently plays a major role in most cases of language obsolescence, it should be stressed that in itself, such contact is not a sufficient cause of language obsolescence. As Nurse and Walsh (1992: 199) have demonstrated, Chifundi and Vumba, two varieties spoken in southern Kenya and northern Tanzania, have undergone widespread phonological and morphological influence from Digo, and yet both have survived, and the myth that extensive lexical mixing precipitates extinction may be dispelled by the most superficial examination of the English language. Moreover, languages may survive with very few speakers, since strong entrenchment can often compensate for a lack of prestige (Cobarrubias 1983: 55). For example, Tucano (spoken in the Vaupes River region of Brazil) has only 4,500 speakers but is not deemed to be obsolescent (Aikhenvald 1996: 81).

Finally, we should note that although we can only be sure a language will die when there remains only one native speaker, usually past child-bearing age (see Chapter 6), during the course of her work on East Sutherland Gaelic, Dorian (1981: 51) introduced the useful notion of linguistic *tip* to refer to the linguistic point of no return, beyond which an obsolescent language will embark upon an inexorable course towards death: 'In terms of possible routes towards language death it would seem that a language which has been demographically highly stable for several centuries may experience a sudden "tip" after which the demographic tide flows strongly in favor of some other language'.

As will be seen in Chapters 5 and 6, language revitalisation and, by definition, *language revival* have both been attempted in communities after tip has taken place, so that even this does not necessarily condemn a variety to extinction. However, the likelihood of the obsolescent variety becoming restored as an everyday language for a significant part of the members of those speech communities is quite remote.

We will now consider the linguistic changes involved in language obsolescence. Since, as we saw earlier, no two case studies of language obsolescence are identical, it is worth stating that the following section identifies observable trends rather than universally present changes.

4.2.2 Linguistic changes

The linguistic changes that occur during language obsolescence are by no means unique to so-called 'dying' languages. Every variety, whether 'healthy' or obsolescent, undergoes linguistic change involving grammatical and lexical innovations so that, from a purely linguistic point of view, the phenomena of language obsolescence and language change are linked by common mechanisms. Indeed, it is often difficult to distinguish the changes involved in language obsolescence from those resulting from the natural development of a language which show no evidence of incursion by a dominant variety. For example, although it has been demonstrated that obsolescent East Sutherland Gaelic is in the process of losing case differentiation (Dorian 1981: 129–36; see Section 4.3.2) Trudgill (1983a: 104) has shown that Norwegian has also undergone a reduction of cases, noun declensions and verbal inflections with respect to Faroese, despite the fact that it is a 'healthy' language.

The notable features about the changes inherent in language obsolescence are the *amount* and *rate* of change. Whereas in 'healthy' languages, a few changes will occur almost imperceptibly over quite a considerable period of time, with language obsolescence it is possible to witness many different types of innovation over a matter of generations. We now turn to a brief discussion of some of the most common types of change that have been found on examination of different language obsolescence case histories. These changes are also all widely attested in 'healthy' languages. The changes described below have been divided into those attributable and not necessarily attributable to the dominant language, but it is worth noting that it is often difficult to tell definitively in every case whether we are dealing with internal or external change. It is therefore often necessary to acknowledge the principle of multiple causation (Thomason and Kaufman 1988) or 'ambiguous change' (Mougeon and Beniak 1991: 218) (see Chapter 2).

We begin with changes commonly found in obsolescent languages but not necessarily attributable to the influence of the dominant language. One such change is *simplification*. If a language has, for instance, three ways of expressing a particular concept, then two of these will be redundant. In obsolescent languages it is common for speakers with incomplete acquisition histories to generalise one of these constructions at the expense of the others.

For example, as in standard French, in Ontarian French many verbs do not show a distinction between the third-person singular and the third-person plural in the present indicative (e.g. *parler* 'to speak' has *il parle* 'he speaks' and *ils parlent* 'they (m.) speak', which are both realised in speech as [il paʀl]. However, Mougeon and Beniak (1991: 91–109) found that, where Ontarian French did make a distinction between these forms, for example in the case of verbs such as *il veut* [il vø] 'he wants' – *ils veulent* [il vœl] 'they want', the morphologically marked forms tended to give way to the unmarked third-person singular forms (hence *ils veulent > ils veut*). This represents an instance of simplification in that only one pattern now had to be learnt for the third person (singular or plural). This phenomenon was found to be most widespread in the speech of semi-restricted and restricted speakers of Ontarian French.

Reduction is another commonly found change. Whereas the changes involved in simplification modify a system without having any effect on the speaker's ability to express a particular concept, reduction, on the other hand, involves the 'actual loss of some part of the language – or more precisely a loss of some part of a component of the grammar without resulting complication of another component to make up for this loss' (Mühlhäusler

1974: 22). In the pronominal system of Warlpiri, for instance, there exists a distinction between inclusive (of hearer) and exclusive (of hearer) in the first person but not in the second or third persons. There exists, therefore, an asymmetrical system. However, in a survey of Warlpiri speakers ranging in age from nine to sixty it was found that a merger was occurring between the inclusive and exclusive categories (Bavin 1989: 280), an indication that this pronominal distinction will eventually be lost altogether. Another instance of reduction is provided by Sasse (1992: 77) who cites the case of Elmolo, a now extinct language but one whose records show that one of the changes that occurred prior to its death was the abandoning of gender distinction in the third person.

In another typical pattern of change, an obsolescent language may demonstrate (if relevant) a movement from synthetic to analytic morphological type. Synthetic forms are often opaque, whereas analytic forms are comparatively transparent. Dimmendaal (1992: 119), for example, mentions the development in Kore from inflectional and agglutinating structures towards analytic and isolating ones and Schmidt (1985: 61) comments on the loss of morphological ergativity and the regrouping of core elements on a nominative-accusative type pattern shown by word order in young people's Dyirbal.

Finally, in areas of language such as the gender-marking system, a distinction between marked and unmarked categories, in which the latter is the commoner or 'default' option, often exists. There seems to be a general tendency in obsolescent languages for the unmarked category to be generalised to contexts that historically require the marked feature. This generalisation of unmarked categories is observable in obsolescent languages such as Kore, where the unmarked feminine gender is being generalised within the language's demonstrative system (Dimmendaal 1992: 126). Jones (1998: 64–71, 170–6) demonstrates a similar pattern of generalisation – of masculine gender – in many contexts in modern Welsh.

It is noteworthy that, although precipitated in the context of language death, the types of change described above are also in evidence in 'healthy' languages. For example, Miller remarks that case endings are being omitted (a type of simplification) by young speakers of obsolescent Shoshoni (1971: 119) (see also Section 4.4) – but case syncretism is also found in many areas of northern Germany and in Rhenish areas (Keller 1961). It is worth reiterating that in language obsolescence it is the *rate, amount* and *context* of the linguistic change that is noteworthy, rather than the specific nature of the change.

We now turn to types of change typically deemed to be attributable to interference from another language.

Grammatical interference is often observable in obsolescent languages, as can be seen in the influence of English on the development of Dyirbal instrumental case-marking devices. In English, *with* has both instrumental and comitative functions. Traditional Dyirbal, on the other hand, distinguishes these functions with an ergative-instrumental affix marking instrumental functions and a comitative suffix *-bila* marking the comitative function. Schmidt (1985: 57) remarks that young Dyirbal speakers analogise on the English model, using *-bila* to cover both instrumental and comitative functions. This development may, quite appropriately, be interpreted as an instance of reduction as it results in the elimination of instrumental marking. However, it has not been classed with the examples of linguistic change not necessarily attributable to the dominant language because, unlike in those examples, the change has clearly been precipitated through contact with English.

Jones (1998: 253) found instances of syntactic calquing in young people's Welsh. In Welsh, a noun directly following a cardinal numeral is always singular – for example:

4.2.2.a

y	*saith*	*merch*	
the	seven	girl	'the seven girls'

4.2.2.b

y	*deg*	*tŷ*	
the	ten	house	'the ten houses'

The noun may be plural only when preceded by the preposition *o* 'of'. For example:

4.2.2.c

saith	*o*	*ferched*	
seven	of	girls + **soft mutation**[4]	'seven girls'

4.2.2.d

deg	*o*	*dai*	
ten	of	houses + **soft mutation**	'ten houses'

However, many younger speakers translated the phrase 'your two . . . cats' with

4.2.2.e

eich	*dau*	*cathod*
your (**polite form**)	two [masc.]	cats [fem.]

where the syntax is based on the English model. Note also the use of a masculine numeral with a feminine noun in this sentence: an instance of the increasing generalisation of the masculine gender in modern Welsh (mentioned above).

In a truly bilingual community one often finds a certain amount of lexical interference in both languages. As seen in Chapter 2, Timm (1975: 473–82) and Ma and Herasimchuk (1971: 347–464) have demonstrated this phenomenon in relation to Spanish–English bilinguals in the USA. This code-switching must, however, be kept distinct from the prolific lexical borrowing occurring in language obsolescence for two reasons. First, in obsolescent languages the lexical movement is asymmetrical, occurring mainly from the dominant language to the variety under threat, with only a limited amount of movement in the opposite direction. Second, whereas in a 'healthy' language code-switching is acceptable (such as the situation in Puerto Rico, for example, where, as seen in Chapter 2, the phenomenon is considered as nothing more than people making full use of the resources of a bilingual situation), such borrowings are criticised in communities facing potential language death. Dorian mentions that in East Sutherland, a few individuals are reported as being 'notorious for speaking "darn' leth Gàidh-lig, darn' leth Beurl" ' 'half Gaelic, half English' (1981: 98).[5] Thus, as seen above, the same linguistic phenomenon must be considered differently according to whether it occurs in 'healthy' or obsolescent languages. The distinction is undoubtedly affected by a language's sociopolitical situation: the fact that Spanish is not perceived to be in any danger of extinction in the USA means that code-switching is seen to be less threatening than if it were occurring in, for example, the Celtic languages, which are facing precisely this threat from the variety used in the code-switch.

An obsolescent language may also display the effects of *phonological interference*. When a non-indigenous language first becomes used in a speech community, speakers will be conscious of the different phonological systems belonging to each variety and any loans occurring will tend to be adapted to the phonotactics of the indigenous language. However, as more and more loans enter the indigenous language, they tend to be adopted 'wholesale' to the point where new phonemes may enter that language. Schmidt (1985: 194), for instance, comments on the progressive introduc-tion (from English) of fricative sounds, which do not occur in traditional Dyirbal, in the pronominal system of young people, who make use of forms such as *wifela* ('we' plural). However, again, this type of interference is also found in 'healthy' languages. For example, as we saw in Chapter 2, due to the influence of English, French has acquired the /ŋ/ phoneme via loans such as *le smoking* 'evening jacket'.

Lexical borrowing (an extremely common result of language contact between 'healthy' languages; see Chapter 2) also occurs in obsolescent lan-guages. Although not in itself therefore an automatic herald of language obsolescence, lexical borrowing becomes an indicator of the phenomenon when it is prolific, asymmetrical and occurs in conjunction with a particular sociopolitical context. As with code-switching, borrowing is more stigma-tised in obsolescent languages then in 'healthy' ones. For example, Dorian (1981: 101) comments how, in her presence, one man corrected his wife's use of the English borrowing *tiun* 'tune' to the Scots Gaelic equivalent, *port*.

Borrowing may result in *lexical substitution*. Bavin (1989: 275–6) remarks on the replacement of traditional words in Warlpiri with English borrowings and the subsequent assimilation of these loanwords into the

Warlpiri system, for example [pipi] < *baby*; [pata] < *fat*. Schmidt (1985: 182) provides examples of the same phenomenon in both traditional Dyirbal and young people's Dyirbal: [bujigan] < *pussycat*; [ŋandi] < *aunty*. Words may also be borrowed in an unmodified form: English intrusion in young people's Dyirbal speech is noted by Schmidt (1985: 183) in, for example, sentences such as *ŋanaji happen to bura-n bayi helicopter waymban-gani-nyu* 'We happened to see a helicopter travelling around' and Rouchdy (1989b: 262) remarks on the way in which Arabic numerals are 'imported' into Nubian *ay wili talata wi isrin sabati sokka kagis* 'I yesterday three and twenty baskets carried along'; *talata wi isrin* being 'twenty-three' in Arabic.

Borrowing may also lead to the use of calques (see Chapter 2). Schlichter, for example, notes the instance of 'many loan and literal translations from English' in the speech of two of his Yuki-speaking informants in California (see Elmendorf 1981: 41). Mougeon and Beniak (1991: 177) also mention the presence of calquing in Ontarian French, where the periphrasis *à la maison de* (a literal translation of the English phrase 'in the house of') is commonly used for the more idiomatic form *chez*.

In its terminal stage, with the cessation of regular communication in the language, all that remains of the obsolescent variety is a handful of words and phrases, set expressions and idioms, which are often learned by heart by their last speakers. These frequently have no understanding of the syntactic and other rules that govern them, and are unable to use them as building blocks to create new grammatically acceptable sentences of the language.

4.3 Case study: East Sutherland Gaelic

As mentioned above, no two cases of language obsolescence are identical, and for this reason it is difficult to select one instance as a representative study. Dorian's (1981) study of East Sutherland Gaelic (ESG) does, however, merit note given its significance to the field as an early attempt to study both the social and linguistic conditions in which language death takes place. The following summary only provides a brief outline of the study, which should be read in full.

The county of Sutherland lies in the Highlands, in the north of Scotland. Dorian notes that at the time of her study only three villages in the county (Brora, Golspie and Embo) had any native speakers of the East Sutherland variety of Gaelic and that these were disappearing rapidly. In 1972, speakers of ESG constituted only 1.6 per cent of the population of Brora (twenty-three out of 1,436), 3 per cent of the population of Golspie (forty-two out of 1,374) and 30.4 per cent of the population of Embo (seventy-nine out of 260). No ESG monolinguals remained by this date and the most of the speakers came from the older half of the population. Younger people did not speak Scots Gaelic.

Dorian demonstrates how the decline of ESG has happened against the backdrop of the general decline of Scots Gaelic throughout the Highlands.

Although Scots Gaelic has a long history in Sutherland, having been spoken there since before AD 900, by the fourteenth century it was ceasing to be socially acceptable, with English used increasingly by the ruling aristocracy (the Earls of Sutherland) and by the Scottish mercantile class. By the time of the Act of Union, the earls lived mostly in London and in the late eighteenth and early nineteenth centuries they were funding their lifestyles by removing the peasants and small farmers from their lands (the infamous Highland Clearances) to make way for more profitable sheep-farming. The Clearances therefore forced thousands of Scots Gaelic speakers to resettle in coastal towns, where many took up fishing, and at the same time brought English speakers up from the south to run the sheep farms. This helped reinforce the image of Scots Gaelic as the language of the poverty-stricken labouring classes.

By the nineteenth century, Scots Gaelic had begun to give way to English in East Sutherland due to a combination of in-migration of English speakers and increasing bilingualism among the indigenous population which occurred in the wake of the 'opening up' of the county as a result of extensive road-building. A diglossic situation emerged (see Section 4.2) with English being used for all official functions, including education. As the remainder of Sutherland acquired English, the Scots Gaelic-speaking fishermen, living together in their own neighbourhoods and rarely marrying outside this tight-knit community, were slow to adopt the incoming language and this served to increase the segregation that, by virtue of their trade, already existed between them and the rest of society. Scots Gaelic served as a further badge of their stigmatised identity. By the twentieth century, they were the only remaining Scots Gaelic speakers in the area. Although Scots Gaelic was therefore widely spoken in fishing communities at the turn of the century, this was to work against the language: the fact that the fisherfolk were stigmatised and considered inferior by the remainder of the community meant that the Scots Gaelic they spoke also acquired this negative image.

After the First World War, fishing started to decline as a livelihood in the area. As many of the fisherfolk entered new jobs, their segregation from the remainder of the community gradually lessened. Intermarriage increased as they no longer maintained their separate social networks and became more integrated into the (predominantly Anglicised) communities. However, since Scots Gaelic had become one of the features that characterised the fishers, at this time there was a tendency to abandon the language along with other fisher characteristics. The language therefore lost one of its last strongholds and its decline was swift.

Dorian's investigation of linguistic change in ESG examined the nominal and verbal systems by means of translation tasks that focused on the categories of gender, number, case and voice. Dorian commented in particular on the language use of three groups, the older fluent speakers (OFS), the younger fluent speakers (YFS) and the semi-speakers (SS) (cf. Section 4.2) and her work revealed the existence of a proficiency continuum of Scots Gaelic

speakers. Some of Dorian's findings on tense usage and the case system will
be briefly outlined below in order to illustrate some of the tendencies found.

4.3.1 Tense usage

Traditional Scots Gaelic has three recognised tense forms: past, future and
conditional. Example 4.3.1.a illustrates the forms for the regular verb /kʰur/
'to put'.

4.3.1.a Forms for /kʰur/ 'to put'

	root (=also imperative singular)	/kʰur/
Past	root + lenition[6]	/xur/
Future	root + suffix	/kʰuri/, /kʰurəs/
Conditional	root + lenition + suffix	/xuru/

Among fluent speakers, the tense system is totally intact. However, in SS
usage, although the past tense was formed correctly in 90 per cent of constructions, there is evidence of deviation within the tense system as a whole
in that seven out of eleven SS showed a collapsing of the distinction between
the past and future tenses due to the confusion of mutated and non-mutated
forms. Confusion was also apparent in SS use of the conditional tense, where
54 per cent of the forms produced were unrecognisable.

4.3.2 Case usage

Traditional Scots Gaelic has four cases: one form shared for the nominative/
accusative and a distinct form for each of the genitive, dative and vocative
cases. The contrast is greatest in the singular: the only distinctive form in the
plural being the vocative, with the genitive plural only present as a
rare, fossilised form. As 4.3.2.a illustrates, the different cases are indicated
chiefly by the definite article and initial consonant mutation, which change
according to case:

4.3.2.a The ESG case paradigm for masculine and feminine nouns

Masculine singular

nom./acc.	/ə(n) gatʰ/ 'the cat'
dat.	/ə xatʰ/
gen.	/ə xatʰ /
voc.	/xatʰ /

Masculine plural

nom./acc./dat.	/nə kʰačʰ/
[gen.	/nə(n) gatʰ/]
voc.	/xačʰ /

Feminine singular

nom./acc.	/ə xalag/ 'the girl'
dat.	/ə xalag/
gen.	/ə xalag /
voc.	/xalag/

Feminine plural

nom./acc./dat.	/nə kalagən/
[gen.	/nə(n) galagən/]
voc.	/xalagən /

In ESG, the genitive case was found to be moribund, with prepositional phrases usually being preferred to indicate possession. The dative case was found only to be distinguished in masculine nouns beginning with a labial or velar stop. Nouns beginning with other initial consonants, and which show this case distinction in standard Scots Gaelic, were found not to have a distinctive dative form in ESG.

In ESG, where it is marked, the dative is conveyed by the article losing its final consonant and the noun being lenited. This stands in contrast to the nominative/accusative case where the noun is nasalised. As seen in 4.3.2.b and 4.3.2.c, the use of the dative in prepositional phrases illustrated clearly the difference in usage between OFS and YFS.

4.3.2.b Mutation used in the dative environment: results for Brora and Golspie

	Lenited		Nasalised	
	Number	Percentage	Number	Percentage
OFS	42	98	1	2
YFS	–	–	–	–
SS	35	80	9	20

4.3.2c Mutation used in the dative environment: results for Embo

	Lenited		Nasalised	
	Number	Percentage	Number	Percentage
OFS	33	77	10	23
YFS	45	51	43	49
SS	27	50	27	50

(after Dorian 1981: 132)

In the dative environment, the OFS used the appropriate mutation (lenition) 98 per cent of the time (Brora and Golspie) or 77 per cent of the time (Embo). However, the Embo YFS (there were no YFS in Brora or Golspie) nasalise 49 per cent of the masculine 'dative' nouns.

The chief signal of the vocative case in the singular and plural is the lenition of the initial consonant. Two OFS and two YFS lenited for the vocative in 100 per cent of the vocative test sentences. But although one YFS showed only a very weak retention of the vocative lenition (20 per cent) no fluent speaker is entirely lacking the phenomenon. However, by contrast, three SS showed no lenition at all in the vocative and of the eight who did lenite in this context some of the time, none did so consistently (see Section 4.3.2.d).

4.3.2.d Use of lenition to signal the vocative

	Number of speakers	Number of opportunities	Number of lenitions	Percentage of use
OFS	4	40	38	95
YFS	6	53	40	75
SS	11	88	23	26

(after Dorian 1981: 135)

In terms of case usage, therefore, there seems to be a conservative OFS system which gives way to an increasingly undifferentiated noun phrase among YFS. The most deviant usage of all, however, is recorded for SS.

The departure from OFS norms exemplified by these variables was reproduced in the case of numerous other variables examined in this and other studies of ESG made by Dorian. However, although some of the changes recorded are clearly due to the influence of English, Dorian's work reveals that the type of changes noted are not exclusive to the language death scenario. Indeed, as we saw in Chapter 3, the loss of case distinctions was part of the process which 'gave birth' to Proto-Germanic from Proto-Indo-European. Rather, Dorian shows ESG to be obsolescent by portraying the widespread and accelerated linguistic change occurring in the variety while stressing its particular sociopolitical environment.

As a final point, Dorian's study shows that the occurrence of language death does not automatically entail widespread morphological breakdown. In this and other studies (such as Dorian 1978a) she concludes that a great deal of morphological complexity is found even among the most halting speakers of ESG, and even very near the point of its extinction. The simplification found appeared to be relatively minimal and although some of the devices most alien to English showed a marked weakening, there was no 'wholesale' dropping of devices not found in English, nor any wholesale importation of high-frequency English elements, even in the usage of the very weakest SS. For example, in discussing the complex noun plural morphology of ESG, Dorian (1981: 136) notes the existence of eleven different pluralisation devices. Her data reveal a marked movement in the direction of simplification by the extension of the process of simple suffixation to nouns that would normally require some other device in fluent-speaker usage. It is significant that of the eleven different ways of nominal plural marking, the one being generalised in ESG is that bearing the closest resemblance to the device used in English. However, it is not the English plural morph which is being borrowed but rather the tendency of English to realise most of its plural marking by the single grammatical device of suffixation, and ESG does this using indigenous material. Moreover, as we have seen, some case morphology was retained by even the weakest SS. In other words, ESG may be dying, but it is doing so 'with its morphological boots on' (Dorian 1978a: 608).

4.4 Case study: Pennsylvania German

The study made of Pennsylvania German by Marion Lois Huffines illustrates how language death studies may also be made of languages spoken
beyond the geographical frontiers of the territory occupied by its original
native speakers. The language known today as Pennsylvania German (PG)
was brought to America as early as 1683 by German immigrants, many of
whom came from the Rhine valley area and were seeking to escape economic
hardship and religious persecution. During colonial times, many of these
immigrants settled initially in farm communities across south-eastern and
central Pennsylvania and later in parts of Ohio, Indiana, Illinois and the
Virginias (Huffines 1989: 211). Despite the fact that many of these communities have since become assimilated into American society, the language
is still spoken natively in Amish and Old Order Mennonite communities and
can still be heard amongst the older generations in non-sectarian communities in central and eastern Pennsylvania. The sectarian communities
usually live in isolation from mainstream US society and culture, wearing
distinctive clothing and shunning the modern way of life and many of its
trappings. English is learnt at school and is used in the sectarians' limited
transactions with the 'outside world'. Although all those interviewed were
bilingual, PG is the everyday language of the community. High German is
only used in Bible readings and in some religious rites. In the non-sectarian
communities, however, there is a situation of impending language death as
PG is not being passed on to future generations. English is the native language of all except the oldest members of society, and in these communities
the oldest members are the only people who really use PG on an everyday
basis. English is also used more in religious services than in the sectarian
communities. It is impossible to pick out one sole reason for the impending
demise of PG in the non-sectarian communities, but some of the contributory causes are, undoubtedly: there is no one domain where PG is the
dominant variety; speaker numbers are small, and the speakers themselves
operate within the (English) social and cultural life of the mainstream USA;
there are no official establishments (such as schools or churches) that
support PG; and, lastly, PG-accented English is stigmatised (Huffines 1980:
46–52).

   In her study, Huffines examined the 'dying' variety of PG spoken by the
non-sectarians in relation to that of sectarians. Although the distinct back-
grounds of the two communities (the sectarians living in relative isolation,
the non-sectarians more integrated in US society) might have led to the
expectation that greater evidence of innovation and change would be found
in the PG spoken in the non-sectarian community, Huffines's results
revealed that, in fact, this was not the case, as will now be illustrated with
reference to two of the variables studied.

4.4.1 *Case usage*

Unlike in standard German, in PG there is no nominative/accusative distinction for nouns. However, in the pronoun system, the nominative, accusative and dative are all distinguished. Informants were asked to translate a number of English sentences into PG and their results are reproduced in 4.4.1.a.

4.4.1.a Case of personal pronouns in dative functions

Group	Dative	Accusative
Non-sectarian	83	22
Mennonite	1	86
Amish	2	90

(after Huffines 1991: 129)

As can be seen, despite the fact that PG traditionally distinguishes between dative and accusative pronouns, use of the dative is virtually non-existent among sectarians, whereas even though some variation exists among the non-sectarians, this group generally maintains the use of this case. Some examples of this are given in 4.4.1.b.

4.4.1.b Examples of pronouns in dative functions (translation task)
Non-sectarian: /əs ghɛrt nɛt tsu dir/
Mennonite: /əs ghɛrt nɛt tsu dıç/
Amish: /əs hɛrt nɛt tsu dıç/
'It doesn't belong to you.'

(Huffines 1991: 129)

As a final point, it is also worth reflecting with Huffines (1991: 133) that, in fact, there may even be other factors at play here. For example, the accusative and dative cases have been merged in the German of Berlin without any intimate contact whatsoever with English. This is an example of the internal/external ambiguity discussed in Chapter 2.

4.4.2 *Word order*

In independent clauses involving an adverb, the PG past participle traditionally occupies the final position: /əs hat gɛsdər gərɛɣərt/. This contrasts with English word order where, in the corresponding sentence, *It rained yesterday*, the past participle would not be in final position (Huffines 1991: 134–5). In free conversation, however, the non-sectarians positioned past participles in final position far more frequently than the sectarians.

4.4.2.a Position of past participle in independent clauses (free conversation)

Group	Total number of participles	Non-final (number)	Non-final (percentage)
Non-sectarians	678	94	14
Mennonite	496	117	24
Amish	357	11	28

(after Huffines 1991: 134)

Evidence from Huffines's work therefore suggests several interesting findings. First, we see that although PG is still being used on a daily basis by the sectarians, it is showing evidence of change, the direction of which suggests an apparent English influence. The speech of the non-sectarian native speakers, on the other hand, is more conservative: the dative is used for dative functions and more past participles are positioned word finally. Even though PG is undergoing a decrease in speaker numbers and a decline in usage typical of a dying language, Huffines's work shows that, as was seen in Section 4.3 above, the language is dying relatively 'intact'. We can also see that language death does not necessarily involve convergence to the dominant variety (see Chapter 2), even in the presence of a large amount of contact (although Huffines (1989) reveals that in fact more variation is apparent in the PG spoken by native English-speaking non-sectarians).

The sectarians, on the other hand, although living apart from mainstream US culture and refusing to integrate linguistically by maintaining PG as their everyday language, do, paradoxically, accommodate to the linguistic environment, not by switching to English, but by making their PG more like English. Hence, despite the fact that the norms governing community life dictate that PG is to be used as the everyday language of the community, it does not prescribe the form of the language used. Although it might initially have been expected that, due to the different lifestyles of the two groups, it would be the variety spoken by the non-sectarians which would have shown more of a tendency to converge with English, Huffines (1991: 135–6) suggests that the results may be explained in the following way. Non-sectarians speak PG to their linguistic peers, but if they have difficulty in expressing themselves, they have the option of switching to English. In the sectarian communities, however, switching to English is not appropriate. Since the sectarians have no real exposure to standard German, it is claimed that they are only able to elaborate and develop their language by using resources from English (remember that all the sectarians interviewed were bilingual). This dependence upon English in a context that does not allow switching paradoxically leaves their PG open to English influence. Switching to English therefore protects the PG of non-sectarians from this influence, although it hastens its death in the non-sectarian communities. In the sectarian communities, then, PG is maintained as an everyday language via – paradoxically – the ability of its speakers to elaborate it with English elements.

4.5 Dialect death

As we have seen, the term *language death* has been used to refer not only to obsolescent languages (such as Breton or Shoshoni) but also to the demise of dialects (such as East Sutherland Gaelic). Although this may initially seem surprising, it is entirely appropriate since, as Dorian (1981: 8) has pointed out, if a dialect dies out and is replaced by some form of a different language altogether (see Section 4.3), then the dialect loss in question is also a case of language death – in other words, one distinct language being superseded by another in the regional context. In this framework, therefore, language death and *dialect death* are virtually synonymous. However, as we will see in this section, it is also possible to focus on dialect death from another perspective, namely, when the rise of a standard language precipitates the demise of its related dialects.

It should be pointed out, of course, that the standardisation of a language does not automatically entail the loss of its associated dialects: English dialects are still spoken today, many centuries after the emergence of standard English. However, we will see that the rise of a standard is mainly the result of sociopolitical and cultural factors and that its purpose is to unite the speech community, through knowledge of a codified, uniform variety. The rise of a standard is therefore likely to have a hand in dialect death for although the elevation on one variety to the standard leaves the other dialects intact, the fact that the standard language is the only one deemed appropriate for 'official' functions such as the media, education and government and is ultimately regarded as a symbol of loyalty for the whole community means that its associated dialects are often felt to be 'inferior' by their speakers and come to be reserved for non-official functions, such as for use with family and friends. As upward mobility comes to be attached to the standard language, dialects cease to be transmitted to the next generation and eventually stop being spoken. This second type of dialect death, therefore, contrasts from that mentioned in Section 4.3 in that although the dialects in question may disappear altogether from a region, the associated language survives in that area.

There are two main ways in which standardisation can occur. These will now be outlined briefly.

4.6 Case study: French

Many sociolinguists tend to reduce the process of standardisation to four separate stages: *selection, codification, elaboration of function* and *acceptance* (Haugen 1966). The selection of one form as a prestige variety has little to do with linguistic considerations and is frequently influenced by factors such as political centralisation, with the language of the power base often gaining in importance as it becomes the medium of political transactions and commercial dealings. The Latin brought to Gaul in the wake of the spread of the Roman Empire had, by the ninth century, fragmented into a number of dialects (see Chapter 3). Linguistically, these were all the equal of another, but the economic and cultural pre-eminence of the dialect spoken in the Île-de-France (the area of modern Paris) as the variety used by the king increased the prestige of this variety and its influence consequently extended first throughout northern and then southern France (Lodge 1993).

As its influence increased, the Paris dialect started to be used in domains hitherto reserved for Latin and, for example, from the fourteenth century onwards it became used in medical, legal and even religious texts. It thus started to undergo an elaboration of function. Between 1490 and 1539, a series of Royal Edicts were announced, which had the main purpose of enshrining French (as this dialect was called) as the language of government and administration. The most famous of these was the Ordinance of Villers-Cotterêts (1539), which stipulated that 'all legal decisions and all procedures pertaining to either the highest courts or to the lower or inferior ones . . . should be pronounced, registered and delivered to the litigants in the French vernacular language and in no other way' (translated in Lodge 1993: 126).

As it became used for an increasing number of official functions, French began to be codified by lexicographers such as Estienne (in his *Dictionnaire françois–latin* (1549)), grammarians such as Vaugelas (*Remarques sur la langue française* (1647)) and Arnauld and Lancelot (*Grammaire générale et raisonée* (1660)) and by the establishment of institutions such as the Académie française (1635). This helped set down a model of what was deemed to be good usage: prescriptive norms that contained the 'rules' of the language.

The final stage, acceptance, is deemed to be complete when the language is considered as the principal language of the community by the relevant population. During the revolution of 1789, French was declared to be the sole official language of France and was promoted as such via a number of decrees, for example that of 1794 which ordered the establishment of a French-speaking teacher in every district of those areas of France where the inhabitants normally expressed themselves in other languages, such as Breton, Italian, Basque and German. Through the process of standardisation, French has therefore risen to a position of 'first among equals'. This clearly has had adverse effects on the remaining dialects of France. Today, standard French alone represents the prestige variety, the linguistic norm to be aspired to within the speech community. People have therefore striven to acquire this variety and have consequently turned their back on the other French dialects.

4.7 Case study: Welsh

Although the proliferation of a prestige dialect is the most common way in which standardisation can take place, it is not the only one. There are also instances whereby the process involves a conscious attempt to divest the different dialects of their regional, idiosyncratic features, thereby seeking to arrive at a 'common core' variety. This is the process that occurred in Wales.

As in Gaul, widespread dialectal fragmentation occurred in Wales very early on, resulting in major dialect areas. However, because of its broken terrain, Wales historically never had a single easily recognisable power base. This meant that there was no prestige dialect immediately available as a candidate for elevation as the standard, so that when it did occur, the process of standardisation differed from the conventional pattern.

By the twelfth century, the country's literature was based firmly on the bardic tradition, whose strict regulations led to the development of a highly specialised, poetic language that was far removed from the spoken language of the day. No dialectal features appeared in the work of the bards and it was impossible to tell from the language used which part of Wales a poet was from. In other words, it was an early literary standard.

The dissolution of the bardic schools brought in its wake a relaxation in the implementation of the rigorous poetic conventions, but although the standard fell largely into disuse during this period, its existence was not forgotten. When called upon, therefore, in 1563 to undertake a translation of the New Testament into a Welsh which would be understood by the whole of the country, William Salesbury turned to this old bardic language as an available literary variety. A similar policy was adopted by William Morgan who, in 1588, produced the first complete Welsh Bible. The importance of the translation of the Bible into Welsh cannot be underestimated as it re-established the bardic language as the literary standard, and the fact that it was used in such a significant text enabled the standard to gain widespread currency throughout Wales.

Standard literary Welsh underwent codification by means of dictionaries, such as the *Dictionarium Duplex* (1632) by Dr John Davies, Henry Salesbury's *Geirfa Tafod Cymraeg*, published a few years later, and by grammars such as that of Dr Gruffydd Robert, *Gramadeg Cymraeg* (1567) and Dr John Davies, *Antiquae Linguae Britannicae nunc Communiter Dictae Cambro-Britannicae a fuis Cymraecae vel Cambricae ab alys Wallicae Rudimenta* (1621). Although the Welsh of the 1588 Bible has undergone subsequent modification by scholars who have aimed to make it suitable for use in a greater variety of contexts, both the modern literary language and standard spoken Welsh are still based more on the variety used by William Morgan than on anything else.

This second type of dialect death, therefore, can be considered as a by-product of standardisation, and its linguistic processes have been examined by Jones (1998). One of the dialects included in this study was the Welsh spoken in Rhosllannerchrugog, a large village situated in north-east Wales. According to the 1991 Census, Rhosllannerchrugog had, at that time, a population of some 9,169 residents, 38.1 per cent of whom were Welsh-speaking. Despite the fact, therefore, that Welsh speakers formed a minority, the speech community was sufficiently large for Welsh to be used in Rhosllannerchrugog as an everyday means of communication and Welsh was heard frequently on the street. The dialect spoken in the village was highly distinctive and incorporated many idiosyncratic phonological and lexical features (Jones 1998: 367–79).

Analysis of the spoken Welsh of ninety-six native speakers of the area revealed the marked loss of dialect features. For instance, in standard Welsh, final [ð] is commonly found as a noun ending (*bwrdd* [bʊrð] 'table'; *gardd* [garð] 'garden'; *ffordd* [fɔrð] 'road' and so forth). In Rhosllannerchrugog, final [ð] is usually lost when it forms part of the cluster [rð], hence [bʊr]; [gar]; [fɔr] and so forth.

Analysis of this variable demonstrated that a tendency to include final [ð] (as in the standard language) was progressively emerging in the Welsh of Rhosllannerchrugog. As Figure 4.7 shows, the schoolchildren produced final [ð] in nearly all the possible contexts. It was also apparent that the introduction of word-final [ð] rose with the age of the speaker, with those aged seventy-five and over showing least inclination towards the realisation of the phoneme in this context. Although Welsh is therefore still a living language in Rhosllannerchrugog, from the trend outlined in the graph, it seems that the type of Welsh spoken by older and younger speakers differs significantly. The Welsh spoken by the former is primarily dialectal in nature, whereas that of the latter is far more standardised. The increased contact between the speech community and standard Welsh (via, for example, education and the media), coupled with the enhanced prestige attached to the variety is leading to the progressive loss of the dialect.

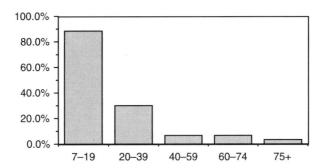

Age-group	7–19	20–39	40–59	60–74	75+
Number of opportunities	66	46	58	42	63

$\chi^2 = 153.65 > 9.49$ $p = 0.05$

Figure 4.7 Introduction of final [ð] in certain contexts

4.8 Discussion

In this chapter, we have seen that language obsolescence is a linguistic process precipitated by contact with another variety that may ultimately culminate in language death. It has been demonstrated that analyses of this type of linguistic change should consider the sociopolitical setting as well as the linguistic changes themselves, for the latter alone may not be sufficient to distinguish language death from change occurring in 'healthy' languages. We have also seen that although, in certain contexts, the loss of dialects may also be considered to be cases of language death, due to their particular sociopolitical characteristics, dialects may also disappear as a consequence of the spread of an associated standard language. As we have seen, this means that dialect death may be divided into two distinct and identifiable subtypes.

As a final point, it is interesting to consider what happens when language death and dialect death both occur simultaneously within the same speech community. In Wales, for example, at a superordinate level, there is evidence of language obsolescence, resulting in a decline in the number of speakers and in linguistic change (Jones 1998) and, at a subordinate level, the loss of dialect features in the wake of the spread of standard Welsh. It may be that within the context of language obsolescence these two phenomena are somehow linked – the loss of dialect features providing the means of establishing a more uniform type of speech throughout Wales. This, in turn, may enable the Welsh language to put up a stronger defence against the threat of language death posed by English. This last point is, however, entirely speculative and what little evidence there is to date suggests that the Welsh situation is by no means borne out in all speech communities, Breton being a case in point (Jones 1998: 296–333). However, this remains an interesting avenue for future exploration.

Our discussion of change and its potential realisation in instances of language birth and death has so far assumed that speakers, despite ultimately being the controlling force behind such processes, are generally unaware of the 'linguistic decisions' that they make. While this is indeed true in the majority of cases, there are in fact instances in which '(socio)linguistic decisions' are deliberately taken with a view to influencing the fate of a language and indeed, in some cases, that of the community with which it is associated. We consider attempts at such types of change in the following three chapters, and do so in the context of *language planning*, a phenomenon which we first explore in detail in Chapter 5. Chapter 6 considers strategies of language planning aimed at reviving obsolescent languages and Chapter 7, at those involved in the deliberate creation of new languages.

5 Language planning and revitalisation[1]

5.1 Introduction

Language planning is a relatively new addition to the discipline of linguistics. The term was first introduced in 1959 by Einar Haugen, and the field has become increasingly important as awareness of the sociopolitical nature of language choices in multilingual/multidialectal communities has grown. The definition and aims of language planning have been the subject of much discussion and debate (see, for example, Cooper 1989; King 1999: 111; Gorman 1973: 72; Nahir 1984: 294; Rabin 1971: 277–9; and Hornberger 1989: 7), but there is a general consensus that it essentially involves 'deliberate efforts to influence the behaviour of others with respect to the acquisition, structure or functional allocation of their language codes' (Cooper 1989: 45). Fasold (1984: 246) underlines the deliberate nature of the undertaking (the very term *language planning* implies that certain choices will be made about language behaviour), and we would emphasise here too the ideological: whatever choices are made and implemented by language planners will be done in conformity with a particular set of beliefs and principles, which are not necessarily shared by the subject community.

The ideology or ideologies that underlie language planning strategies are often at least partly attributable to what has been described as *language policy*, or 'the set of positions, principles and decisions reflecting [a] community's relationships to its verbal repertoire and communicative potential' (Bugarski 1992: 18; cited in Schiffman 1996: 3). The strategies of language planning are therefore often formulated 'within language policy to act on linguistic communication in a community, typically by directing the development of its languages' (Schiffman 1996: 3). The fact that policy and planning can, and often do, feed into each other means that they are sometimes 'treated as one' in the relevant literature (Schiffman 1996: 3). However, Schiffman rightly points out that there are important distinctions between the two, and that language policy is a complex entity in itself. For example, language policy can have conflicting manifestations at different bureaucratic levels, which can make holistic language planning difficult. Thus, the individual cantons of Switzerland, for example, may have different 'federal' language policies, which in turn may differ from those exhibited at municipal level, in educational institutions, judiciaries and even in non-governmental organisations such as churches and labour unions. In polities such as these (which include areas such as the Indian states, the USA, the provinces of Canada and so on), the result is often 'a hodge-podge of rules, regulations and policies that may be in conflict with other state, local or even federal rules, regulations and policies' (Schiffman 1996: 4). In addition, the existence of a policy on language use does not necessarily imply its implementation. For example, a government's educational plan may state that schools are to encourage 'respect for and appreciation of' an unofficial, indigenous vernacular, but the planning strategies which would facilitate this are not necessarily put into place. This is often attributable to the coexistence of overt and covert language policies. A community may have an overt '(explicit, formalised, *de jure*, codified, manifest)' language policy that conflicts with covert '(implicit, informal, unstated, de facto, grass-roots, latent)' policies (Schiffman 1996: 13). Thus, even though the USA as a whole has no overt language policy that promotes the use of English over other languages, a covert policy – or a grass-roots ideology – has in fact ensured that it is the primary and in many cases, exclusive, language in many domains. As Schiffman (1996: 15) points out, covert policy does not become apparent until it is challenged: if American citizens insist on their right to carry out business in a public forum in a language other than English, then 'we would hear that "everybody knows" that the default language is English'. Thus, the covert language policy of the USA 'favours the English language. No statute or constitutional amendment or regulatory law is necessary to maintain this covert policy – *its strength lies in the basic assumptions that American society has about language*' (Schiffman 1996: 15; our emphasis).

We agree that the distinction and relationship between policy and planning is a complex one and shall return to this in the case studies. Before doing so however, we consider in more detail the aims and strategies of language planning itself.

5.2 Strategies and aims of language planning

As stated in Section 5.1, the overarching aim of language planning is to direct and influence the use of language codes within a particular community. In other words, language planning generally aims to set a speech variety on its feet, and it is worth noting that, in fact, language planning movements in different societies tend to follow and make use of similar patterns and methods of implementation. However, despite such parallels, the specific aims of planners will differ from context to context. Thus language planners in a community that is home to a obsolescent variety (for example, Jèrriais, see Section 5.4) could be said to have the same aim as those in a community with a native creole (such as Seselwa, see Section 5.5);

namely, their promotion as 'acceptable' codes in official domains. Both groups of planners are likely to channel most of their endeavours through language bills, educational activities and reform, and the media. Both campaigns are also likely to stress the cultural importance of the languages. However, there are considerations that will be specific to each context: in cases where reversing language shift is an issue, planning strategies centre on *revitalisation* (see Chapter 4 and Section 5.4) and *acquisition planning*. In ex-colonial societies that formulate official pro-creole policies, language planners are said to aim for *vernacularisation*. Thus, even though we can identify certain general aims and areas of implementation, effective assessment of planners' goals, problems, successes and failures must take account of the sociopolitical context of each situation.

Language planning strategies tend to be manifested within two particular areas, *status planning* and *corpus planning*. In the words of Kloss (1969: 81), who initially defined these subdivisions, status planning involves those 'primarily interested in the status of the language, whether it is satisfactory as it is or whether it should be lowered or raised'. Bartens (2001: 29) maintains that status planning is today used as a cover term for 'all the cultural and legal actions which can be taken to promote a language'. Indeed, status planning has often provided the impetus for corpus planning, which modifies 'the nature of the language itself' via changes in vocabulary, orthography and structure (Kloss 1969: 81). For instance, introducing a language into a new (modern) domain may well precipitate the creation of new vocabulary. Corpus planning therefore involves changes in the language itself, whereas status planning is sociopolitical in nature and hence extra-linguistic. However, although in theory it may be possible to treat these two as distinct, in practice, the boundary between them may often be blurred: a corpus planning change, such as a spelling reform for instance, could also have the effect of changing a language's status.

Despite this complementary relationship, both types of planning tend to be undertaken by different groups: status planning by politicians and administrators and corpus planning by linguists. Since 'linguists ... have no political power' and politicians 'generally have no (socio)linguistic knowledge' (Arends et al. 1995: 68), the necessary interchange of ideas between the two groups is often un-coordinated or non-existent. This often results in the 'language promotion process being slowed down in a significant manner' (Bartens 2001: 29).

In terms of aims, Cobarrubias and Fishman (1983: 63–6) identify four underlying objectives of language planning strategies, namely: the achievement of *linguistic pluralism, assimilation and purism, vernacularisation* and *internationalism*. Strategies that aim for pluralism support the 'coexistence of different language groups and their right to maintain and cultivate their languages on an equitable basis' (Cobarrubias and Fishman 1983: 65). A well-known example is that of Belgium, where French is the official language of the south, Flemish that of the north and German that of the east. French and Flemish are both officially recognised in the capital, Brussels.

Planners who have linguistic assimilation as their goal seek to ensure that all members of a speech community have the ability to use the dominant language. As we shall see in Section 5.3, this often means that the needs of linguistic minorities to maintain or gain official recognition of their native tongues are ignored. In 1938, for example, the government of the former Soviet Union stipulated that all non-Russian schools had to teach Russian as a second language. Even though schools were later granted the right to choose their language of education in 1958, Russian essentially retained domination in the schoolroom, so much so that pupils in most Russian republics received their primary and secondary schooling in this language, with little or no concession made to their respective mother tongues (Daoust 1997: 442).

According to Cobarrubias and Fishman (1983: 65), linguistic purism and assimilation are shaped by the same principles and achieve similar results. In the case of the former, an 'ideal' language variety that exists primarily in the written medium (and which is therefore somewhat estranged from the variation that characterises everyday speech) is promoted. 'This form of language is associated with specific aesthetic and sometimes moral values which represent the speech community's social ideal and norm' (Labov 1972). The belief that competence in this form guarantees social recognition and progress (despite the existence of social inequalities based on gender, ethnicity and suchlike) is also perpetuated by institutions such as the education system, the media and, in some cases, language academies. Thus, non-'ideal' forms of that language come to be seen as deviant, and their use in domains where the 'ideal' form dominates is discouraged or repressed.

A well-known historical example of the search for linguistic purism is that of France. The Académie française was set up in 1634 to oversee and regulate the development of standard French (see Chapter 4), a variety that existed (as standards tend to) mainly in the written form. The post-Revolution government of eighteenth-century France decreed that this standard (partly codified by a dictionary of usage) was to be the sole language of primary schools and also of the law. In addition, the orthographic conventions devised by the Académie were made compulsory in 1832. In passing such laws, the government hoped not only to make knowledge of standard conventions as widespread as possible, but also to wipe out use of what they believed to be 'impure' varieties of French.[2]

Language planning strategies whose goal is vernacularisation have indigenous languages or those that are widely known in a community officially recognised instead of, or alongside, an international language of wider communication. In Haiti, for example, the indigenous French-lexifier creole now carries official status, along with French. Similarly, Bislama, the Melanesian Pidgin English spoken in Vanuatu, is one of the island's three official languages, the other two being English and French. Section 5.5, as mentioned earlier, explores the vernacularisation of Seselwa.

Internationalism is the final category discussed by Cobarrubias and Fishman (1983). They state that strategies with this aim in mind usually result in the adoption, or maintenance, of a language of wider communication in an official capacity. The reasoning behind this is to allow for socio-economic participation at an international level. However, the promotion of this international language often entails the marginalisation of indigenous languages and their speakers, since it is typically a socially powerful elite minority who are competent in the use of the international language. Their 'hold' on the language not only invests it with prestige but also maintains their sociopolitical power.

Finally, Cooper (1989: 33) argues that another aim of language planning can be revitalisation (the relevant strategies are known as acquisition planning), which is specifically aimed at increasing the number of speakers of the language or variety in question. This is frequently seen in situations of language obsolescence (see Chapter 4), where the process may be an integral part of reversing language shift. Section 5.4 looks at this type of planning in more detail.

We now turn to our case studies, which consider three different instances of language policy and planning. Section 5.3 explores the language situation in the USA, demonstrating the complexities and contradictions in overt and covert language policy as well as the resultant difficulties in formulating language planning strategies. As we will see, the situation is perhaps inevitable in such a huge and somewhat decentralised polity, which seems to generally aim for assimilation to English despite its multilingual status. Section 5.4 considers planning in Jersey, one of the Channel Islands lying off the coast of Normandy, which is home to an obsolescent dialect, Jèrriais. Here, planning strategies are mainly aimed at revitalisation; in other words, making Jèrriais an attractive and 'useful' resource for modern users. Finally, in Section 5.5, we look at the vernacularisation of Seselwa, a French-lexifier creole spoken in the Seychelles. For this Republic, gaining official status for the indigenous language and promoting it as equal to languages institutionalised under the colonial administration has been a vital part of establishing political, and psychological, independence. As implied at the beginning of this section, the strategies and issues that planners dealing with Jèrriais and Seselwa have grappled with respectively are sometimes quite similar; something that will become clearer in the case-study discussions themselves. As we will also see, even though the aim of the planners is to set two long-suffering tongues 'on their feet', it is not at the expense of losing competence in languages which have international clout, such as English. This is of course not a consideration raised in Section 5.3 which demonstrates that, in the USA, the underlying assumption in language issues seems to be the achievement of competence in English above all else.

5.3 Case study: language policy in the USA

Language is not mentioned at all in the US Constitution. When the founding fathers were laying down the foundations for their new country, they chose not to single out any national or official language but seemed, rather, to intend it to be a matter of personal choice (Heath and Mandabach 1983: 87–105). As Gleason (1980) has pointed out, American national identity was conceived mainly in abstract, ideological terms, as the majority of early Americans shared the cultural traditions, language and religion of the nations against which they rebelled. Being American, therefore, was based around a particular mindset – the pursuit of freedom – rather than on any considerations of ethnicity. Furthermore, although colonies such as Plymouth, Pennsylvania, Maryland and others were founded by people escaping religious persecution, no one came to them in order to escape linguistic oppression (Schiffman 1996: 258). It is worth considering that even if language had been mentioned in the Declaration of Independence, it is by no means certain that English would have prevailed, as a significant proportion of the then population spoke German (Madrid 1990: 63). In fact, one apocryphal myth about this early federal period is the so-called 'Muhlenberg legend', according to which German failed to become the official language of the USA by one vote (Schiffman 1996: 219).

It is of course impossible to give a detailed linguistic history of the USA in the space of a few pages. We therefore highlight some of the landmarks in US language policy over the past century and, in so doing, illustrate the de facto promotion of a language (English) within the framework of equal linguistic rights for all.

In the early days of the Federation, although the bulk of settlers were of English descent, other European languages were also widely spoken – for example German in Pennsylvania, Dutch in New York and New Jersey, French in Louisiana, Spanish in New Mexico and California and Russian in Alaska. At the time, linguistic tolerance seems to have been widespread, although this was not extended to Native American languages. Bilingual and minority language schooling flourished in the nineteenth century, especially in German, French, Spanish and Norwegian, but even then English-only restrictions were also in operation. For example, California, a state which, as we will see, was to gain a highly prominent place in the history of US language planning, officially discontinued Spanish-language schooling in 1855 (Leibowitz 1969) and its constitution (drawn up in 1878–9) declared that 'All laws of the State of California and all official writings, and the executive, legislative, and judicial proceedings shall be conducted, preserved and published in no other than the English language' (Crawford 1992: 52). This declaration was made despite the fact that the Treaty of Guadalupe Hidalgo (1848), which ended the Mexican–American War and brought California into the Union, had seemed to imply the right of Spanish-speaking citizens thereby annexed into the USA to maintain Spanish without restriction.

Crucially, however, despite such restrictions, which were apparent to some degree in many parts of the Federation, it was never proposed that English should be favoured as the official language of the USA. Indeed, the first official-language measure ever considered by the US Congress was a rather tongue-in-cheek proposal in 1923 to declare 'American' (versus English) the national language. The Bill pleaded for American writers to 'drop their top-coats, spats, and swagger-sticks, and assume occasionally their buckskin, moccasins, and tomahawks'. It failed in committee, although it was adopted later that year by the state of Illinois.

Under the American Constitution, the overall rights of all Americans are protected, and one of the arguments against an overt national language policy is that this would favour one subset of American citizens above others. However, Schiffman (1996: 211) argues that it is often assumed that

> because the US has no overt stated policy regarding . . . language, the statement that the US 'has no official policy' is equivalent to 'has no policy' or is 'neutral' with regard to English or any other language. This totally ignores the very strong *implicit* policy with regard to the English language (and other languages) that is obvious to any casual observer.

Indeed, Hornberger (1990) outlines a number of developments in twentieth-century US educational policy that support this perspective. For example, in 1923, German Lutherans filed a suit against the state of Nebraska (*Meyer* vs. *Nebraska 1923*), after it legislated that only English could be used in its schools. The Meyer mentioned in the title of the case was a teacher who, in spite of the legislation, taught German to pupils, claiming that this was not in violation of the state regulations since he did so outside of school hours. He was, however, accused of breaking the law, hence the Lutherans' suit. The Supreme Court found for the Lutherans, ruling that forbidding teaching languages other than English until the eighth grade violated the Fourteenth Amendment (which precludes any state-imposed distinction based on race). However, although its ruling seemed to strike a blow for minority-language tuition (in private if not in state schools), the decision seems to have been based on the right of a child to learn any 'foreign' language, rather than on the rights of a national minority to be educated in their native language. The petitioners had won, but it was clear that they had not done so on the language maintenance ticket.

The mindset that English is primary and all other languages 'foreign' can also be seen in the thirty-four-year history of the Bilingual Education Act, initially proposed in 1967. It was originally intended as an attempt to address 'the special educational needs of the large numbers of students in the United States whose mother tongue is Spanish and to whom English is a foreign language' (Cazden and Snow 1990). Although its title seems to imply that the aim was to protect the minority languages of the USA, before it was approved in 1968, the Act was expanded from a primarily Spanish focus to cover other languages spoken in the USA, and its text was modified so that it referred to the individuals it was legislating for as 'children of limited English-speaking ability'. The use of this term therefore effectively changed the Bill's focus into a remedial programme for children who were deficient in English-language skills, rather than one which catered for those who were proficient in another tongue (Lyons 1990: 68). Instead of furthering a child's native language skills, it mainly set out to ensure that all children, whatever their linguistic background, would become literate in English. The Bill was amended several times, but never was its aim stated more explicitly than in the 1978 amendment, which declared that 'the objective of the program shall be to assist children of limited English proficiency to improve their English language skills, and the participation of other children in the program must be for the principal purpose of contributing to the achievement of that objective' (Cazden and Snow 1990). Subsequent revisions did go some way towards redressing the balance – for example, the 1994 version included among its goals 'developing the English skills . . . and to the extent possible, the native-language skills' (Crawford 2002) of LEP [limited-English-proficient] students'. However, in 2002, the Act was abolished and the name of its replacement, the English Language Acquisition Act, demonstrated clearly the thinking behind federal policy. This was also highlighted by the renaming of the Federal Office of Bilingual Education and Minority Language Affairs, which as a consequence of the Act became the Office of English Language Acquisition, Language Enhancement and Academic Achievement for Limited-English-Proficient Students.

In 1974, another landmark case, *Lau* vs. *Nichols*, was brought by the parents of nearly 3,000 Chinese pupils against the San Francisco Unified School District. It was filed on the basis of Title VI of the 1964 Civil Rights Act, which prohibited discrimination on the basis of race, colour or national origin in federally-assisted education programmes, and of the Fourteenth amendment to the US Constitution. The plaintiffs argued that, in this District, some two-thirds of the Chinese students received no extra special tuition in English and that this was in violation of both the above pieces of legislation. The Supreme Court found for the plaintiffs, ruling that there was no equality of treatment to be had merely by providing students with the same facilities, textbooks, teachers, and curriculum, since those who did not understand English were effectively foreclosed from any meaningful education. This decision had repercussions for the entire US school system, and in 1975 a series of guidelines was announced by the US Commissioner for Education that spelt out steps to remedy such linguistic inequality. These were known informally as the 'Lau Remedies'. These guidelines were further developed under President Carter (1976–80) and took on the title of 'Lau Regulations', but they have never become law.

Such cases and bills clearly illustrate the de facto belief, shared also by non-native speakers, in the primacy of English. An attempt to turn this into a *de jure* assimilationist policy was made in 1981, with the submission of an

English Language Amendment to the US Constitution. Its proposal that 'The English Language shall be the official language of the United States', would have had the effect of virtually banning the use of all other languages by federal, state and local governments. The measure has been before Congress several times but has never come to a vote.

Powered by the same underlying ideology as the English Language Amendment proposal, a movement known as English Only came to the fore in the mid-1980s. Its members advocate the promotion of English as the official language of the USA at the expense of multilingualism, arguing that English is the unifying force of America and, as such, facilitates the social assimilation of ethnically diverse groups. Two of the movement's main mouthpieces are the national groups English First and US English. English First, founded in 1986, aims to make English America's official language and to eliminate what it sees as costly and ineffective multilingual policies. US English encompasses two organisations, the US English Federation and US English, Inc. The former is based in Washington DC and works to promote the use of English in education, contending that 'learning English quickly and learning it with English-speaking peers is the best way for English learners to get ahead academically and socially'. Its stated goal is 'to ensure that English continues to serve as an integrating force among our nation's many ethnic groups and remains a vehicle of opportunity for new Americans', and stresses the necessity for immigrants to learn English in order to 'enjoy the economic opportunities available in this country' (US English 2002a).

US English, Inc. is a legislative organisation founded in 1983, with 1.7 million members worldwide. It works at the state and federal levels in order to pass legislation to make English the official language of government and to reform bilingual education. It too stresses that speaking English is 'the single greatest empowering tool that immigrants must have to succeed' (US English 2002b).

A more recent organisation, English Plus, which advocates that additional language support is essential for equality of opportunity, has emerged as the main policy alternative to the English Only movement. It does not deny the importance of being proficient in English but also advocates the preservation of other languages and cultures. To date, a non-binding English Plus resolution (H.Con.Res.9) has been introduced in the 107th Congress (2000–1) (by Rep. José Serrano) and similar measures have been introduced at the state level in New Mexico (1989), Oregon (1989), Washington (1989) and Rhode Island (1992). The English Plus Information Clearinghouse (EPIC) is a coalition of more than fifty civil rights and educational organisations opposed to the campaign for Official English. It was established in 1987 under the auspices of the National Immigration Refugee and Citizenship Forum and the Joint National Committee for Languages.

It is perhaps appropriate at this point to consider a related issue: the nature of the English being promoted. Given the highly diverse nature of the

US population, this is not a straightforward matter. Alongside standard English, for example, there exist several, distinct varieties of ethnic English, such as Indian English (Leap 1992) and African American Vernacular English (AAVE) (Rickford 1992). It seems that in the USA an ideal of linguistic purism holds: the promotion of English effectively means the promotion of standard English. As a result, speakers of other varieties may be, in practice, as disadvantaged as those who speak completely different languages as their native tongues. Lippi-Green (1997: 112) cites an essay by Winsboro and Solomon (1990: 51–2) who state that 'we must . . . teach those who speak with a dialect [meaning AAVE] that a realistic chance of success in American society is frequently based on mastery of Standard English'.

In fact, there is clear evidence that speakers of other varieties of English are all too aware of this. In 1979, African-American parents of children attending the Martin Luther King school in Ann Arbor, Michigan won a landmark court case which alleged that the school prevented their children from making normal academic progress by ignoring the fact that their native AAVE was radically different from standard American English (Schiffman 1996: 241–4). This was the first time a judge had ruled that a language barrier did not have to be caused by a foreign language. The decision highlights the complexity of the issues that need to be addressed when attempting to formulate a coherent language policy in a country such as the USA. It is extremely unlikely, for example, that proponents of English First intend to include AAVE within the scope of their campaigns.

We have, so far, focused on the promotion of English in education. In the remainder of this section, we shall briefly outline US language policy outside the classroom, mainly by focusing on recent developments in California, a state which, as mentioned earlier, has made language planning decisions throughout the twentieth century. In November 1986, the voters of California passed Proposition 63, a constitutional amendment that made English the official language of the state, by a 74 per cent margin. Its acceptance meant that any law passed in the state would have to take this into account. California was not the first to make English its official language, having been preceded by Nebraska (1923) (the only other state to do this by constitutional amendment), Illinois (1969), Virginia (1981), Indiana (1984), Kentucky (1984) and Tennessee (1984). However, the decision was noteworthy in view of California's sizeable Spanish-speaking population and was undoubtedly a measure of the support enjoyed by the growing English Only campaign.

On 2 June 1998, this was followed by Proposition 227, which was passed by 61 per cent. The proposition arose as a result of a 1996 action whereby a group of Spanish-speaking parents pulled their children out of school as a protest against what they saw as the failure of bilingual education to teach English properly. The boycott came to the attention of businessman Ron Unz, who subsequently bankrolled a state-wide ballot initiative requiring that 'all children . . . be taught English by being taught in English' (Unz and

Tuchman 1997: Chapter 3, article 2). Proposition 227 had the repercussion of virtually outlawing all classes taught in languages other than English for children under the age of ten, replacing them with a class aimed at enhancing the English language skills of children with mother tongues other than English. It was estimated that the measure affected nearly one in four Californian students and allowed parents to sue any teacher who violated the English-only provisions. As with *Lau* vs. *Nichols* two decades before, it is noteworthy that it was non-native English speakers whose action initiated this measure. Moreover, the situation is also indicative of the fact that the Lau Remedies were either not being applied or were failing to produce the required results.

The repercussions of Proposition 227 were also felt outside California: on 7 November 2000, Proposition 203 was adopted by the voters of Arizona by 63 per cent to 37 per cent. This campaign was also bankrolled by Unz and, as a consequence of its adoption, all public school instruction in the state henceforth had to be conducted in English, with children not fluent in the language being placed in an intensive one-year English immersion programme.

On 24 April 2001, Oakland launched California into the headlines once more by becoming the first city in the state (and probably in the USA) to introduce a policy establishing equal access to city services and programmes on the basis of language. This was achieved by requiring city departments to offer bilingual services and materials if a substantial portion of the public utilising city services did not speak English effectively because it was not their primary language. In other words, the Oakland decision guaranteed bilingual services where needed in order to provide equal access to local government. This, then, was very much a pro-English Plus resolution and illustrates how, in the USA, a local ordinance may be diametrically opposed to state language policy.

As Schiffman (1996: 246) states, 'though the last 30 years have witnessed a number of statutory laws, initiatives and Supreme Court cases, a coherent and explicit policy about language and language rights has not emerged, despite the high hopes of some and the fears of others'. Language rights have not been seen by legislative organisations, such as the courts, as fundamental; instead, they are annexed to other rights, such as 'due process, educational equity', or are seen as rights possessed by individual adults (cf. *Meyer* vs. *Nebraska* 1923). Indeed, Schiffman (1996: 247) maintains that 'the courts have stopped short of interpreting the US constitution to mean that language rights are a fundamental American right'. Perhaps the only real attempt to address this was the 1990 Native American Languages Act, whose goals included the promotion, protection and preservation of the indigenous languages of the USA. In view of the federal government's treatment of Native Americans in recent centuries, however, this was a case of too little much too late.

It is highly likely that the reason behind the lack of a centralised policy that guarantees language rights is that the basic, crucial ideology that favours English as the language of the 'melting-pot' has not changed. While there are occasional challenges to this myth, and while some states, local institutions and jurisdictions will officially recognise that not all of their individual speech communities are monoglot English users, there is still an underlying, strongly held belief that there is only one American language: 'antipathy to any expanded role for "foreign" language [*sic*] in American life is strong, and allied perhaps to xenophobia, racism and other unsavoury attitudes, it does not wish to tolerate something that it sees as dangerous, untrustworthy . . . perhaps even un-American' (Schiffman 1996: 247).

Kloss (1977: 284) importantly highlights the flip side to the 'antipathy to "foreign" languages' coin; namely, the 'absorbing power of the highly developed American society'. In other words, native speakers of languages other than English (and indeed, of other American varieties such as AAVE), also come to believe that the language of success, progress, and also of everyday life, is the English that is promoted. Thus, linguistic assimilation has informally happened, and continues to do so, because 'the manifold opportunities for personal advancement and individual achievements which [American] society offer[s-are] so attractive' that significant numbers of the relevant groups 'sooner or later voluntarily [integrate] themselves into this society' (Kloss 1977: 284). Movements such as English First and English Only, therefore, are unlikely to have any real ideological battle on their hands; their challenge will lie in attempts to get their proposals officially recognised, since there is still a reluctance to make such restrictions on language explicit, despite their covert acceptance. Thus, the USA, a country which superficially prides itself on tolerance of diversity, continues ahead with the 'murkiest of language policies' (Schiffman 1996: 278), and the American dream continues to be dreamt in English.

5.4 Case study: language planning in Jersey

A form of Latin and, subsequently, Romance, speech has been spoken on Jersey for some two millennia. As mentioned in Chapter 2, Jèrriais is the name given to the contemporary Norman French dialect of the island. Although the dialect is closely related to the French of northern France and, in particular, to the dialects spoken in Normandy, politically Jersey has not formed part of the Duchy of Normandy since 1204 when King John of England lost the territory to France. The Channel Islands, however, elected to continue their allegiance to the British Crown, and from then on have been attached politically to the British Isles.

In spite of this, the English language did not arrive in Jersey overnight. However, Anglicisation – although slow – was steady, and as links with Britain strengthened throughout the centuries and transport improved, the presence of English on Jersey increased considerably. Gradually, the Jèrriais speech community began using English more and more often in domestic situations with family and friends and, in the twentieth century, the inter-generational chain of transmission started to break. Today, most of the island's inhabitants are monolingual speakers of English and no Jèrriais monoglots are still alive. The 2001 Census revealed that, at that time, only 2,874 inhabitants (or some 3.2 per cent of the population) were able to speak Jèrriais. Based on these figures, it is likely that, today, around 90 per cent of the dialect speakers are aged fifty and above and that fewer than 1 per cent are under twenty-five. English has become Jersey's dominant variety and Jèrriais is obsolescent.

The decline in the fortunes of Jèrriais has prompted the establishment of a revitalisation movement, which has been instrumental in initiating a series of language planning measures in favour of the dialect. These will now be outlined.

The situation in Jersey is of interest in that, unlike the case of Welsh (Jones 1998) no official state-controlled body exists to contribute to either status or corpus planning. Instead, both of these areas lie in the hands of small non-linguistically trained groups. The oldest society established for the promotion of Jèrriais – L'Assembliée d'Jèrriais ('the gathering of Jersey people') – was founded in 1951 with the aim of preserving the use of Jèrriais. Since 1952, it has published quarterly bulletins which contain poems and short stories in the dialect, and its membership has grown from twenty-two founder members to more than 160 today. The Assembliée's contribution is to status planning rather than corpus planning. It organises social events on a monthly basis, has forged close links with its counterpart on Guernsey (L'Assembllaï d'Guernesiais) and has brought Jèrriais into the religious domain by organising an annual carol service in Jèrriais. Although not a dynamic force in revitalisation, in that there is little attempt to be pro-active on the part of Jèrriais, the Assembliée provides a regular opportunity for its members to speak the dialect and a context in which Jèrriais is, for once, seen as primary.

The Island's biggest society, La Société Jersiaise ('The Jersey Society'), has existed since 1873 and boasts many branches focusing on different areas of island life. No specific provision was made for Jèrriais by the Société during most of the twentieth century, but this changed in 1994 when four members decided to found a branch of the Société, called the Section de la Langue Jèrriaise ('The Jersey Language Section'), which would 'encourage the use and study of the native language and culture' (Annual Report 1995).

The Section de la Langue Jèrriaise has had a role in both the status and corpus planning of the dialect. In the domain of status planning, it has lobbied successfully for the presence of Jèrriais on signs in the airport and harbour (achieved in 1998). It also helped to petition for increased Jèrriais air time on BBC Radio Jersey (achieved in 1997, see below) and for bilingual milk cartons to be delivered to the island's schools (achieved in 1999). Although such measures will not, in themselves, have an immediate effect on speaker numbers, by giving the dialect a presence in such high-profile locations, they help to render it familiar to non-Jèrriais speakers, and also to reinforce the image of Jersey as a bilingual island. Although initially, the presence of Jèrriais in these 'new' domains may be seen as a novelty, the higher the frequency of occurrence, the more the inclusion of the dialect will be considered 'normal'. It is hoped that, ultimately, there will be a reversal of norms, with the exclusion of Jèrriais becoming the exception.

The Section de la Langue Jèrriaise has also sought to present the dialect on a wider stage. It was prominent in the campaign for Jèrriais to feature in the opening ceremony of the 1997 Island Games, has forged links with other societies engaged in the promotion of Norman French and has ensured that Jèrriais has been represented in minority-language conferences (such as Visionet (1996) and the fourth European Conference on Immersion programmes (September 1998)). A recent project has been to launch Jèrriais on the World Wide Web[3] and to date, there are over 2,000 Jèrriais pages to be found at this site.

As far as corpus planning is concerned, the Section de la Langue Jèrriaise has also produced a Jèrriais volume in the First Thousand Words series, a vocabulary book for children providing essential terminology. The book has two aims: to supply children with many of the basic words of Jèrriais in a user-friendly way and also to show that Jèrriais can be used to talk about all aspects of modern life. To this end, it has been necessary for many of the terms found in modern domains such as computer terminology to be coined (examples of these would be *maitre-pêtre* for 'webmaster', *distchette* for 'floppy disk' and *la page d'siez-mé* for 'homepage'). The Section de la Langue Jèrriaise has, therefore, set itself the task of modernising the dialect's vocabulary. In the absence of professional assistance and governmental support, this is no mean task. Words are created during special meetings by individuals united by their concern to preserve Jèrriais but who have no actual linguistic training. This may seem an unsatisfactory way to proceed but, given the lack of support, there is no other option currently available.

Another organisation active in promoting Jèrriais is the Don Balleine Trust, which was created from a substantial legacy left by Arthur E. Balleine (1864–1943) for the study of the dialect. By publishing books in Jèrriais, the Trust has contributed to status planning but, as will be seen, by supporting the publication of novels in Jèrriais and metalinguistic works on the dialect, it has also been one of the main agencies behind the standardisation of Jèrriais.

As with the Section de la Langue Jèrriaise, no trained linguist oversees the work of the Trust. Its executive committee consists mainly of Jèrriais authors and others interested in the promotion of the dialect. Over the past thirty-five years, as well as its quarterly *Chroniques du Don Balleine* and *Nouvelles Chroniques du Don Balleine*, the Trust has published a number of works with the aim of promoting Jèrriais and, at the same time, providing a record of the dialect for posterity. Its first major publication was the *Dictionnaire*

Jersiais–Français (Le Maistre 1966), a Jèrriais–French dictionary containing some 20,000 words.

The *Dictionnaire* was a significant milestone in the history of Jèrriais in that, for the first time, it enabled spelling to be fixed and the forms of words to be determined definitively. But perhaps more valuable than this was the fact that by setting down the dialect in this way, the *Dictionnaire* gave Jèrriais the status it had hitherto lacked, enabling its speakers to consider it as a variety in its own right rather than a mere variety of French. The codification of Jèrriais was carried further in 1985, with the appearance of *Lé Jèrriais Pour Tous* ('Jersey French for All') by Paul Birt, a translator in the University of Wales, Bangor. This doubled as both a grammar of Jèrriais for the existing speech community and a textbook for beginners. *Lé Jèrriais Pour Tous* followed the lead of the *Dictionnaire* in adopting a western variety of Jèrriais known as St. Ouennais as the basis of standard Jèrriais. Although the fact that Jèrriais is not used in any official capacity means that the existence of a standard variety is not particularly relevant for the existing native speech community, in language planning terms, it was essential if any hope was to be entertained of this; for example, teaching the dialect at school.

In terms of status planning, the publication of work in and about Jèrriais has been successful in enhancing the prestige of the dialect. More recently, advocates of Jèrriais have built on this new positive awareness, and focused their attention on revitalisation, or increasing the existing pool of speakers as well as taking the dialect into new domains. A major contribution in this area on the part of the Don Balleine Trust has been the appointment of a Jèrriais language teaching co-ordinator, whose remit has been the introduction of Jèrriais into the primary school as an extra-curricular subject (see below). By expanding its role in this way, the Trust has now placed itself firmly at the heart of the revitalisation movement. We will now look at new developments in the fields of education and the media, the areas where the revitalisation effort is concentrated.

In terms of education, evening classes have been held in Jèrriais at both beginner and advanced levels since 1967. Although numbers are not high it could be argued that the culture spread by the evening classes is, in many ways, more important than the actual classes themselves in that their influence extends far beyond those who actually attend them. For example, the students play an active part in promoting Jèrriais in cultural events in the island.

Despite the structured approach to the acquisition of Jèrriais offered by the evening classes, in practice these have been insufficient to produce a significant increase in speaker numbers. Moreover, the students attracted tend to be predominantly adults. In order to target large numbers of younger students, there has therefore been a clear need to teach Jèrriais in school.

The idea of teaching Jèrriais as a fully fledged school subject has never received any official backing. However, in 1996, after seeing a report on how

Manx was currently being taught to schoolchildren on the Isle of Man (despite the fact that the last surviving native speaker had died in 1974) supporters of Jèrriais started to lobby the island's Education Committee for its teaching in primary school. An overwhelmingly positive response was obtained from parents, which led to the establishment of a two-year pilot programme to teach Jèrriais, under the direction of a Jèrriais language teaching co-ordinator. Jèrriais would be taught on a voluntary, extra-curricular basis, for thirty minutes per week, to pupils in their last two years of primary education (nine- to eleven-year-olds). The teaching programme was to be run jointly by the Don Balleine Trust and the island's Education Department. The first Jèrriais language teaching co-ordinator, a staunch supporter and promoter of the dialect who had himself learnt Jèrriais as a second language, began work in January 1999. Classes started the following September at twenty schools throughout Jersey and were attended by some 170 children. The teaching materials used were adapted from Manx. At the end of its first full year, the general feeling amongst schoolchildren and their parents was that the Jèrriais education programme had proved both desirable and a success. As a result of this, in the year 2000, the programme was awarded a further five years of funding, which has enabled Jèrriais to be introduced on the same basis into the secondary school (eleven-year-olds upwards).

In terms of the media, the position of Jèrriais has been slow to develop. Although regular columns and other articles have been published in the *Jersey Evening Post* for many years by advanced students of Jèrriais and the Don Balleine Trust, BBC Radio Jersey showed no desire to increase its provision for Jèrriais broadcasts from five minutes per week. However, in 1997, the support given to a survey about increasing the existing air time allocated to Jèrriais was such that in November of that year a new programme, *Les Crapauds Avanchent* ('The Toads Progress') was launched.[4] This twenty-minute transmission was broadcast once a fortnight, thereby more than doubling at a stroke existing Jèrriais air time. In addition to this, since 1998, Jèrriais has been given a weekly, half-hour Jèrriais slot within a popular magazine-type programme.

Jèrriais television-broadcasting is still almost non-existent. Channel Television's licence demands that sixty minutes of air time per year be allocated to the dialects of the Channel Islands, which means that, in practice, Jèrriais and Guernesiais (the Norman dialect of Guernsey, see Chapter 2) are each given one hour every two years.

Through a combination of status and corpus planning measures, Jèrriais is now in a stronger position than it was ten years ago. It is therefore appropriate to speak of Jèrriais as a variety that is being revitalised via language planning. The position of Jèrriais is somewhat unusual among minority varieties of western Europe in that language planning is occurring with very little support from official bodies. This differs from the situation in places such as Wales or Cataluña (Jones 1998; Ballart 1996) where the process is far better established and more advanced. However, we should not think that language planning is in itself an automatic saviour of obsolescent varieties. We end this discussion by raising a few points which are often critical to its success or failure in these contexts.

One major issue that needs to be considered is the role of the school, which is often given a central place in campaigns to revitalise obsolescent varieties (Jones 1998; McDonald 1989). Allowing a variety to take its place on the curriculum gives it increased status by assigning it a role in an official domain (Hornberger and King 1996: 438). However, it is important to realise that introducing a language or variety in school is not enough to secure its future. For this to be done, it is necessary to strengthen (or, in the case of Jèrriais, to re-establish) the intergenerational transmission chain. Merely increasing the numbers of speakers is ultimately meaningless if these are largely made up of non-native speakers who have neither the motivation nor the opportunity to use the minority form (Bentahila and Davies 1993: 365; cf. Ballart 1996: 15). The school therefore can be a valuable part of any planning campaign, but in the case of an obsolescent variety, it is vital that efforts made inside the classroom be complemented, and reinforced, by opportunities to use that variety outside the learning context. Interestingly, as we shall see in Section 5.5, this is also a consideration in situations where attempts are being made to encourage the use of a 'home language' in official domains.

Another crucial issue for the Jèrriais revitalisers has been the question of standardisation (a consideration that often rears its head in language planning). Because it has undergone dialectal fragmentation, promoting one unified form of Jèrriais, which has the ability to draw together the whole of the speech community (and which makes the production of pedagogical material and teaching strategies much more manageable), is more practical than catering for each individual dialect. In addition, learning a standardised form can also provide a psychological boost: it is often a more attractive proposition to new speakers than the acquisition of a minority form of what is already a minority speech variety (see also Section 5.5).

However, care is needed when planning the process of standardisation. The two main strategies are, first, the Jèrriais model, involving elevating one of the existing varieties to a 'first among equals' status and, second, the path followed by Welsh, which has been to promote a non-geographically locatable variety, divested of all salient regional features (see Chapter 4).[5] The creation and imposition of a standard can often be quite problematic (cf. Richards 1989: 109; Hornberger and King 1996: 433), especially when there is disagreement as to the candidate for elevation under the 'first among equals' model, as has been the case for Irish. For language planning to succeed, therefore, care must be taken to ensure that the variety to be promoted is acceptable to the majority of the speech community. If this is not achieved, the speech community will not identify with it and its symbolic function will be greatly diminished.

Chance has meant that Jèrriais has avoided many of the problems often inherent in the selection of a variety to be standardised. Moreover, given the sociopolitical circumstances of the dialect, it is unlikely that a rival candidate will ever emerge. The fact that speaker reduction is so advanced makes it unlikely that the promotion of St. Ouennais in school will have any detrimental effect on the other varieties, and the fact that the latter are all mutually intelligible means that there are unlikely to be any difficulties with cross-generational communication, unlike those witnessed in Brittany (see Jones 1998: 296–333).

Probably the most important factor to influence the outcome of language planning is the approval of the speech community for the measures taken. If speakers ultimately see no need for a variety to undergo a change in status then, even with considerable official backing, it is unlikely to meet with much success. One need only look at the case of Irish to see that, in spite of the huge amounts of money allocated to revitalisation and the numerous government agencies that were established to this end, lack of enthusiasm on the part of the speech community led to the movement for revitalisation being less successful than might have been anticipated.

Moreover, it is not sufficient to merely approve of the language planning measures proposed: speakers must also engage actively in their support. Of what use is Welsh television if no one watches it? Or a Catalan newspaper if no one reads it? As Fennell (1981: 39) states of language planning in the context of obsolescence,

> a shrinking language minority cannot be saved by the actions of well-wishers who do not belong to the minority in question . . . It can be saved only by itself; and then only if its members acquire the will to stop it shrinking, acquire the institutions and financial means to take appropriate measures, and take them.

Support from outside the speech community is beneficial in that it creates an atmosphere of good will towards the variety and the planning measures but, at the end of the day, this group of speakers cannot be counted on in terms of active support, as witnessed in the Breton *commune* of Plougastel-Daoulas, where many non-Breton-speaking parents declared themselves, in principle, to be in favour of optional Breton classes in school but stated that their sons or daughters were unlikely to take advantage of their availability (Jones 1996: 67; see also Hornberger and King 1996: 432).

Approval of the speech community is also extremely important in the domain of corpus planning, for any new words created will only be used if they are actually understood. Indeed, corpus planners often fail to recognise that merely inventing or introducing a word is not enough to ensure that it will be used and that, if sufficient care is not taken with corpus planning to ensure acceptance on the part of the native speakers, this can actually undermine efforts at the status planning stage. There is no purpose to new words if no one uses them and corpus planners would do well to test new vocabulary on native speakers in order to determine their acceptability, a strategy that is currently being advocated for language planning in several countries (Richards 1989: 113).

A final question concerns whether or not the goals asked of language planning revitalisation strategies are realistic. In the context of language death it is clearly inappropriate to expect that such measures will somehow be able to turn back the clock and to restore the obsolescent variety to its former glory. Promotion at school, in the media and in other 'new' domains will enhance a variety's status but will not guarantee its restoration to the ones it previously occupied. As Bentahila and Davies (1993: 371–2) point out, for pragmatic reasons, language planning in these cases tends to focus outside rather than inside the home when, of course, this very domain has represented one of the constant strongholds of the obsolescent variety. Furthermore, as the middle classes are often the champions of language planning (Macnamara 1971: 85; Jones 1998: 314; Dorian 1987: 63; McDonald 1989: 214) whereas the bulk of the traditional speakers of most obsolescent languages come from the working classes, such measures can even transform the very nature of the speech community in question. In modern Brittany, there even exists a situation whereby much of the impetus for language planning comes from outside the historical territory of the Breton language (Jones 1998: Chapter 5). We therefore need to be realistic in our expectations and see language planning in such contexts not as an attempt to hanker back to some prior 'golden state' of the language (see discussion of the revival of Cornish in Chapter 6) but as a way of equipping a variety with the means to be used in today's world. After all, of what use would nineteenth-century Jèrriais be in the twenty-first century? The dialect has lost its primary *raison d'être*, namely as an islandwide tool of communication, and the restoration of its use will depend upon whether it succeeds in acquiring a secondary function that is important enough, and exclusive enough, to it. One of the most likely candidates to fill this role is ethnic identity (Garzon 1992: 64). If Jèrriais can be identified as a quintessential part of island identity – an emblem of community and a focus of national loyalty on a par with, say, a flag – then this symbolic role may well serve as a springboard for its use. The problem, of course, is to ensure that its practice extends beyond the ceremonial, for this would not be sufficient to change any interpersonal or familial patterns of language use (King 1999: 122–3). Of course, emphasising the link between language and identity will only result in increased use of the former if speakers actually view their ethnicity in a positive light. If they consider a variety as a leash tethering them to a stigmatised self-image, such a course of action will only succeed in hastening its decline (Dorian 1978b: 653) and, as mentioned in Chapter 4, it is for this reason that language planning should also encompass an element of what Pool (1979: 5) terms 'identity planning'.

5.5 Case study: language planning in the Seychelles

The Republic of the Seychelles comprises a small group of islands in the Indian Ocean, about 600 miles north-east of Madagascar. Initially 'discovered' in 1502 by Vasco de Gama, they remained free from European settlement until 1770, when they were claimed by France. The islands were initially settled by French colonists and slaves from Mauritius and became producers of spices such as nutmeg and cinnamon, coffee and cotton. They were pawns in the territorial tug of war between France and England during the Napoleonic wars but eventually became British territory in 1810, a relationship that prevailed until independence in 1976. British ownership and the institution of English as an official language were not enough to erase the Gallic legacy of the islands – the native language, established during the years of French settlement, has continued to be a French-lexifier creole known locally as Seselwa. It is largely mutually intelligible with modern Mauritian French Creole, which is unsurprising given that they are both modern descendants of eighteenth-century Mauritian creole forms.

In 1977, a socialist government came to power in the newly formed Republic and, like many of their ex-colonial counterparts across the globe, began to engage in a 'process of decolonisation' (Arends et al. 1995: 65). In the Seychelles, this manifested itself in a 'people-oriented concept of development: [the government] believed that the majority of the population should participate fully in the economic, social, political and cultural development of the country' (Mahoune 2002: 1; our insertion). As such, it was felt that the population had to be educated into a new perspective; namely, one in which they abandoned the 'colonial hangover' (Mahoune 2002: 3) and instead viewed themselves as a viable, independent nation that could also hold its own on the global stage. The government therefore focused much of its energies on revamping the education system, but also simultaneously concentrated on validating and promoting many aspects of local culture. Thus, a positive sense of Seychellois identity was to be fostered through as many channels as possible.

Education had not been a priority for the colonial administration. After the British takeover, Roman Catholic and Anglican churches had established schools in their parishes where possible, but governmental input had been limited. The 1960 Census report states that about 70 per cent of twelve-year-olds attended schools (very likely on an irregular basis), but because of limited opportunities for secondary-level schooling, this fell to 25 per cent by the age of fifteen (ADEA 1999: 4). Ernesta (1988; quoted in ADEA 1999: 4) states that the major reasons behind poor enrolment lay in the fact that parents did not see education as necessary, as well as in a certain cultural ideology (and perhaps necessity) that children of a certain age were more useful as potential breadwinners or carers for younger siblings. Overall, it would seem that little or nothing had been done before independence to enamour the population to the idea that education could play a pivotal role in the development of the region. Instead, it was largely viewed as a system in which 'the rich go further and the poor lag behind' (ADEA 1999: 8).

The 1977 government therefore instituted far-reaching educational reforms on the basis of their three guiding principles: 'education for all, education for life, education for national and personal development' (ADEA 1999: 9). In fact, education receives the biggest share of the annual budget: between 1985 and 1990, 17 per cent of the country's total budget was allocated to the Ministry of Education (ADEA 1999: 6). Thus, 'the school has been integrated into the socialist concept of the nation': its remit is not only to foster intellectual and technical development but also, in keeping with the government's socialist doctrine, to be the main official channel through which promotion of local culture takes place.

Bartens (2001: 30) points out that, in the relevant territories, pro-creole language policies are typically formulated by socialist governments, and the Seychelles has been no exception. In 1979, Seselwa was made one of the country's official languages alongside English and French, and in 1982, the creole was declared the first official language of the Republic. By 1981, the National Institute of Pedagogy (NIP) had been formed, charged with the task of developing 'educational programmes relevant to the needs of the country' as well as co-ordinating the in-service training of teachers (ADEA 1999: 14). This was also the year in which proposals (first made in 1978) for a suitable orthography for Seselwa were ratified, and a large part of the codification was undertaken by the NIP. When Seselwa was made the main language of the classroom at Primary 1 level (ages five to eleven) in 1982, the NIP had already begun the process of corpus planning that would later be shared by the Creole Institute (formed in 1986). This latter organisation is today home to a documentation centre that oversees academic research into cultural and linguistic aspects of Seselwa. It is also actively involved in ministerial language policies, and promotes and monitors 'a Seychellois Creole Literature which [assists] the teaching of Creole in schools and in the Adult Literacy Program' (Mahoune 2002: 1).

As mentioned earlier, the government's ideology of 'creole development' here was essentially that of vernacularisation. The 'home language' of Seselwa, which had been denigrated under the colonial administration and restricted to oral, informal everyday use was to be given the same status as the ex-colonial languages of French and English. As such, it was to be standardised and developed for use in formal and written domains. Corpus planning was therefore vital, and status planning had to be closely linked: people would have to be encouraged to use it in the new domains.

As mentioned in relation to Jèrriais, standardisation can have positive psychological and practical effects. Codification and all it entails, such as the development of an orthography, dictionaries, grammars and teaching materials, not only fulfils a practical purpose in facilitating a language's use in certain media, but also imbues it with a sense of authority and legitimacy. In many creole territories, speakers have been inculcated into the belief that their native language is no more than an unstable and incompetent rendition of an 'established' language and, as such, is fit only for everyday, non-serious, oral interaction. The fact that 'serious' writing, such as that of academic, governmental, legal, ecclesiastical and literary works, may not consistently be carried out in the unstandardised creole, which may also not have a stable orthographic system (so that written representations vary), reinforces this belief. Alongside this exists the conviction that the standard varieties of languages such as English and French are 'correct' and 'proper', an idea bolstered by the official status they typically have in these communities, as well as by exposure to the traditions of scholarship and the literary canons which make use of and therefore promote these forms. Creating a standard form of a creole is therefore the first step towards giving it the same measure of viability, although it must be noted that this in itself is not enough: the creole-speaking community needs to *accept* its potential equivalence with the standard forms that have long been seen as primary.

The Creole Institute has undertaken much of the corpus planning work involved in standardising Seselwa and oversees its use in schools, the media and general administration. The government has actively sought to raise the status of the creole by encouraging the use of Seselwa in local literature and music, as well as by generally promoting awareness of the local 'creole culture'. An important milestone was recently reached with the first publication of the entire New Testament in Seselwa in January 2000, 'a date to write in golden letters in the church history in Seychelles and in the Creole culture [*sic*]' (*L'Echo des Îles* 2000; quoted in United Bible Society on-line newsletter). Indeed, the article states that all 6,000 copies of the translation were sold out within the month.

The plans for the role of Seselwa bring to mind Brathwaite's (1984) positive reconception (and renaming) of a creole as *nation language*; namely, a language that authentically expresses the individual identity of its people with the authority that is perceived as belonging to longer-established languages such as English and French. Indeed, Pitts (undated; quoted in Mahoune 2002: 1) stated that the Seychellois 'have made their language, formerly an instrument of subordination an instrument of their liberation'. But to what extent have they been successful?

Mahoune (2002: 3) argues that the cultural promotion of Seselwa has been quite successful, largely because of a good 'deployment of financial and human resources' (Bartens 2001: 41), as well as the implementation of profound educational reforms. Under the patronage of the Creole Institute, fiction written in the creole has become widely available, as well as more 'functional' literature such as research material and governmental reports and leaflets. Local newspapers and magazines also print a substantial proportion of their articles in Seselwa. The Ministry of Culture has sponsored the formation of a National Cultural Troupe, which stages theatrical productions in creole (original works by local playwrights as well as translations of Shakespeare and Molière, for example). Local musicals are also being performed, and one of the Ministry's upcoming projects concerns the adaptation of successful stage productions for film. Local music is also widely promoted – popular creole songs are available and sold on CDs and cassettes 'in large numbers', and there is also demand for recordings of *moutia*, a local genre of extemporaneous musical composition. Local artists Jany de L'Etourdie and Patrick Victor have also taken Seychellois music to international audiences (Mahoune 2002: 2–3).

In terms of education, the use of Seselwa at primary level seems to have helped raise levels of academic performance and, ultimately, of pupil participation in the learning process. Ravel and Thomas's study (1985; cited in Siegel 1999: 520) compared the performance of Grade Three students in 1983, the last Grade Three to be taught in English, with that of same-grade students in 1984, the first to be taught wholly in Seselwa. They found that the latter group performed significantly better, both on standardised tests and in other academic subjects such as English and mathematics. In 1988, Bickerton reported on the findings of a later study which showed that pupils educated in Seselwa gained higher grades in subjects such as mathematics, science, French and social studies. He concluded that 'the prediction by the enemies of the creole, that education in creole would lower scores in English and French, has failed to be borne out' (Bickerton 1988: 3; quoted in Siegel 1999: 520). Mahoune (2002: 3) states that there are plans to introduce the teaching of Seselwa and Seselwa literature at secondary level, for which teachers are currently being trained at the National Institute of Education. The school of Adult and Continuing Education's adult literacy programme also begins initial instruction in the creole, after which students move to literacy in French and English.

The picture painted for the future of Seselwa would appear to be a bright one indeed. Yet, while both highlighting the developments above as positive aspects of a thriving and healthy interest in the linguistic and cultural heritage of the region, Mahoune (2002) and the Ministry of Education report (ADEA 1999) also point to the fact that there is significant opposition to the use of Seselwa in official domains, especially in the classroom. The Ministry of Education report (ADEA 1999: 18), for example, states that one 'barrier that the government has to face was the critic [*sic*] against the introduction of creole as the medium of instruction. There has been a lot of unjustified argument against the introduction of creole in schools'. Mahoune (2002: 3) states that 'many teachers feared that pupils would have difficulties making the transition from Creole to English and French at a later stage' and that a resultant new target (set after 1988) was to introduce English to students at an earlier stage in their education. In addition, even though 'Creole is the language of the most important functions in . . . society', a high percentage of Seychellois still 'subconsciously associate development with French and English' and 'there is a growing tendency to use the latter languages in public functions' (Mahoune 2002: 4). Thus, despite continued and financed promotion of Seselwa, there are still challenges to be faced. What exactly are the nature of these, and what possible solutions are there?

Arends et al. (1995: 66), writing specifically about language planning strategies in creole-speaking territories, state that the main processes ideally include:

a1. setting of goals
a2. implementing these goals
a3. evaluating both the attainment of original goals and methods of implementation. This may lead to the formulation of new goals, which is the starting point for a new cycle of language planning activities.

The problems that typically hinder the carrying out of these processes often have to do with:

b1. the nature of the remaining colonial ties
b2. the nature of linguistic diversity
b3. the developmental state of the indigenous languages
b4. the language attitude among the speakers.

The Seychellois government has been actively addressing a1–a3 since the 1970s. The formation of organisations such as the NIP and the Creole Institute as well as the creation of departments such as the Creole Section of the Department of Languages in the Ministry of Education have all been immeasurably useful in the corpus and status planning necessary for Seselwa, particularly its standardisation. In 1994, the Ministry of Education reaffirmed its pro-creole policy in its Language Policy Review, stating that its 'fundamental, immutable tenets' included 'the use of the mother-tongue in the early stages of learning' and 'the continued development of Creole in schools' (Mahoune 2002: 3). Yet the problems identified in b1–b4 (which, it should be noted, are all inter-related) still retain some measure of potency. Although now politically autonomous, the Seychelles is still somewhat economically dependent on other territories, such as Europe and North America, for trade and tourism. The outside world seems to offer many more promising and varied opportunities than are available in the islands, and Seychellois who want to take advantage of these therefore believe that they will be better served by competence in languages such as English (cf. this consideration of 'linguistic worth' in cases of language death; Chapter 4). This is not dissimilar to the situation in other creole-speaking territories such as the Caribbean, where a major consideration is the fact that 'the outside world, the world of the dollar and of international trade, speaks English' (McCrum et al. 1992: 348), and creole speakers therefore become drawn into the 'absorbing power' (see also discussion of Kloss (1977) in Section 5.3) of the English-speaking world, particularly that of the USA.

Mahoune (2002: 3) explicitly states that one of the biggest hurdles faced by the pro-creole planners is the 'colonial hangover' which 'makes it hard for Creoles to accept their own language as one equal to other languages' (see b4). Again, this is a ubiquitous problem in creole-speaking territories, where the (often Eurocentric) perspectives of the coloniser, which denigrated these languages, have been instilled into the general populace (Singh 2000). This is often not helped by the long-held belief that creoles are 'broken', 'sub-standard' forms of more established languages, a perspective that was widely adopted in the early years of creole description and study (for more detail see Singh (2000) and Holm (1988); see also Chapter 3). As mentioned above, the fact that creoles tend to primarily exist in the oral medium and appear variable in writing if they have no dedicated orthographic system (see b3), reinforces this perspective. As we have seen, inconsistency in the written medium is not a problem for the Seychelles (although we will return to b3 below), but the fact that Seselwa shares a proportion of mutually intelligible features with French means that for some speakers, the idea that the creole is an imperfect version of the latter language persists.

In addition, although the government has been successful in promoting the use of the creole in a variety of cultural media, these all have primarily local currency: the success of Seselwa music, literature and theatre on the international stage is limited and non-mainstream, which could reinforce the belief that the language itself has no real validity for potential 'citizens of the world'. In terms of education, although the use of creole in the initial stages of learning has been successful, it may not be sufficient to promote the use of Seselwa in public, formal domains. First, despite its pro-creole policy, the educational system actually seems to advocate the use of French and particularly English over the creole. In fact, the 1994 Language Policy Review also stated that one of its major aims was to oversee 'the progression to English as a medium of instruction when children are ready' (Mahoune 2002: 3). In other words, the fact that Seselwa is only used at primary level, and as part of a transitional bilingual programme to French and English, aids in cementing the view that the latter two languages are the ones that belong to 'serious', formal, public and international communication. Second, most of the pedagogical material produced to promote the use of the standardised variety of Seselwa, which Mahoune (2002: 3, see above) hopes would be more frequently used in public forums, applies to primary and initial literacy strategies. Thus, very little corpus planning with respect to developing registers (and guidance for their usage) has been done for the use of formal Seselwa outside the classroom. As Bartens (2001: 30) states, such 'post-literacy materials are essential for the community not to relapse into illiteracy'. At the same time, relevant registers for the use of French and English in public discourse have long been available and are no doubt taught and supported by a variety of materials. In addition, it must be noted that standardisation measures initially apply to written usage, and it is very difficult, if not impossible, to transfer this wholly to spoken discourse. Indeed, in cases where this has occurred, as in the development of standard English, transference has been an extremely slow and incomplete process, and has happened largely because of an extensive body of prescriptive teaching and guidance. Thus, if speakers do not know how to use, or feel uncomfortable using, the formal Seselwa they once learned in primary school in public intercourse, they will inevitably turn to the forms they feel are relevant (and which they can use) in such contexts. Finally, it should be noted that the standardised Seselwa available is a relatively new creation and its use in spoken discourse may still produce for speakers uncomfortable conflicts with the other forms of creole that have developed 'naturally' in the oral medium. In fact, some speakers have rated the Seselwa learnt in school as 'hard' and different to the creole they speak natively. One speaker (in personal communication with Singh) stated that she would not feel capable of using the 'school creole' because she had made 'many mistakes' when learning it. She therefore felt that she could not speak what she referred to as 'the creole' properly. This is an interesting twist on problem b3: hurdles for creole language planners usually lie in getting the language codified so that it can be taught, accepted and used in public domains, but in the Seychelles a major obstacle to more frequent use may be the fact that the standardised variety creates the misapprehension that there are 'right' and 'wrong' forms, and that the majority of people cannot speak their native language correctly.

There are no easy solutions to these issues. Many creole speakers in the Seychelles, like the speakers of creoles and indeed minority languages everywhere, are all very much aware of their potential as global citizens, which necessitates fluency in a language such as English. At the same time, many also feel that this should not be at the expense of their native language, which retains potency as a symbol of identity. It would seem that McCrum et al.'s (1992: 348) assessment of the 'language paradox' in creole communities such as Jamaica holds true across the board:

> Ask a Jamaican what he or she speaks and you will have the best expression of the paradox that underlies Caribbean attitudes towards English . . . nationalism will prompt them to put as much distance as possible between what they speak and the Standard English of the ex-colonial . . . On the other hand, if you suggest to the Jamaican that he or she does *not* speak English, they will be insulted or outraged.

Thus, even though 'identity planning' (Pool 1979; see Section 5.4) is more advanced in the Seychelles than in Jersey, it would seem that the 'absorbing power' of the English-speaking world has an extremely long reach.

5.6 Discussion

In this chapter, we have drawn a distinction between language policy (Section 5.3) and language planning (Sections 5.4 and 5.5). Although this distinction is not always observed in the literature, following Schiffman (1996), we believe that it is helpful to consider these fields separately, since the formulation of policy is neither always straightforward nor explicit, and does not inevitably lead to planning strategies. Indeed, this is well illustrated in a comparison of the studies. The USA has no explicit and coherent language policy (or planning strategies), but assumes assimilation to ('acceptable') English, thus ignoring its actual status as a multilingual polity. In Jersey, although there is no official and overt pro-Jèrriais policy, there is widespread and significant support for the revitalisation of this variety. Thus, even though status and corpus planning occurs without explicit governmental backing, it is clear that the covert pro-Jèrriais stance carries enough potency to engender overt interest and involvement in its promotion. In the Seychelles, on the other hand, a pro-creole policy has become an official and integral component of the articulation of the post-colonial Republic. Promotion of Seselwa therefore takes place within the framework of explicit and overt ministerial policies. Interestingly, in all three cases, covert and overt policy and planning (i.e., assumptions of assimilation, strategies for revitalisation and vernacularisation) are propagated through the same channels: the school, the media and other cultural establishments. In addition, in all three cases, English is a major player: it is the language of and for Americans, and in Jersey and the Seychelles, is imbued with official status as well as extreme attractiveness as the world language of progress and opportunity. Thus, in the latter two areas, promotion of Jèrriais and Seselwa is not made at the expense of achieving competence in English (and also, in both cases, French). Indeed, in the Seychelles, official language policy for the schools makes provision for an eventual transition to English as the medium of instruction.

Jersey and the Seychelles are also similar in that planning strategies in both areas have had to address standardisation, as well as promote the use of the standard variety in official and public domains. In both cases, the creation of standard forms has facilitated the production of pedagogical material as well as supplied the linguistic basis for the overall promotion of Jèrriais and Seselwa. However, both standards carry little weight outside the domains within which they have become established. In other words, speakers learning St. Ouennais as part of the revitalisation movement willingly receive formal instruction in it and learn to read it, but may find it difficult to make it a part of their everyday usage. In Jersey, this is quite significant, since it is through continued use in a variety of domains, including the informal and domestic, that a dying variety has a chance of regaining a foothold. In the Seychelles, standard Seselwa seems to be perceived by some speakers as belonging primarily to the school and, therefore, not to them. Indeed, as we saw in Section 5.5, it can have the effect of isolating native speakers from a sense of what their 'real' language is. In both cases too, the guidance needed for speakers to use these standard forms in public, oral and official domains (which planners seem to want) is lacking and, very importantly, so is motivation. Overall, speakers have to *want* to use whatever forms, varieties and languages are being promoted. If the community's acceptance is non-existent or weak, then planners face a huge, even insurmountable, obstacle. This is not to say that individual speakers are not for the revitalisation or promotion of their native tongue. Rather, it is a statement about the relative motivation and opportunity that exists for acquiring competence in another language that carries more social promise. Thus, as we have seen in all three case studies, deliberate interventions and attempts to direct the language choices and, in some cases, the language 'development' of communities can enjoy some measure of success, but the fundamental determinant is always people's assumption of what is most useful for them. Without their approval, 'man-made' attempts to influence language use will carry little validity for a speech community.

We now turn to our last two examples of language planning: language revival in Chapter 6 and language invention in Chapter 7.

6 Language revival

6.1 Introduction

As we saw in Chapter 4, language obsolescence should be thought of as a process rather than a state. Many more languages undergo obsolescence than those which reach the end point, which is language death, for as we have seen, language obsolescence may be halted and revitalisation may occur.

Some languages, though, do die. Moreover, as seen in Chapter 4, this is not an exclusively modern phenomenon. If languages do lose all their speakers and become completely extinct then, in most cases, they vanish forever and all their functions are taken over by another language (usually the one with which they were in competition before their death).

However, in the case of a very small number of languages, this is not the end of the story. In this chapter, we will examine how dead languages can be 'revived' or brought back to life, even though they may not have been spoken for hundreds of years.

It is important, at this point, to clarify the distinction between *language revival* and *language revitalisation*. The crucial difference lies in the fact that, (as we saw in Section 5.4) although it may well be obsolescent, a revitalised language will never have ceased to be spoken natively, whereas language revival involves 'resurrecting' a language that is no longer spoken by anyone as a native vernacular. This dichotomy is discussed by Dorian (1994a: 481), who also points out that the time depth concerned is irrelevant: the revived language may not have been spoken for several centuries or may have ceased to be spoken quite recently. The crucial point is that in cases of language revival, the language has no remaining speakers. This means that although revitalisation campaigns depend on the obsolescent language gaining new speakers, who acquire it as their second tongue, there will also exist native speakers who, while not necessarily monoglot, will have a proficient knowledge of the revitalising language. Languages undergoing revival, on the other hand, have no speakers of any kind. Thus those who begin acquiring such a language will all speak it as a second language and have another variety as their native tongue.[1] Language revival is therefore far more ambitious, more difficult and less common than language revitalisation, as no existing community of speakers can be drawn on to support the reviving language. Moreover, as we will see, the absence of a native speech community means that judgements concerning the linguistic make-up of the reviving language (matters such as its pronunciation, grammar and vocabulary) must be made in a rather decontextualised fashion, which sometimes results in conflicting opinions and practices.

Undoubtedly, the most famous case of language revival is that of Hebrew, which was spoken widely by Jews in the Middle East until their conquest and removal to Babylon in 586 BC. By the second to third centuries BC, Aramaic had replaced Hebrew as the everyday language of most of the area and, with the destruction of Judea in the second century AD, Hebrew ceased to be used as a spoken language.

However, despite its death as a spoken language, many sacred texts in Hebrew survive from the tenth to eleventh centuries, indicating that the language was continuing to be studied. There is also evidence that it was maintained as a written language, as it is found in several secular documents from the same period. Moreover, over the centuries Hebrew also served as a means by which Jews in different countries could communicate with one another. It remained too as the formal language of prayer and, as such, was sometimes taught phonetically for use in worship by one generation of Jews to the next. Fishman (1991: 289) even reports that people who had studied Hebrew to the level of actual or potential rabbinic ordination were 'able to write Hebrew freely within the bounds of more traditional subject matter' and that in the nineteenth century a few individuals could even use the language in a variety of modern literary genres, although most (male) Jews had a much more patchy knowledge of the language.[2] When its revival as a spoken tongue was first proposed by Eliezer Ben-Yehuda at the end of the nineteenth century in an attempt to create a Hebrew-speaking speech community in the Holy Land the fact that there were people who had a detailed knowledge of Hebrew was of a tremendous advantage. Today, Hebrew has been successfully revived and is a living, thriving language spoken as a vernacular by approximately 4 million inhabitants of the modern state of Israel (created in 1948). It is the country's official language and is used in all domains of life.

As the most famous example of language revival, the history of Hebrew is extremely well documented.[3] The focus of this chapter, however, is a less well-known case of language revival, namely that of Cornish, a Celtic language spoken in the south-west of the British Isles. As we will see, Cornish died in 1777[4] but today is once more being spoken. Along with Manx (the last native speaker of which died in 1974) it is one of two languages currently being revived in the British Isles.[5] The case of Cornish is less well documented than that of Hebrew, but it is worthy of note since, according to Chaim Rabin, a former Professor of Hebrew at the Hebrew University of

Jerusalem, 'the revival of Cornish is the only real parallel to the Hebrew case' (cited in Ellis and Mac a'Ghobhainn 1971: 62).

6.2 Case study: Cornish

Cornish, an Indo-European language (see Chapter 3, Figure 3.2), was brought to Britain by Celtic migrants from the European continent. With Welsh and Breton, Cornish is a member of the Brythonic subgroup of the Celtic family (as opposed to the Goedelic subgroup, which is formed by Irish, Scots Gaelic and Manx). The relationship between Cornish and other Celtic languages can be seen in 6.2.a, adapted from Sandercock (1996: 4)

Although Brythonic Celtic was originally spoken over most of England, Wales and southern Scotland, increased territorial conquests by Anglo-Saxon invaders in the fifth and sixth centuries began to separate the Brythonic-speaking communities and led to several Brythonic-speaking tribes fleeing their homeland in the British Isles and establishing a colony in Brittany (see Section 3.2). Place-name evidence suggests that in about the eighth century, parts of east Cornwall were settled by the Anglo-Saxons. English kings (such as Alfred, AD 871–99) had control over lands in east Cornwall in the ninth century and English rule in Cornwall was consolidated in the tenth century by Athelstan (924–39) who, according to William of Malmesbury, established the boundary of Cornwall at the River Tamar and gave Cornwall its own bishopric. However, by the mid-tenth century, English kings were also making land grants in the western half of Cornwall. This was the beginning of a gradual process of Anglicisation that took some eight and a half centuries to complete.

As we saw in Chapter 4, it is difficult to pinpoint the exact reason for the obsolescence of any language, and Cornish is no exception. There are, however, a number of developments in certain areas which may have played a role in its demise.

One of these areas was religion. In 1050, the Bishopric of Cornwall was transferred to Exeter and the region became part of the (English-speaking) Bishopric of Devon. (However, the uniting of the bishoprics may also have had some positive benefits for Cornish, see below). The Act of Uniformity of

6.2.a Some lexical cognates in Celtic languages

English	Cornish	Breton	Welsh	Irish
'bad'	*drog*	*drouk*	*drwg*	*droch*
'land'	*tir*	*tir*	*tir*	*tir*
'sea'	*mor*	*mor*	*môr*	*muir*
'black'	*du*	*du*	*du*	*dubh*
'house'	*chi*	*ti*	*tŷ*	*teach*
'clean'	*glan*	*glan*	*glân*	*glan*
'rider'	*marghek*	*marc'hek*	*marchog*	*marcach*

1549 made the use of English in religious services obligatory and imposed an English Book of Common Prayer. Although the Bible was translated into Welsh in the hope of enforcing Protestantism in the principality, the same policy was not followed for Cornish, probably due to the fact that speaker numbers were already dwindling and that the very small proportion of the population of Cornwall who did not understand English by the sixteenth century would have been those at the very bottom of society, and it is possible that translation of the Bible for such a minority was not seen as viable. A Cornish Bible would have given the language both an enhanced prestige and also the basis of a uniform written language. The Reformation also became an important factor in the weakening of the Cornish language. The flow of emigrants from south-west Britain to Brittany during the medieval period had led to the development of close linguistic and cultural ties between Brittany and Cornwall. The fact that significant numbers of Bretons came to western Cornwall to work during the first half of the sixteenth century (choosing this area since they could communicate easily with the locals) must have given Cornish a considerable boost. However, after the Reformation, when Cornwall was Protestant and France Catholic, this kind of frequent interchange was less easy. The Reformation also heralded the demise of Glasney College (discussed below). The production and performance of religious mystery plays, which represented a significant percentage of all Cornish literary output at this time, did not come to an end at the time of the Reformation (for example, the manuscript of the *Creacion of the World*, an important Cornish text, was written in 1611). However, it is unlikely that the performances would have survived the Protestant zeal of the mid-seventeeth century (although it may be that the language was so weak by then that there would have been little call for them).

Political factors may also have contributed to the demise of Cornish. Indeed, from the late ninth century onwards, Cornwall had been absorbed politically by England, and from Athelstan's reign onwards, members of the Cornish gentry were received in Court and returned to Cornwall with the customs, clothes and language of the English. Then, in 1066, the Norman Conquest meant that Cornwall, like much of Britain, came under Norman rule. This relegated Cornish to third place in the linguistic hierarchy, behind French and English. In addition, the political unification of Brittany with France in 1532 led to the ties between them being strengthened and, as a result, the weakening of those between Brittany and Cornwall.

Cultural factors also had a part to play. After the uniting of the bishoprics of Devon and Cornwall, the Bishops of Exeter recognised the importance of having trained clergy who could communicate with their flocks in their native language. In 1270, they founded the Collegiate Church of St Thomas of Canterbury at Glasney (Penryn), with the specific aim of providing a Cornish cultural centre. Glasney had become the centre of literary activity in the Middle Cornish period and was responsible for the production of virtually all extant Cornish literature, so the united bishopric may have actually boosted the language for a time. However, this establishment was suppressed in 1545 as part of the Reformation and the resulting decrease in literary output contributed to a lack of prestige for Cornish.

Finally, industrial factors may also have been influential. From the Middle Ages, commercial links were increasingly fostered with England and, because of their strategic importance, the Cornish ports became important centres of commerce – attracting merchants from England from at least the thirteenth century onwards. The ports therefore became centres of Anglicisation and, as commerce developed, the success of Cornish people became contingent upon their knowledge of English. Psychologically, therefore, English became increasingly linked to notions of success, while Cornish concomitantly became associated with poverty. This attitude was manifest even in west Cornwall from the tenth century onwards, when west Cornish gentry, with Cornish given names and presumably ethnically Cornish, also began taking English given names, presumably in a bid to make themselves 'respectable' at court and with other gentry.

Although no single reason mentioned above was, in itself, sufficient to 'kill off' Cornish, it is clear that, together, they collectively contributed in some way to the language's demise by severing its links with similar ethnic groups, limiting the opportunities for its use and increasing the prestige of English. In the later Middle Ages, the language was already so weakened that there was very little feeling of linguistic identity. The lack of such an identity meant that Cornwall never produced great literary figures, which in turn arguably resulted in the lack of cultural-national sentiment in the sixteenth and seventeenth centuries. It seems that Cornish essentially came to be stigmatised by its speakers who, little by little, ceased transmitting it to their offspring. For instance, although William Hals records having been told by the Vicar of Feock that he had been obliged to administer the communion in Cornish until about 1640 'because the aged people did not well understand English' (Pool 1975: 8), there is also evidence that in the seventeenth century the language was losing ground in its very heartlands: in 1662 the naturalist John Ray visited Land's End and noted 'we met with none here but what could speak English; few of the children could speak Cornish, so that the language is like, in a short time, to be quite lost' (Pool 1975: 8).

The last native speaker of Cornish is traditionally held to be Dolly Pentreath of Mousehole, who died in December 1777. However, it is probably impossible to give an exact date for the language's demise, since there is evidence that Cornish was able to be spoken reasonably fluently by at least one person after her – a letter survives from 1776 written by William Bodinar, who claims to have learnt Cornish as a boy from old fishermen (and hence he cannot be considered a native speaker in the strict sense of the term). This is the last piece of traditional Cornish that has survived. Bodinar died in 1789 and, although there may have been people after this who knew fragments of Cornish, no subsequent record exists of any other person able to hold a conversation in the traditional form of the language.

The most obvious question that springs to mind when we examine the case of Cornish is if the language died, why revive it? Language is first and foremost a tool of communication and, although Cornish had been used for that purpose, the fact that it was allowed to die means that its speakers must have found another language (English) to fulfill this function. As English could be used to talk about anything that Cornish could, it replaced Cornish in all its domains and, quite simply, at a pragmatic level, there was no longer any need for Cornish. Moreover, as Bentahila and Davies (1993: 359) have pointed out 'a revival is a luxury'. Clearly, reviving a language spoken by their ancestors will not be one of the main preoccupations of a speech community occupied with basic subsistence living. It has been noted many times in the literature on language revitalisation that those most actively involved in such movements tend to be the Western, educated middle classes (see, for example, Timm 1980; Jones 1998). Moreover, these campaigns are generally waged not because people need a means for communication but rather because, in these contexts, in the West in particular, dying languages may often take on a very different role, fulfilling the symbolic function of a focal point of ethnic identity, on a par with a national anthem or a flag. The same occurs in language revival. In the case of Hebrew, there was a need for a lingua franca for the new state of Israel, but the reason that Hebrew was chosen above, say, English (which would already have been spoken by many of the citizens of the new state) was due to its symbolic function as the sacred language of the Jewish religion. Thus, the Diaspora could be reunited by the one thing that they had in common and which, at the same time, distinguished them from non-Jews. In Cornwall, however, the situation was considerably less dramatic. Why, then, a century after it had disappeared, did people revive the Cornish language?

In 1904, Henry Jenner addressed this question in his *Handbook of the Cornish Language*, stating 'Why should Cornishmen learn Cornish? There is no money in it, it serves no practical purpose and the literature is scanty and of no great originality or value. The question is a fair one, the answer is simple. Because they are Cornish.' We will return to the importance of these factors in Sections 6.2.4 and 6.2.5.

6.2.1 The revival of Cornish

Although the death of Dolly Pentreath is traditionally taken as synonymous with the death of the Cornish language, Cornish had, in fact, been undergoing processes of obsolescence for some time before this. As mentioned above, by the end of the seventeenth century, it had become quite obvious that time was running out for the language and this had prompted a number of intellectuals such as Richard Angwin, William Scawen and William Gwavas to transcribe the speech of some of the last speakers of Cornish in order to preserve some form of record of the language. When Cornish died, therefore, it was not entirely undocumented and even boasted a grammar (Lhuyd 1707). This documentation helped to serve as a basis on which the revival of Cornish was established.

The person given the title 'Father of the Cornish Language Revival' is Henry Jenner (1848–1934) (see above), a keeper of manuscripts at the British Museum. He had been interested in Cornish since his youth: in 1875, he and Revd. Lach-Szyrma had sought out and visited many old Cornish people in order to note down some of the last traditional scraps of Cornish, and, in 1876, he had read a paper entitled 'The History and Literature of the Ancient Cornish Language' at a Cornwall Congress of the British Archaeological Foundation, thereby provoking a great deal of interest in the language. In addition, Jenner organised a special commemoration service in 1877 for the centenary of Dolly Pentreath's death, and the publicity surrounding this seems to have given impetus to the revivalist movement. At this time, Jenner's interest in Cornish seems to have been purely as an object of historical and philological study. However, by the turn of the century, his ideas had changed and, caught up in the Celtic renaissance that was sweeping the British Isles and Brittany at that time, he and a number of other enthusiasts began to sow the seeds of the Cornish revival. In 1901, L.C. Duncombe-Jewell founded the Cowethas Kelto-Kernuak, the first organisation devoted specifically to the promotion of Cornwall's Celtic identity at an international level. The year 1904 saw the publication of Jenner's Cornish grammar, *A Handbook of the Cornish Language* (see above). This work was to form the linguistic basis of the revival.

The example of Cornish shows the significance that one person can have in the revival of a language, for although Jenner did not revive Cornish single-handedly, and was dependent upon others for support, he was the first to create the enthusiasm for such a revival and also helped to provide the means whereby this could be achieved. The same phenomenon can be seen in the revival of Hebrew, where the pivotal role was played by Ben-Yehuda (see Section 6.1) who, although he has not escaped criticism,[6] undoubtedly provided much of the initial impetus behind the movement to revive Hebrew. Jenner devoted much of his life to promoting Cornish, producing poems in the language, translating work from English to Cornish and generally acknowledging the importance of creating an appropriate climate for the language's revival. For example, in 1904, Jenner delivered a paper entitled 'Cornwall: A Celtic Nation' to the Celtic Congress. This was given a good reception and was probably a factor in Cornwall getting accepted as a member of the Congress in the same year. In 1916, when the London *Daily Mirror* published the soldiers' marching song 'It's a Long Way to Tipperary' in the languages of the British Empire, Jenner supplied a Cornish version. Jenner also played an active role in the Old Cornwall Societies, whose aim was to collect and circulate old Cornish folklore, thereby providing a basis on which future Cornish culture could be built (Hale 1999: 23). He was also instrumental in the creation of the Cornish Gorseth, a bardic circle, on a par with those already established in Wales and Brittany. The Gorseth was established on 21 September 1928 and was an institution that helped modern Celtic Cornwall come of age.

6.2.2 The building blocks of revival

Jenner's *A Handbook of the Cornish Language* was based on Late Cornish, which was the last form of Cornish to be spoken natively. However, there is evidence that, in its terminal phase, Cornish had undergone a considerable degree of influence from English (Jones 1998: 335; Wmffre 1998: 3–5) and other developments characteristic of obsolescent languages (Jones 1998: 334–5). The result of this was that Late Cornish could be considered a somewhat 'corrupt' and 'declining' form of the language.

There consequently emerged an alternative school of thought that advocated the revival of Cornish on the basis of texts dating from the language's heyday in the Middle Ages, when it showed no signs of obsolescence and less (though still very substantial) influence from English. In fact, the extant texts of Middle Cornish are also more extensive than those of Late Cornish and hence offered more resources on which to base Revived Cornish. Basing the revived tongue on the Cornish spoken in medieval times was a radical course of action and, of course, would not be possible in a case of language revitalisation, where the continued presence of (albeit few) native speakers means that the revitalised language must necessarily bear a form that resembles that which is still being spoken. However, since the speakers of Revived Cornish would never need (nor indeed be able) to speak with anyone but each other, this presented the opportunity of reviving Cornish as it had been in its 'golden age'. Indeed, in the words of Smith (1947: 20):

> The decline of Cornish in the eighteenth century need not be regretted. Had the language survived into modern times, it would inevitably have lost much of its own idiom owing to the overwhelming influence of English and its vocabulary would have become more English than Cornish. As it is, we have a compact medieval language whose idiom is Celtic and little likely to undergo any further changes.

In 1929, therefore, Robert Morton Nance published a work entitled *Cornish for All*, based on the surviving Middle Cornish literature. After Jenner, Nance is probably the second most notable important figure in the revival of Cornish. In 1919, he had founded the first Old Cornwall Society, which undoubtedly contributed to putting Cornish culture on a popular level and probably helped create a climate conducive to the establishment of the Gorseth. Nance's work introduced a spelling system for Revived Cornish known as Unified Cornish, which he had designed together with A.S.D. Smith, another prominent revivalist (see above). Unified Cornish was a rationalisation of the different spellings found in the Middle Cornish texts and was based mainly on the based on the language of the *Ordinalia*, an early fifteenth-century cycle of three mystery plays, and the sixteenth-century play *Bewnans Meriasek* – in Nance's view (1929: 6), Cornish at its best. The importance of Unified Cornish to the revival movement as the first properly standardised spelling system of Cornish was paramount. It was, for decades, the established spelling system of Cornish, accepted by the Gorseth and the Cornish Language Board, which had been founded in 1967 to oversee education, publication, research and examining in Cornish. In its policy statement, the Board declared that it considered Unified Cornish to be an acceptable common basis for spelling modern writings in the language, a basis which was essential if the revival was to secure any degree of public acceptance. Nance used the spelling system in the work for which he is now best known, his Cornish–English dictionary of 1938.

Although Nance's work established a basis on which Cornish could be revived, using Middle Cornish as its main source meant that this work was open to controversy on two fronts. First, no one could know for sure exactly how Middle Cornish had been pronounced and, second, there were those who questioned the validity of using centuries-old texts – written mostly in verse and therefore probably including features such as non-standard word order or poetic vocabulary – as the basis for revival. According to Price (1984: 144), this would be comparable to reviving a defunct English on the basis of little more than the fifteenth-century York mystery plays. One of the most influential critics of Nance's work, Kenneth George, agreed with using Middle Cornish as a basis for revived Cornish, but argued that the pronunciation of Unified Cornish should be based on the contemporary English dialect of West Penwith (in the extreme western tip of Cornwall). This pronunciation had been advocated on the basis that this was the region where Cornish had been spoken longest (and most recently) and that, consequently, the phonology of the English dialect of the area represented that of Late Cornish and could also be used to arrive at that of Middle Cornish. (In practice, this was unlikely to be the case, as Late Cornish, but not Middle Cornish, had been affected by the English Great Vowel Shift (see Section 1.3).) George therefore suggested an alternative system of pronunciation and spelling, based on the phonology of the language around 1500, which he worked out systematically by a detailed computer-based analysis of spellings and rhymes found in the extant Cornish texts and by philological comparison with Breton and Welsh. The proposed new system, known as Kernewek Kemmyn, was adopted by the Cornish Language Board in 1987 as a replacement for Unified Cornish. However, Kernewek Kemmyn was not adopted by all the revivalists and indeed today, the Gorseth accepts work written in both spellings.

Richard Gendall is probably the most prominent of the proponents of revival on the basis of Late Cornish. He proposed his own form of revived Cornish, called Modern Cornish, which is mainly based on his own research into the surviving texts of Late Cornish. Gendall's supporters argue that Late Cornish forms a better basis for the reconstruction of the language for two main reasons. First, since some of the surviving texts are in prose, they are more likely to reflect a more natural spoken word order and vocabulary. Second, since Gendall follows Nance's thinking and advocates a pronunciation for Late Cornish that is closely related to the English dialect of West Penwith (see above), it is felt to be endowed with a certain authenticity.

Another system was proposed by Tim Saunders, a student of Celtic studies, who rejected much of Nance's Unified Cornish and proposed instead an etymological system in which he used terms derived from the other Brythonic languages. Carnoak Tithiack is a system that favours Late Cornish pronunciation, grammar and spelling and is based on the work of a seventeenth-century writer named Wella Kerew. Another hat was thrown in the ring in 1995 by Nicholas Williams who, in his book *Cornish Today*, dismissed Modern Cornish as 'pointless' given that, in his view, Late and Middle Cornish were essentially the same language. In the same work, Williams also made twenty-six criticisms of Kernewek Kemmyn and proposed an alternative orthographical system, which he called Unified Cornish Revised. This was a modernisation of the system devised by Nance and Smith, which eliminated some of the ambiguous spellings found in the *Ordinalia* and attempted to shift the emphasis from there to the later writings of John Tregear (*c*.1570) and William Jordan (1611). Williams's criticisms were rebutted in a 1997 publication by Ken George and Paul Dunbar, entitled *Cornish for the Twenty-First Century*, where the bitterness between the Unified Cornish and the Kernewek Kemmyn camps was revealed for all to see, with Dunbar writing: 'Kernewek Kemmyn is the preferred spelling system of almost all fluent Cornish speakers. To anyone wishing to carp about this but who is not willing or able to work their objections into a reasoned argument, I can only suggest origami as an alternative pursuit' (1997: 176). Such overt squabbling amongst the revivalists who, at the end of the day, share the same common goal, namely the revival of Cornish, has led one commentator to note, 'If some of the tremendous energy the Celts have used to belittle each other's ideas of "the truth" was directed towards working for more resources to support research, teaching and media use of Celtic languages and arts, people would not need to talk so much about survival' (Kuter 1989b: 40). Dorian (1994a: 489) also comments that 'Revival leaders might do well . . . to concede that more than one kind of authenticity exists and to begin the more productive work of establishing a compromise version of Cornish which sacrifices a modicum of each form of authenticity in favor of learnability', adding that ultimately 'it may prove the wiser course to accept considerable compromise rather than make a determined stand for intactness, where threatened languages are at issue' (1994a: 492).

Unlike revitalisers therefore, revivalists are offered the apparent luxury of being able to draw on the whole corpus of the language over time, rather than on its more recent (and arguably 'degenerate') stages. However, in the case of Cornish, this luxury has become something of a two-edged sword. Due to the lack of plentiful evidence of its latter states, revived Cornish has at least six different forms, and the lack of unity among proponents of the different systems surely cannot be conducive to their common ultimate aim of setting Cornish back on its feet. The situation of Cornish therefore stands in contrast with that of Manx, for although the last native speaker of Manx died in 1974, the extensive recordings that were made before this date have allowed the language to be revived with far less disagreement with regard to its form.

6.2.3 *The problems of reconstruction*

In the previous section, we saw that the absence of native speakers allowed revivalists the choice of which state of the language they should revive: a choice that has inevitably led to come conflicting opinions. The present section touches on more issues that can be contentious within the context of language revival but which are less so for language revitalisation.

6.2.3.1 *Pronunciation*

As seen above, the question of whether the pronunciation of Revived Cornish should be based on the medieval period has led to some disagreement. Moreover, Shield (1984) demonstrates that William Pryce's 1790 survey of Cornish, which contains the rudiments of the variety in a Cornish grammar and Cornish–English vocabulary, is often at odds with Nance's system.[7] She concludes (1984: 333) that despite the fact that Nance claimed the pronunciation of Unified Cornish to be relatively authentic, 'the diphthongs at least appear to be based on post-Great Vowel Shift English pronunciation rather than that of Late Cornish or another closely-related Celtic language'. However, leaving that aside and merely deciding to adopt the pronunciation of recent (Late) Cornish is by no means as straightforward as it might appear, simply because no speakers exist on whose language this pronunciation can be modelled, and although the efforts of Jenner and others ensured that some fragments of the language were noted down for posterity, these are not sufficient to give us an idea of the complete phonology of Cornish at this stage.

Shield (1984: 332) also notes how Jenner, like Nance and, more recently, Gendall, believed that the pronunciation of Cornish should be based on the contemporary English dialect of West Penwith (see above). Indeed, Jenner believed that the peculiarities of this dialect, compared to the English of other parts of Cornwall, was due to interference from Cornish. However, as we have seen, George does not agree with this belief. In fact, the claim that the pronunciation of the English dialects of Cornwall did not faithfully represent that of Cornish is also supported by Pryce's (1790) account of

Cornish pronunciation and, more recently, Thomas has remarked that the 'various spoken English dialects in Cornwall derive most of the phonetic quality from the late Middle English of Wessex' (1973: 9).

Then, of course, there is the likelihood that pronunciation varied across different parts of Cornwall. Williams (1990: 255) claims that, on the basis of place names, we can divide Cornwall into, at the very least, East and West regions. However, whether or not these differences can be recreated in Revived Cornish is another debatable point: Climo-Thompson (2001: iv–v) agrees with this and discusses some of the differences, deciding to base his course, *Kernuak Es*, on the pronunciation and spelling variation of west Cornwall as this was the last form of the language to be used. Climo-Thompson also provides guidelines on how to 'convert' forms from west Cornish to east Cornish. However, the grammarian Wella Brown claims that, although it is likely that differences did exist, given the fact that English is spoken in a variety of accents in modern Cornwall, very little is known about dialect variation in Cornish (Brown, in personal communication with Jones). Dialect differentiation is used by some authors to account for certain 'irregular' developments in the language (Jenner 1904: 8; Fudge 1982: 26; Williams 1990: 244, 254, 258), but others, such as George, claim that these are imprecise and seldom pinpoint exact areas (George, in personal communication with Jones). However, Oliver Padel, one of the foremost authorites on the place names of Cornwall, disagrees completely with Williams, Fudge and Jenner and argues that the variation found in place names is a chronological rather than a dialectal one (Padel, in personal communication with Jones).

6.2.3.2 New vocabulary

Another problem facing a language that has been dead for a long time is that we are entirely dependent upon extant texts for our knowledge of that language's vocabulary. In the case of Cornish, given that most of the surviving literature is religious drama, it is clear that this does not contain a complete record of all the then-contemporary vocabulary of Cornish. In addition, since many of the extant plays are in verse, it is possible that some of the vocabulary is poetic in nature. Furthermore, since the language's demise, many new concepts have been invented, concepts for which the traditional language had no words. For both these reasons, when reviving Cornish, it has been necessary to create new words.

The second of these reasons is, of course, also an issue in language planning and revitalisation: witness the creation of new Jèrriais words for its use in new domains (see Chapter 5). However, in cases of revitalisation native speakers can play a role in such lexical augmentation for, as Bentahila and Davies note (1993: 365) 'Even if many such individuals rarely use the language, they can at the very least be felt to constitute part of a reservoir which may be called into service at some later stage'. Thus, revitalisers on Jersey have, for instance, been working with native speakers for several years in order to compile lists of flora and fauna, primarily for use in the classroom. No such resource, however, is available to the revivalists. Revival therefore necessitates the creation of many more words than revitalisation and it is always possible that a new coinage bears no resemblance to one that was used in the traditional language. Thus, if a new text comes to light, which contains an example of that 'older' word, the language would need to be modified accordingly.

In the case of Cornish, different strategies for word creation have been advocated at different times. For instance, the problem of lexical gaps was addressed by Nance in his 1938 dictionary. As a work aiming to provide a basis for the revival of Cornish, the dictionary had to supply words where either no form was recorded in the available texts or where no word had hitherto existed in Cornish. In the introduction to his work, Nance (1938: III) states his aim quite clearly: 'This new Cornish–English Dictionary aims at including every known word of the Cornish Language, but as chance must have prevented many of its words from coming down to us ... it also includes many words which can only be *presumed* to have formed part of the language'.

The dictionary introduced several hundred new words into Cornish, and Nance filled lexical gaps in Cornish on the basis of certain principles. For example, where Welsh and Breton had cognate forms, but none existed in Cornish, it was assumed that the Cornish form was unrecorded and the deduced form of this word features in the dictionary (Nance 1938: IV). For example, the verb *menegy*, 'to point out, mention, report, declare', is set up on the basis of Welsh *mynegi* and Breton *menegiñ*. Similarly, what Nance terms 'new Celtic compounds' were introduced on the basis of words current in Welsh or Breton, for example *march-tan*, 'locomotive', was calqued on the model of Breton.

Nance (1938: IV) notes that his dictionary incorporates 'local dialect survivals'. Although he gives no further details of these words, a perusal of his dictionary reveals entries such as *collenky*, 'to swallow down', which he notes has been created on the basis of the form *clunk* in the English dialect of Cornwall. Given that this form has cognates in Welsh (*llyncu*) and Breton (*lonkañ*), Nance has clearly taken the existence of the word *clunk* in the contemporary English of Cornwall as evidence that a similar form may have existed in Cornish.

Nance also notes that Middle Cornish borrowed readily from Middle English and thus incorporates some new Middle English adaptations: for example *adamant*, 'diamond', and *scochon*, 'coat of arms'. However, he adds 'we may shun those of them which most resemble current English' (Nance 1938: IV). This practice is found in many contexts of language obsolescence (see Chapter 4), where there seems to be a general reluctance to borrow from the contemporary dominant language (Hewitt 1977: 38–9).

Richard Gendall's *Practical Dictionary of Modern Cornish* (1997, 1998), on the other hand, adopts different strategies for lexical augmentation. Unlike Nance, Gendall tries to avoid what he calls 'the temptation of inventing new words from so-called Celtic roots', as he feels that it damages the 'genuine historical character of Cornish' (Gendall 1997: C). He therefore advocates filling lexical gaps by various other means such as, for instance, the incorporation of loanwords. Gendall prefers borrowing words from English than creating completely new Celtic words on the basis that this is consistent with the practice adopted in Middle Cornish (1997: IV). He also justifies this decision with reference to Welsh, and cites examples of Welsh words which have been borrowed from English.

Gendall (1998: B) also prefers the semantic extension of existing Cornish words over the creation of new Celtic compounds. He justifies this practice on the basis of Middle Cornish, citing the example of *scute* (itself a borrowing from Latin) which, as well as a 'shield', means 'coin', 'shoe-protector' and 'offcut of wood'. However, despite his reluctance to invent words on the basis of other Celtic languages, Gendall has used Welsh and Breton cognates as a guide in semantically extending Cornish words. This, he argues, has been necessary given the paucity of recorded Cornish which does not generally indicate the 'full use that can be made of them [Cornish words]' (Gendall 1998: C; our insertion). He therefore advocates consulting Welsh and Breton dictionaries in order to 'make the fullest use of our own words' (Gendall 1998: C). This might arguably be seen as a compromise of his principles, as there is no reason why we can assume that semantic extension would have taken place in a particular word in Cornish merely on the basis of a similar extension of its cognate.

Gendall continues Nance's practice of adopting words that occur in the contemporary English dialect of Cornwall when these can be shown to have cognates in other Celtic languages (Gendall 1997: IV). In addition, he advocates using words from this dialect even when there are no cognates when these have a form peculiar to Cornwall and when they fill a lexical gap in the language. For example, on the basis of the forms *crow, craw, crou* (meaning 'hut'/'sty'), the form *krow* is set up for Cornish (Hodge 1997: 6).

It will therefore be seen that, although both the neologising strategies of Nance and Gendall are aimed at making the vocabulary of Cornish more extensive, the means by which this is achieved differ to some degree. They do, however, draw on vocabulary from all periods of Cornish, which gives rise to interesting (but ultimately moot) speculation as to the extent to which a native speaker of Cornish – if one were able to be resurrected – would be able to understand the vocabulary of modern Cornish, even if we were to discount terms referring to modern concepts and inventions.

6.2.3.3 *Grammar*

Revival efforts also necessitate attention to grammatical forms, which may be incompletely recorded in textual data. The latter are unlikely, for instance, to contain a complete set of paradigms for each of the language's verbs (especially since writing usually favours third-person forms). In the case of Cornish, it has often proved necessary to piece together such paradigms on the basis of several different texts and, in the absence of an example of a particular person of a particular verb, a suitable form has sometimes been invented on the basis of the paradigm of other verbs. While this is not an unreasonable way to proceed, new evidence can, from time to time, cause invented forms to be revised. For example, Wella Brown (2001: vii) mentions how he has revised the parts of his 1984 grammar dealing with the subjunctive on the basis of a more recent work (namely George 2001).

Moreover, if new texts came to light which contain examples of a verb form (or an item of vocabulary) that had previously been deduced, this will also introduce changes into the language which must then be adopted by all speakers. An instance of this occurred in 2000, when a manuscript came to light which contained a previously unknown Middle Cornish verse play called *Bewnans Ke*. Its discovery increased the corpus of known Middle Cornish literature by about 20 per cent and it may contain some hitherto unknown forms.

Reviving a language on the basis of texts is a difficult task. As we saw in Chapter 5, revitalisation is easier since, even if only a handful of native speakers remains, these can still supply forms which, in the context of revival, are simply irretrievable unless they feature in the extant literature.

6.2.4 *The goals of revival*

As we have seen, when Cornish died, it was replaced by English in all its speech domains. It therefore seems reasonable to ask what exactly the goals of reviving Cornish are. In the case of Hebrew, we saw that there has been a desire to revive the tongue as a focus of ethnic identity and (from the mid-twentieth century) the main everyday language of the state of Israel. This meant that the goal was the creation of new native speakers and the transformation of Hebrew from a language of religion to one which could be used in all domains. The revival of Hebrew, then, had both a symbolic and a pragmatic aim. The case of Cornish is, however, rather different. The need for English on both local (to England) and international fronts puts Cornish at a tremendous practical disadvantage and means that the creation of a Cornish-speaking Cornwall cannot be seen as a realistic goal of the revival campaign.

Native speakers of Cornish can only be created by children being born to parents who use it (despite it being their second language) as their everyday means of communication within the family setting. While such a scenario is not impossible to envisage, such cases are likely to be few and far between. Even though an individual might have a strong commitment to Cornish, speaking exclusively to one's child in a language one has learnt as an adult – especially given the lack of vocabulary for many everyday twenty-first-century concepts – is no mean task.

If the use of Cornish as the main language of Cornwall is therefore not the goal of the revival, then we can conclude that Cornish is being revived for symbolic reasons which, as we saw earlier, is the other value that can be attached to language. Jenner felt that Cornish people should speak Cornish 'because they are Cornish', and indeed the most significant function of Cornish today is as a badge of sociocultural and socio-historical 'otherness' (particularly in relation to England). By reviving Cornish, therefore, people are emphasising the fact that Cornwall is different and that they, the Cornish people, belong to a different tradition, culture and mindset from their English neighbours. Language, then, can be a vehicle for the promotion of a distinct self-image. Ellis and Mac a'Ghobhainn (1971: 144) state that 'a language cannot be saved by singing a few songs or having a word printed on a postage stamp', but in fact all the trappings of Cornishness that become more visible in the wake of the revival of the language – such as Cornish greetings on Christmas cards, its use on commemoration stones and in rugby club mottoes – are important as they are highly visible and widely found markers of 'otherness'. Moreover, they can be used by people who do not speak Cornish but who nevertheless wish to subscribe to this feeling of 'otherness' from the rest of the UK. The acceptance and use of Cornish in such apparently trivial contexts all contributes to the establishment of the region's distinct self-image.

Reviving the language also gives added impetus to movements that promote Cornish culture. Here, we have something of a chicken-and-egg situation, since the promotion of a language and its culture often go hand in hand: it is difficult to promote a language in a contextual vacuum, and such promotion is likely to be more successful with the support of a cultural framework. For example, we have seen that Jenner's work to establish a Cornish Gorseth gave added status to Cornish as a literary language but at the same time gave Cornwall an important cultural institution, one which placed it firmly in the Celtic – as opposed to the Anglo-Saxon – tradition.[8] Furthermore, the revival of Cornish has also brought in its wake the revival of Old Cornish traditions and customs such as Midsummer Bonfires and wrestling. Hale (1999: 26) mentions how raising the profile of Cornwall's cultural and political 'difference' by means of events such as a Celtic film and television festival (1997) and, in the same year, a month-long march commemorating the 1497 Cornish rebellion has provided added attention and support for the Cornish language. Using the language as a vehicle for the cultivation of a distinct Cornish identity is therefore probably the most realistic goal of the revival movement.

6.2.5 *Will revival work?*

In order for its revival to be successful and for Cornish to be heard once again throughout Cornwall on a daily basis (even if it is unrealistic to expect that this will be as the dominant language of everyday discourse), the language needs to have a role that it alone can fulfill. It may be used as a means of communication by revivalists but since English already performs this function within the speech community, we have seen that it is the symbolic value of Cornish as the vehicle and hallmark of a distinct Cornish identity that is therefore central to the revival campaign, and the degree to which this role is accepted by the speech community is central to the success of the campaign.

Cornish will survive if it is felt to be relevant to the present-day speech community, and this brings us to the question of how ethnically distinct Cornwall feels itself to be. We have seen that Hebrew acted as a powerful force to bind together the ethnically diverse population of Israel. However, the fact remains that Cornwall is not perceived as a nation, even by the majority of its inhabitants. Whereas the other Celtic countries of the British Isles all have some measure of devolution, Cornwall is devoid of any national infrastructure or any national sports teams or national mass-appeal associations that could become the focal point for any sense of national identity. Both inside and outside its borders, Cornwall is generally seen as merely a part of England. Moreover, many of Cornwall's 400,000 inhabitants are not Cornish at all but English people who have decided to move or retire to Cornwall. To this extent, therefore, the revivalists seem to be battling in isolation.

The make-up of the current Cornish speech community is also likely to influence the success of the revival. As mentioned above, in the Western world, the champions of endangered languages are most likely to be found among the educated middle classes (Jones 1998: 314; Macnamara 1971: 85). In the early twentieth century, the establishment of the Old Cornwall Societies signalled a significant change in revivalist ideology by 'shifting the focus away from an intellectual to a popular footing' (Hale 1999: 23–4). The cause will be helped in the twenty-first century too, by making Cornish of interest to all sectors of the community.

Clearly, the degree of official backing the language receives must also be of some importance here for, as seen in Jersey, although the efforts of revitalisers (or revivalists) can put the movement on its feet, the state alone has sufficient resources to develop and sustain adequate measures in vital areas such as education and to provide economic incentives for its use (see Chapter 5). In November 2002, it was announced that Cornish had been granted official protection under the provisions of the European Union Charter on Minority Languages (see Section 3.4), which was ratified by Britain in 2001 (Elliott 2002). This was undoubtedly an important step forward for the language but, as yet, the degree of official backing the respective languages receive represent a major difference between Hebrew and Cornish.

Finally, Cornish seems perpetually destined to be a second language. Although this was initially the case with Hebrew, there was sufficient impetus at the grass-roots level to ensure that, even after one generation, it was on its way to becoming restored as a native language. Although it is possible that a few children may grow up with Cornish as their native tongue, the impossibility of living in what is politically a part of England without being able to speak English means that numbers of Cornish-dominant bilinguals are likely to remain few and far between. A further point to consider, then, is whether this matters, or indeed whether the revival of Cornish can be felt to have succeeded even if its survival is as a second language.

Cornish will never be the same as it was before. As Bentahila and Davies (1993: 376) point out, the restoration of a language often involves using it in domains in which it has never been used before, standardising its grammar and expanding its vocabulary. Thus, with any reviving or revitalising language, it is perhaps more appropriate to speak of 'transformation' than 'restoration' and a simple return to past norms. We should not, though, be tempted to use Hebrew as a benchmark for the success of the Cornish revival, since their sociopolitical contexts are worlds apart. The success of the Cornish movement can best be judged by setting realistic goals for the particular context in hand.

6.2.6 How authentic is revived Cornish?

We now come to the question of how authentic Revived Cornish really is. As seen above, the question of authenticity has led to disagreement among revivalists, some of whom feel that the language should be revived in its 'golden state' of the fifteenth century, while others feel that the revived language should resemble the variety that died in the eighteenth century.

The question of authenticity has been specifically addressed in relation to Cornish by Price, who distinguishes what he calls 'the traditional and authentic language of Cornwall' from 'modern pseudo-Cornish', referring to the former as 'Cornish' and the latter as 'Cornic' (Price 1984: 141).[9] As we have seen, the creation of a spoken form of the language on the basis of rather meagre textual evidence has meant the filling of lexical and grammatical gaps on the basis of deduction and invention. Moreover, in the absence of native speakers, the authentic Cornish pronunciation of vowels and consonants is practically irrecoverable. For these reasons, Price (1984: 144) has claimed that:

> Cornic is not Cornish – or to use the traditional terminology, 'revived' Cornish is not real Cornish. It could perhaps be compared to a painting so heavily restored as no longer to qualify as an authentic work by the

artist who originally painted it, or to a piece of music found in fragmentary form and arranged some centuries later by another composer.

We should note that Price's comment is not meant to suggest that Revived
Cornish should be abandoned but instead that, due to its very nature, we
cannot expect it to be identical to the language that was spoken natively in
Cornwall for many centuries, nor should we pretend that it is. If we could
resurrect a speaker of Cornish, it is likely that he or she would be able to
converse with one of the fifty or so modern-day fluent speakers of revived
Cornish, but it is unlikely that this would be wholly unproblematic.

We cannot turn back the clock. In sociopolitical terms, Cornish will
never be the majority language of Cornwall, nor even a native language to
more than a small handful of its inhabitants. In linguistic terms, its true
nature can never be recaptured in terms of grammar or pronunciation, and
dialect differences that may once have existed have largely been lost. As we
have seen, several different views are currently held as to what constitutes
authentic Revived Cornish, and Payton (2000: 102) has welcomed debate
about the nature of the revived language as part of the 'quest for authenticity'. However, we should not lose sight of the fact that, at the end of the
day, the debate about authenticity is a luxury and its only real importance is
on academic grounds. The fact of the matter is that in the twenty-first
century Cornish does once more exist as a spoken tongue. Although some
Cornish scholars may feel that Revived Cornish can only enjoy equal status
with other languages by establishing its authenticity, to the average learner,
such questions are not of primary concern. For them, the main consideration
is choosing whether or not to learn and speak Cornish and not the authenticity of this variety.

6.3 Discussion

In this chapter, we have seen that it is possible for corpus and status planning
to operate on a language from 'beyond the grave', making it possible for a
language to be promoted – and to change – even after it has 'died'. As
mentioned above, language revival is a far less common process than language revitalisation and, as we have seen, its success is contingent upon non-
linguistic factors, the most prominent of which are the existence of a separate ethnic identity (which can by crystallised in the shape of the language),
its relevance to the modern speech community and the degree of official
backing this receives. To date, Hebrew represents the only example of a
successful revival as both a native tongue and as a medium of public life and
administration (Ellis and Mac a'Ghobhainn 1971: 72), but the example of
Cornish usefully demonstrates the fact that language revival can be undertaken even with the most meagre tools, no real infrastructure and within the
territory of a world language.

Fishman (1991: 315–16) states that after the revival of Hebrew had been completed and the language had come to be used widely and effortlessly as a native tongue, the sentiment attached to its use began to diminish. He reports that, on the occasion of the proclamation of the Hebrew year 5750 (1989/1990) as the 'year of the Hebrew language', the Israeli Minister of Education lamented 'If only we loved Hebrew as much as Yiddishists love Yiddish or Ladinoists love Ladino'. The best-loved languages, it seems, are dead or dying ones.

7   Language invention

7.1 Introduction

In this chapter, we have chosen to consider instances of a phenomenon not typically examined in analyses of language change – the creation and promotion of artificial or invented languages. The label *artificial/invented* is in fact a superordinate term for a plethora of conscious constructions including computer languages, magic languages, potential lingua francas such as Esperanto and Pasilingua, and even the non-human languages of Middle Earth in Tolkien's *The Lord of the Rings*. The fact that such entities have generally been excluded from mainstream linguistic discussion is neither surprising nor unjustifiable: many are not 'full' systems, are not used natively or even frequently by speech communities and are therefore not dynamically involved in processes of change typical of natural languages, such as grammaticalisation or borrowing (see Chapters 1 and 2). Furthermore, as we have seen previously, a great deal of modern linguistic research has been focused on ascertaining the properties of the innate and 'natural' language system (Saussure's *langue*, Chomsky's *competence*): an approach that necessarily marginalises deliberate and conscious linguistic generation.

   We do not intend to take issue with these stances: it is indeed true that the nature and purpose of many inventions preclude them from detailed and illuminating linguistic discussion. We have, however, included select discussion of such systems here primarily because invention constitutes part of the natural and normal spectrum of human linguistic ability and behaviour and, as such, merits acknowledgement in our general discussion of language use and language change. At the most obvious level, linguistic inventions are, despite their tag of artificiality, ultimately products of the human linguistic competence and, indeed, *creativity*, that produces their natural counterparts. In many cases, they are also often born of the arguably human impulse to influence and change linguistic behaviour, an impulse which, as we have seen in Chapter 5, fundamentally underlies strategies of natural language planning. Thus, as we will see in this chapter, languages may be invented to reflect particular world views, promote and foster solidarity among certain groups or even potentially for the purpose of preventing natural linguistic obsolescence as a result of the domination of one particular language. It is in such real-life purposes that our interest in linguistic invention lies and, as such, our primary focus will be on *invented auxiliary languages* (abbreviated here as IALs), relatively developed systems which have been created for the express purpose of serving as lingua francas (or at the very least as the basis for lingua francas) for particular groups of users. We will focus specifically on two such creations, one 'fact' and the other based in fiction – Esperanto and Láadan respectively – but begin with a brief contextual history of deliberate invention.

7.2 Inventing language

Deliberate linguistic invention takes place of course against a ubiquitous backdrop of unconscious creation and change and, as such, is perceived and judged in relation to the latter. The inevitable, resultant polarisation of *artificial* (which also carries connotations of *unnaturalness*), and *natural* linguistic behaviour has typically led to questions about the merit of deliberate, 'synthetic' creation. Do not, for instance, enough linguistic resources exist 'naturally' to fulfil every function we desire, from the expression of ideology to the practical use of a lingua franca? Can such issues not be settled without conscious deliberation? Such perspectives have long been current in academic debates and general thought about linguistic invention. For instance, Sapir (1925), writing in favour of the development of an invented international language, noted (somewhat prophetically in relation to English) that:

> the crucial differences of opinion lie not so much between one constructed language and another as between *the idea of a constructed language and that of an already well-established national one* . . . It is not uncommon to hear it said . . . by those who stand somewhat outside the international language question [that] English is already de facto the international language of modern times . . . and that the precise form of it as an international language may well be left to historical and psychological factors that one need not worry about in advance.
>
> (Sapir 1925: 1; our emphasis)

Sapir (1925: 7) also noted that deliberate invention therefore had 'a somewhat cliquish and esoteric air' for many of those uninvolved in the process. This is not without salience some eighty years later: for many, deliberate creation still smacks of the quasi-academic and the 'geeky'; a fringe and fantasy-based pastime that produces 'eccentricities' such as Klingon and Esperanto. The fact that the Internet has given visible shape to communities of invented language proponents through web sites and chat rooms for enthusiastic *conlangers* ('language constructors') has probably done little to dispel its reputation as a somewhat unusual and, to all intents and purposes, intangible undertaking.

Yet while deliberate invention has long been nothing more than a game for many,[1] it has also been seriously considered as an ideal solution to what have been characterised by some as (linked) linguistic and social 'problems'. Eco (1995: 1), for example, argues that the perception of linguistic diversity as an unsatisfactory 'confusion of tongues' which upholds social distance and difference has long been current in practically every culture, as has been the notion that this 'Babel' can be redeemed through 'the rediscovery or invention of a language common to all humanity'. In European thought, this has prompted various linguistic projects throughout the centuries, such as those listed in 7.2.a (adapted from Eco 1995: 2–3):

7.2.a Typology of 'language projects' in European scholarship
1. The rediscovery of languages postulated as original or as mystically perfect, such as Hebrew, Egyptian or Chinese.
2. The reconstruction of languages postulated, either fancifully or not, as original or mother tongues.
3. Languages constructed artificially for one of three ends:

   (a) Perfection in terms of either function or structure, such as the a-priori philosophical languages of the seventeenth century, designed to express ideas perfectly.
   (b) Perfection in terms of universality, such as the a-posteriori international languages of the nineteenth century.
   (c) Perfection in terms of practicality, if only presumed, such as the so-called polygraphies.

4. Magic languages, discovered or invented, whose perfection is extolled on account of either their mystic effability or their initiatic secrecy.

We will focus our discussion on languages which fall into category (3).

Eco's sub-categorisation of language types in 3(a)–(c) perhaps implies, somewhat misleadingly, that the three axioms of deliberate creation are discrete. This is, however, not the case: in a perspective that sees natural languages as imperfect media of communication and as divisive social forces, a language that is structurally and functionally 'perfect' is inevitably judged as also having universal and practical appeal. As an example, consider the a priori philosophical languages mentioned in 3(a); 'a priori' meaning formation on the basis of logic without reference to natural language forms. The germ of these languages lay in a philosophical problem: specifically, the existence of *idola*, or false ideas arising from a variety of sources including established philosophical dogma, human nature and, interestingly, the way in which language is used (*idola fori*) (Eco 1995: 211).[2] *Idola*, and particularly *idola fori*, was not however just an issue in the abstract: it was believed to have real-world effects, 'clouding the minds of men' (Eco 1995: 209) and hampering intellectual thought and progress. It is therefore unsurprising that the creation of a linguistically 'perfect' system –

importantly, grounded in a priori principles so as to, in theory, escape the failings experienced by natural languages – was seen as a primary means of arresting *idola fori*.

There were, however, other potential benefits to such new linguistic creations. Eco (1995: 209) states, for example, that support in Europe for linguistic invention was initially strongest in seventeenth-century Britain, where a new language seemed to offer a range of practical advantages both within the country and in its external dealings. It was felt, for instance, that a new language could replace Latin (a language typically and derisively viewed by the Protestant majority as 'popish'). In this scholarly context, a new a-priori language was also endorsed as a potentially more appropriate medium for scientific writing than Latin had been – new discoveries were being made in the natural and physical sciences, and 'adequate nomenclature' needed to be found 'in order to counteract the symbolic and allegorical vagueness of alchemical terms' (Eco 1995: 210). In addition, an a-priori language had the potential to serve as a commercial lingua franca across Europe and within Britain's expanding colonial empire, where it could also be used for evangelical purposes, conveying the word of God in a medium that, in its 'perfection', was as close as humanly possible to the ideal of pre-Babel Language.

A-priori systems, therefore, were not simply the result of philosophical and religious musings, but were also meant to have real-world salience as commonly used, practical languages. Cave Beck, writing in 1657, expressed this blend of practicality and universality when he stated that the invention of a common language would be 'of advantage to mankind as it would encourage commerce as well as saving the expense of hiring interpreters' (*The Universal Character*; cited in Eco 1995: 211). This ideal captured the imagination of many seventeenth-century minds, including British scholars such as Frances Lodwick (*A Common Writing*, 1647; *The Groundwork Laid (or So Intended) for the Framing of a New Perfect Language and a Universal Common Writing*, 1652), George Dalgarno (*Ars signorum*, 1661) and John Wilkins (*Essay towards a Real Character, and a Philosophical Language*, 1668). A-priori systems also later surfaced in nineteenth- and early twentieth-century scholarship: examples include Vidal's Langue universelle et analytique (1844), Dyer's Lingua-lumina (1875), Maldant's Langue naturelle (1887), Hilbe's Zahlensprache (1901) and Dietrich's Völkerverkehrs-sprache (1902).[3]

However, in their remove from features of natural languages and basis instead on logical conceptualisations personal to their inventors, a-priori systems by and large remained individualised creations, opaque to outsiders and difficult to learn. Indeed, Lorenz (1910: 2) remarked that years of experimentation with such languages had shown 'with absolute certainty that a priori systems cannot be spoken. The learning of any natural language, with all its irregularities, peculiarities and anomalies, is child's play compared to the learning of an a priori system'. Nonetheless, the ideal of either rediscovering or inventing a universal, practical and of course, as perfect as possible language remained, and towards the beginning of the twentieth century, gained new momentum with the advances in transport and communications technology that would increase and encourage international communication, especially in economic and scientific forums.

The emergence of the multilingual global village was seen by some as potentially problematic: Couturat and Leau (1907; cited in Eco 1995: 317) wrote, for example, that deliberate linguistic decisions needed to be made 'sous peine de revenir à la tour de Babel' ('on pain of returning to the Tower of Babel'; our translation). Lorenz (1910: 1) argued that fixing on a language with 'internationality of vocabulary and logical precision of expression' was vital for communication within the scientific community. While the adoption of one natural language as the international lingua franca in these domains seemed an obvious choice (and also carried certain psychological and practical advantages in being established as a 'normal', learnable and hence functional medium of communication), it was also an extremely problematic one. The selection of one natural language immediately introduced, for instance, a dimension of inequality into interactional contexts idealised as egalitarian. In addition, such a deliberate linguistic decision was likely to be resented by many not just as the imposition of a language per se, but also of the values and ideologies with which it had become associated (incidentally, a perspective evident today vis-à-vis the spread of (American) English). Even the revival of an unused language would not provide respite from such issues. Latin, for instance, was an obvious candidate with its historical pedigree as the one-time lingua franca of European scholarship. However, this in itself, plus its continuing use in the Catholic church, made it a partisan choice in the international context. In addition, Latin was fundamentally unsuited to the job in the twentieth century, being 'totally incongruent with modern life and modern requirements' (Jespersen 1931: 1). Above all, proponents of language invention argued, natural languages – living and 'dead'[4] – possessed 'irregularities, peculiarities and anomalies' (Lorenz 1910: 2) which made them difficult for non-native speakers and inappropriate as international media of clear, precise and unambiguous communication.

Thus was made the case for the widespread adoption of new, invented auxiliary languages, free from the structural 'failings' and ideological associations of natural languages, international in flavour, easy to learn and psychologically accessible. The lack of success of a priori languages in relation to the latter point proved to be a salutary lesson and the late nineteenth to early twentieth centuries saw the emergence of a virtual Babel of a-posteriori systems (Eco 1995: 321), or languages ultimately devised from a synthesis of natural language features, including creations such as Universal sprache (1868), Pasilingua (1885), Lingua (1888), Mondolingue (1888) and Anglo-Franca (1889). Also surfacing in this spate of linguistic concoction were mixed systems, or languages formed on both a priori and a posteriori principles.[5]

Perhaps the most well known of such mixed inventions is Volapük, devised in 1880 by a German Catholic priest, Johann Martin Schleyer. Volapük was primarily modelled on English and German, and made use of rule-governed processes and features generally paralleled in natural languages and often familiar to speakers of Indo-European tongues. Thus Volapük has, for example, vowel and consonant qualities found in some Indo-European languages and phonological rules governing stress placement (such as that primary stress falls on the last syllable in polysyllabic words). The major parts of speech each have their own inflectional morphology: singular nouns become pluralised through the addition of -s (*blod* 'brother' > *blods*) and adjectives express degrees of comparison through the suffixation of -*um* (comparative) and -*ün* (superlative), as in *nulik* 'new' ~ *nulikum* 'newer' ~ *nulikün* 'newest'. Verbs in the infinitive carry the suffix -*ön* (as in *löfön* 'to love'), the prefix *ä*- in the past tense (with omission of -*ön*) as in *älöf* 'loved', and the suffix -*öl* in the present participle form, as in *löföl* 'loving'. The pronoun system distinguishes between first, second and third persons, and forms are marked for number (*ob* 'I', *obs* 'we'), gender (*om* 'he', *of* 'she', *on*/ *os* 'it'; *oms, ofs, ons,* 'they' (masculine, feminine and neuter respectively)), possessive case (*ofik/ofsik* 'her'/'their' (feminine), *obik/obsik* 'my'/'our') and in the case of some of the second-person pronouns, familiarity and politeness, echoing the *tu/vous* distinction of the Romance languages. Thus, *or/ol* 'you' (singular) serve both functions, as do their plural counterparts *ors/ols*, but differentiation is observed in the use of *olik/olsik* (singular and plural respectively) for familiar 'your' and *orik/orsik* for polite 'your'.

In addition to its inflectional rules, Volapük also possesses derivational affixes used in familiar Indo-European patterns: adjectives are derived from nouns through the addition of the suffix -*ik* (*flen* 'friend' > *flenik* 'friendly'), and adverbs from adjectives with -*o*, as in *badik* 'bad' > *badiko* 'badly'. The language also has certain syntactic rules governing processes such as question formation and negation. In the former, a statement can be turned into a question through the suffixation of -*li* to the verb, as in *voboms ko flens*, 'they are working with friends' > *voboms-li ko flens* 'are they working with friends?'; and in the latter, a statement becomes negative through the addition of pre-verbal *no*, as in *löfob fleni olik* 'I like your friend' > *no löfob fleni olik* 'I don't like your friend'.

Volapük does, however, also possess rules whose purposes have been judged to be, in the context of deliberate invention, somewhat opaque and arbitrary (although we should of course note that a measure of opacity and arbitrariness is characteristic of natural languages). For instance, the language has no definite and indefinite article(s), so *tood*, for example, translates as '(a/the) car'. However, loanwords must be modified by *el* 'the', as in *el Sputnik*. Not only is the benefit of this one particular rule unclear (since all words foreign and 'native' to Volapük appear to otherwise be treated identically in terms of inflection and derivation), but its inclusion also smacks of ultimate artificiality, in being at odds with what is cross-linguistically observable about the treatment of loans in 'natural' languages; namely, that speakers adopt and adapt them as part of an integrative process of change (see Chapter 2). The decision to curb such a 'natural' process through a consistent signification of otherness seems distinctly a priori in principle.

Another such rule concerns agreement between nouns and adjectival modifiers (illustrated in Section 7.2.b.(i)–(iii)). In Volapük, adjectives may precede or follow a noun. If they are used as pre-modifiers, then they must carry case and number agreement (see 7.2.b.(i)). However, if nouns precede their adjectives, the latter remain invariable in terms of number and case marking, as in 7.2.b.(ii). If, in this post-modifying construction, one adjective is separated from others by an intervening element such as a conjunction, the separated adjective *only* must agree in case and number with the head noun (7.2.b.(iii)).

7.2.b Adjectival modification of Volapük nouns

(i) | *labob* | *smalikis* | *nitedikis* | *bukis* |
     I have   small   interesting   books
     bukis = *buk* 'book' + *-i* (accusative case) + *-s* (plural)

(ii) *labob bukis smalik nitedik*
     'I have small, interesting books.'

(iii) *labob bukis smalik e nitedikis*
     'I have small and interesting books.'

The advantages of such rules are difficult to ascertain. Why, for example, should consecutive pre-modifying adjectives carry inflectional agreement and post-modifying ones none? Why does the introduction of a conjunction transform the adjectival constituent into a mix of uninflected and inflected forms? Once again, such decisions appear to have been based on a priori conceptions that remain opaque to the language learner.

Schleyer has also been chastised for his 'deformation' of natural language vocabulary in Volapük. Thus, the Volapük word for 'room' was based on English (originally from French) *chamber* but turned into *cem*. Similarly *bel* ('mountain') was based on German *Berg* and *fils* on English *fire*. Indeed, the name of the language itself derived from such transformation: *vol* and *pük* are modifications of English *world* and *speak*. Such decisions attracted severe criticism and eventually, catalysed proposals for reform. Jespersen (1918: II) for instance, wrote that one of the primary failings of the language was that words from European languages had been 'massacred and deformed past recognition', and that the eventual failure of Volapük as an IAL was due to such 'qualities of the language itself'. Eco (1995: 321) concluded that in its creation, Volapük lost 'all resemblance to any natural language', which made it difficult for any speaker, regardless of their mother tongue, to learn.

While such criticisms were not without basis, it is worth noting that they were also not completely objective assessments of the language as an autonomous system. As an invented, auxiliary tongue Volapük could no more escape comparison with natural language models (hence criticisms of 'deformation' and 'massacre') than evaluation against IAL ideals (hence judgements about its difficulty and opacity). Its typical evaluation as both a failure of 'good' language invention and a parody of extant tongues is therefore unsurprising. It was, however, not irredeemable. Despite falling short of the ideals of transparency and logical rigour expected of an IAL, it did also significantly conform to transparent, rule-governed processes paralleled in natural languages. The language therefore had enough potential to be rescued through deliberate reform or actual adoption by speakers, who would subconsciously begin the process of 'naturalising' it. Schleyer, however, opposed both, seeing reforms as ' "heretical" modifications which further simplified, restructured and rearranged' the language (Eco 1995: 319), and worried that the adoption and 'naturalisation' of Volapük by speakers would ultimately result in another case of 'Babelisation'. It is arguable that it was such resistance to change, rather than the language's 'imperfections' per se, which contributed to its marginalisation. As we will see later, this paradoxical (and in this paradox, doomed) expectation that invented systems will be used, but remain untouched by that use, is perhaps one of the biggest stumbling blocks for linguistic invention.

Despite Schleyer's reluctance to lose control over his creation, Volapük enjoyed a period of immense popularity in approximately the first two decades of its introduction. Jespersen (1918: I) noted that 'for the first time it was seen to be possible to get one's self understood in international relations both spoken and written by the help of a man-made language'. By 1889, 283 Volapük clubs had been established in Europe, America and Australia, all actively involved in promoting the language. Today, a sizeable Volapük presence also exists on the Internet. Its popularity did however, decline significantly in the early twentieth century, partly because of tensions within the movement itself: discussions on reform appear to have resulted in disagreement and intractability on the part of those involved, and the overall effect was 'confusion and dissolution' (Jespersen 1918: II). We should note, however, that the Volapük model also gave rise to a number of other mixed system projects, including a reworking of Volapük known as Idiom Neutral (1886), and others such as Bopal (1887), Spelin (1886), Dil (1887), Balta (1893) and Veltparl (1896).

The other major reason for the decline of Volapük, however, as well as for the lack of support for other mixed systems, was the rise in popularity of a contemporary language, Esperanto; an a-posteriori system created in 1887 by Polish-born Dr Ledger Ludwik Zamenhof. We will discuss Esperanto in detail in Section 7.3, but suffice to say here that support for it spread quickly throughout Europe, with 'philanthropists, linguists and learned societies [following] its progress with interest' (Eco 1995: 324; our insertion). Today, a Universala Esperanto-Asocio (UEA) exists in all principal cities of the world, and over 100 periodicals are published in the language, which is also a medium for a significant amount of original and translated work. In addition, it also has a significant Internet presence.

Eco (1995: 326) notes that in its first few decades of existence, Esperanto, like Volapük, was in danger of being 'torn apart' by debates over proposed reforms and the adequacy of new, offshoot versions. In 1907, however, Couturat, as co-founder and secretary of the Délégation pour l'adoption d'une langue auxiliaire internationale,[6] declared Esperanto to be the best IAL in existence. There was, however, a proviso – the version that actually gained approval was Ido, a modified form of Esperanto. In an echo of Schleyer's anti-reform stance, the majority of Esperanto enthusiasts resisted this decision, preferring to adhere to the principles set down by Zamenhof in his *Fundamento de Esperanto*. Ido nonetheless continued to garner support (including from linguists such as Jespersen) and work on reform continued in the early years of the twentieth century. The advent of the First World War, however, essentially halted activities in the invented language movement: the promotion of a common language had much more salience in a time of peace than of (inter)national hostility.

Towards the end of the war, scholars such as Jespersen and Sapir once again began to advocate the promotion of IALs. While the commercial and administrative practicality of such a language remained a given, a new – or perhaps, more greatly emphasised – element of the pro-IAL argument was that it could be potentially beneficial in rebuilding relations between nations, and also in combating the nationalistic tendencies which were seen as an inevitable but problematic fallout of the war. Thus, Jespersen wrote in 1918 that:

> When, after the end of the war, the whole relationship between the nations as it was before 1914 is renewed, – and it will be renewed, just simply because the nations can't do without each other – then the question of a world-language, or let us rather say of an art-made means of communication between the peoples, will again become a burning one.
>
> (Jespersen 1918: I)

Groups of allies consolidated by the war (such as England, America, France, Italy and Russia), Jespersen (1918: I) argued, would need an auxiliary language, since none of them 'possesses a single language which appears naturally as the sole means of getting understood among the different members of the group'. In addition, the 'poor neutrals with their smaller populations' would also need such a language at the very least for commercial transactions with bigger nations.

Familiar arguments against the use of natural languages in an auxiliary capacity once again resurfaced but in the contemporary sociocultural context, had a sense of immediacy not present in their earlier manifestations. Sapir (1925: 2), for example, stated that potential choices such as French,

Latin and English were now even more 'involved with nationalistic . . . implications which could not entirely be shaken off'. Indeed, he argued, the choice of any national language was problematic since they were 'all huge systems of vested interests which sullenly resist critical inquiry' (Sapir 1925: 6). Indeed, Jespersen's writings a few years later on the subject have an increased sense of urgency in their explicit stance against the choice of a natural language as a lingua franca:

> Linguistic conditions in Europe are desperate . . . The worst of it is that at the same time as technical inventions render communications between countries easy . . . nationalism is everywhere raising its head and making each nation feel and maintain, even aggressively maintain, its own value. National jealousies are nowadays so strong that it is out of the question to have one of the existing languages adopted everywhere as the recognised means of international communication.
>
> (Jespersen 1931: 1)

The obvious solution, therefore, was an invented language which could not be interpreted as 'the symbol of any localism or nationality' (Sapir 1925: 2). This 'neutral' state, Sapir believed, could be attained and maintained through its strict promotion as an auxiliary system (and not as a competitor to the 'many languages of the folk' (Sapir 1925: 2)), as well as through a process of 'democratic formation'. At the best of times, he argued, people are resentful of linguistic impositions; much more so in a post-war context of 'tightening nationalisms' (Sapir 1925: 2). Only a system which was truly a synthesis of natural languages – in a sense, 'a creation of all' – would be easily accepted: 'a common creation demands a common sacrifice, and perhaps not the least potent argument in favour of a constructed international language is the fact that it is equally foreign, or apparently so, to the traditions of all nationalities' (Sapir 1921: 2).

Sapir's ideal of an IAL was truly universal in its scope. He stated, for example, that such a system should serve as 'the broad base for every type of international understanding, which means, of course, in the last analysis, for every type of expression of the human spirit' (1925: 2). And, once again, aspirations of 'perfection in terms of universality' (see 7.2.a; type 3(b)) not only overlapped with notions of practicality (as indicated in the above discussion) but also with those of structural perfection. Indeed, in a very general sense, inventors envisaged a successful invented system as working in the same way as the much later Generativist school (see Chapter 1) would conceptualise the mechanisms of natural language use: namely, in terms of a finite, rule-governed entity from which emerged an infinite number of linguistic possibilities. The inventors, however, conceived of their fundamental 'language kit' in terms of qualities that are notoriously difficult to quantify objectively, such as *simplicity, precision, logic, richness, creativity* and *universal appeal*. Thus, Sapir (1925: 3) stated that:

what is needed above all is a language that is as simple, as regular, as logical, as rich, and as creative as possible; a language which starts with a minimum of demands on the learning capacity of the normal individual to do the maximum amount of work; which is to serve as a sort of logical touchstone to all national languages.

Similarly, Jespersen (1931: 1) postulated that in adherence to principles such as the attainment of simplicity, precision and the other qualities mentioned above, it should not be problematic to construct an artificial language 'that is so easy that everybody can master it in far less time than it usually takes to learn one of the ordinary languages'. Overall, these overlapping aspirations of universality, practicality and structural/functional 'efficiency' were summarised in the 1930 Declaration of the International Auxiliary Language Association (IALA) that recognised the need for a 'universal auxiliary language, simple in form, politically neutral and destined to facilitate relations between peoples' (Jespersen 1931: 5).

The notion of (sociopolitical) neutrality has, so far in our discussion, surfaced consistently as a requirement for auxiliary languages. We should note, however, that there is no reason why the opposite may not occur; that is, the deliberate invention of a system in order to give shape to particular ideologies or world views. Granted, this is not at all a common occurrence – indeed, in the contexts we have been considering, such an invention would be an impossibility – but such creation for use by a group who, for various reasons, may have no real voice in their natural native language would not be an unimaginable undertaking. One such attempt was made in 1984 by linguist and popular author Suzette Haden Elgin who, in her science-fiction novel *Native Tongue*, put forward the possibility and potential of a language invented by and for women, Láadan. We will explore Elgin's creation in more detail in Section 7.4, but suffice to say here that, like inventors such as Schleyer and Zamenhof, she hoped that it would have some practical real-world effect, influencing linguistic (and by extension, social) behaviour. Indeed, despite differences in their target audiences and ideological standpoints, languages such as Esperanto and Láadan were both conceived in the idealistic hope of promoting solidarity among certain groups of speakers while providing them with a means of communication allegedly free of the dominant sociopolitical associations and ideologies of natural tongues. We will discuss the success of such hopes more fully in Section 7.5 but first turn to more detailed consideration of the real-life creation Esperanto (Section 7.3) and in Elgin's terms, the 'linguistic experiment' of Láadan (Section 7.4).

7.3 Case study: Esperanto

As mentioned earlier, Esperanto was devised in 1887 by Zamenhof, who made the initial proposal in a book entitled *The International Language:*

preface and complete manual (for Russians), under the pseudonym Dr Esperanto (meaning 'Dr Hopeful'). Zamenhof was born in 1859 to a Jewish family living in Tsarist-ruled Polish Lithuania, and grew up in 'a crucible of races and languages continually shaken by nationalistic ferment and lasting waves of anti-Semitism' (Eco 1995: 324). He appears to have been fascinated by the idea of an international language from early adolescence and, given his experience and observation of sociopolitical hostility and oppression, it is unsurprising that he would see such a language as a medium through which peace and solidarity could be promoted. Esperanto, therefore, was born of that impulse. Indeed, in the same years that the language began to spread throughout Europe, Zamenhof also published an anonymous pamphlet setting out a doctrine of international brotherhood known as *homaranism*. Many Esperanto supporters, however, argued that the potential success of the language lay in its ideological neutrality: 'if Esperanto were to succeed, it would do so only by attracting to its cause men and women of different religious, political and philosophical opinions' (Eco 1995: 325). Nevertheless, the language did inevitably come to be associated with particular, idealistic perspectives that were often considered dangerously subversive by authorities. Eco (1995: 325) states, for example, that the language had the 'fortune/misfortune' to be embraced by Tolstoy, 'whose brand of humanist pacifism the government regarded as a dangerous form of revolutionary ideology'. Overall, the fact that the language was typically embraced and promoted as part of a utopic, democratic ideology meant that Esperantists all over Europe frequently suffered persecution at the hands of their governmental detractors.[7]

Zamenhof planned the corpus of Esperanto primarily on the basis of a posteriori principles, drawing features and processes from a synthesis of Indo-European tongues. For instance, although some vocabulary items were constructed from scratch (such as *abelo* 'ape' and *apud* 'next to'), in cases where words were clearly cognates (as in *lingwe, lingua, langue, lengua, language*) Zamenhof derived forms that could be justified as a 'common root' (as in *lingvo*). Zamenhof also transferred what appeared to be relatively common Indo-European patterns to his creation such as, for example, the derivation of feminine-denoting forms via suffixation (as in *patro* 'father' > *patrino* 'mother'; cf. English *waiter* > *waitress*, Latin *rex* > *regina*, Russian *tsar* > *tsarina*); and the signalling of repeated activity via prefixation (as in *konstrui* 'build' > *rekonstrui* 'to rebuild'; cf. English *send* > *resend*).

Overall, Esperanto works on the basis of a finite, transparent set of 'rules' (sixteen, its supporters boast, although 'subrules' make the actual count much higher) that allegedly generate a language as functional and as productive as any natural system. A simplified précis of some of the basic rules, and an example of their output, are given in 7.3.a.[8]

7.3.a Sample rules of Esperanto

(i) **articles**: there is only one definite article, *la*, in Esperanto, and no indefinite article. Hence *libro* means 'book/a book', but *la libro*, 'the book'.

(ii) **nouns**: all nouns end in -*o* and form plurals through suffixation of -*j* (*la hundo* 'dog' > *la hundoj*). In accusative case, nouns carry the suffix -*n*, and other cases such as the genitive and dative are expressed by the use of prepositions:

la hundo	*persekutis*	*la katojn*	*de la knaboj*	*al la domo*
the dog	chased	the cats	of the boys	to the house
		(accusative)	(genitive)	(dative)
		(plural)	(plural)	

(iii) **adjectives**: all adjectives end in -*a* and carry the same case and number markings as nouns: *La bruna hundo persekutas la nigrajn katojn.* 'the brown dog is chasing the black cats'.
The comparative and superlative degrees are formed with *pli* 'more' and *plej* 'most', respectively, as in *pli granda* 'larger' and *plej granda* 'largest'.

(iv) **pronouns**: the pronoun forms are *mi* 'I', *vi* 'you', *li* 'he', *ŝi* 'she', *ĝi* 'it', *si* 'oneself', *ni* 'we', *ili* 'they', *oni* 'they-one-people'.
Possessive pronouns are formed by addition of the adjective ending -*a*: *mia hundo* 'my dog'.
Declension is as for nouns, as in *mia hundo amas vian katon* 'my dog loves your cat'.

(v) **verbs**: infinitives marked by -*i* do not inflect for person or number, but carry tense and mood affixes. Thus, present tense is signalled by -*as* (*mi amas vin* 'I love you'), past tense by -*is* (*mi amis vin* 'I loved you') and future by -*os* (*mi amos vin* 'I will love you'). The suffix -*us* marks conditional (*se vi gajnus la loterion mi amus vin*, 'If you were to win the lottery I would love you'), and -*u*, imperative (am*u min* 'love me!').

(vi) **adverbs**: these end in -*e*, as in *la kato rapide kuris* 'the cat ran fast'.

(vii) **prepositions**: when followed by nouns (or pronouns), the latter are always uninflected for case, as in *la libroj de la knabo* 'the boy's books'.

(viii) **stress placement**: in speech, primary stress always falls on the penultimate syllable.

(ix) **word formation**: the primary means of lexical augmentation is compounding, as in *amoplena* 'full of love' (*ami* 'to love' + *plena* 'full'), *pagipova* 'able to pay' (*pagi* 'to pay' + *povi* 'to be able').

(x) **borrowing**: loanwords are taken into Esperanto, but internally created alternatives are preferable. Thus Esperanto *malbona* 'bad, miserable, nasty, poor', is promoted over borrowed *mava*, and *mallakso* over *konstipo* 'constipated'.

(xi) **negation**: sentences are negated with pre-verbal *ne*, as in *mi ne faris tion* 'I didn't do that'. When another negative word is present, *ne* is omitted, as in *Mi **neniam** faris tion* 'I never did that'.

Despite the persecution suffered by Esperantists (or perhaps because of it, since persecution 'only reinforces an idea' (Eco 1995: 325)), the language has had, and continues to have, a significant following which includes academic support. Meillet (1918: 268), for example, gave it an explicit seal of approval when he stated that 'toute discussion théoretique est vaine: l'Esperanto fonctionne' ('all theoretical discussion is pointless: Esperanto works'; our translation). Many supporters of the language typically point to its alleged structural 'superiority' (relative to natural languages), claiming in effect that the language is logical, simple and rich (cf. Sapir 1925, quoted earlier), easy to understand and learn and completely adequate for every purpose. It is also said to be capable of 'growth' (making it as adaptable a system as a natural language) although, interestingly, this process of change is actually officially monitored by an Esperanto Academy. Indeed, Esperantists claim that the success of the language as an invented system can be measured by the fact that it has moved beyond auxiliary status and gained significant numbers of native speakers.[9]

In terms of auxiliary language use, however, Esperanto has garnered significant support from internationally recognised bodies. In 1954, an official relationship was established between Unesco and the UEA, when the Unesco General Conference (UGC) 'recognised that the achievements of Esperanto match Unesco's aims and ideals' (UEA: 5). Collaboration between the two has continued, and the UGC consistently promotes the teaching of Esperanto in schools and its use in international affairs to member states and international organisations. More recently, concerns about cultural and linguistic endangerment, and for upholding the rights of cultural and linguistic minorities in the face of the increasingly global use of one-time colonial languages such as English, has brought the use of Esperanto firmly into international language planning agendas. In 1996, the Nitobe Symposium of International Organizations called for the inclusion of Esperanto in discussions on language rights and language policy, and produced the Prague Manifesto, 'a modern restatement of the values and goals underlying the Esperanto movement' which emphasises 'linguistic democracy and the preservation of linguistic diversity' (UEA: 1). Even more recently, Phillipson (2003: 141), in an examination and critique of language policy in Europe, states that there is currently a 'clear need, at a time of intensifying europeanization, and when an increased use of English is impacting on other languages, to clarify principles of equity in communication, and to identify criteria that can guide language policy in the new multilingual Europe that is emerging'. One solution, he proposes, is the establishment of a level linguistic playing field, which may be achieved through the use of Esperanto (see Phillipson 2003: 169–74).

Thus, Esperanto appears to have been quite successful on the levels of corpus and status planning. While, as mentioned earlier, Esperantists attribute this to the language's properties, others not so enamoured of its alleged attributes have pointed instead to the timeliness of its emergence (contemporaneous with Volapük), and its cohesive, sustained promotion as a simpler, more recognisable system. Similarly, Chandler (1997: 1) notes that:

> Nowadays, Esperanto still enjoys by far the widest support of any IAL but whether this success is based on linguistic superiority is open to some doubt. It is more likely that other factors such as propaganda and organization by the various national and international Esperanto societies have secured its relative success.

The language has also been criticised in terms of its structure, although it must be noted that this has sometimes been based on intuitive comparisons with the perceived properties of natural languages, and not on objective evaluations of the system itself. Thus, Chandler (1997: 5) claims that the plural noun and adjective endings (-*oj* and -*aj* respectively) are 'heavy and unnatural', as is the construction of various words from smaller independent elements, as in *mansanulejo* 'hospital' (< *man-san-ul-ej-o* 'place for people who are the opposite of well'). Interestingly, other criticisms revolve around the fact that, in some instances, the language is 'too natural': marked and unmarked pairings for example, often display the ideological biases found in real-world languages. For instance, as mentioned earlier, terms denoting female referents are derived via affixation of a base which, by default, is gendered masculine (cf. *patro* > *patrino*). The Esperanto movement has not officially addressed complaints about this androcentric slant – Chandler (1997: 5) notes that Zamenhof's *Fundamento* would prevent change in this area – but masculine suffixes have been unofficially created (that is, without the sanction of the Esperanto Academy) and are in ad hoc use.

Another example in this vein concerns the formation of antonymic pairs. Once again, one Esperanto 'root' is taken as a base, and the formation of its antonym is achieved through the prefixation of *mal-*, meaning 'opposite'. And once again, the choice of what constitutes a root form in such pairs has been argued to reflect real-world, normative perspectives. Hence in the pair *good/bad*, *bona* ('good') is the root, and *mal-bona* the affixed form. Similarly, *dekstra* ('right') is the base from which *mal-dekstra* ('left') is derived. It is worth noting here too, that the negative meaning that *mal* carries for many speakers of European languages also means that such pejorative connotations can potentially be transposed onto Esperanto's allegedly neutral system.

Finally, in terms of structure, critics have argued that the corpus of Esperanto is not necessarily the successful synthesis of diverse natural language features its supporters claim. The model for the language, as we have seen, was Indo-European (more specifically Romance) – an unsurprising and perhaps inevitable decision, but hardly one that is completely representative and truly international. Indeed, Martinet (1991: 681; cited in Eco 1995: 330) succinctly observed that 'the situation would have been different if the language had been invented by a Japanese'.

The bias towards European languages in Esperanto also raises issues around the notion of *linguistic relativity* (discussed more fully in Section 7.4). Eco (1995: 330) notes that inventors and supporters of IALs have never been unduly concerned by the possibility that 'different languages present the world in different ways, sometimes mutually incommensurable'. This has certainly been the case for Esperantists, who point to the high level of translation into this language from various natural tongues as proof of its 'effability' (Eco 1995: 330). Yet, given the difficulties inherent in, and the skill required for, successful translation of material from one natural language to another, it is hard to believe that Esperanto captures every nuance, subtlety, metaphor, idiom; in short, every *sense* possible in every language of the world. If this is indeed the case, then it is a remarkable feat of engineering: a language tied to nothing, but capable of expressing everything.

In this general context, we may also look critically at the claims of ideological and sociopolitical neutrality in its use as an auxiliary language. Arguably, neutrality is in itself an ideological and political stance, as is the promotion of a language such as Esperanto in the name of 'linguistic democracy'. This has not, however, been the main focus of criticisms of Esperanto's neutrality, which have instead concentrated on 'structural biases', such as those mentioned above, as well as on the fact that the language, in echoes of its early association with pacifist principles, has come to be used by various groups and individuals with particular political agendas and, as such, associated with certain ideologies. For instance, Jespersen (1918: II) claimed that during the First World War, Esperanto was used for propaganda in Germany through a monthly review, paid for by the German government and containing 'a defence of German methods and spiteful attacks on other nations'. This complaint highlights one aspect of the 'purity' that IAL inventors have idealistically, and unrealistically, hoped to maintain once their creations enter real-world use. Indeed, the social history of Esperanto use is a salutary reminder that the creation and maintenance of complete neutrality is, in a sense, inhuman: a system created by humans and used by humans will always be governed by and susceptible to human thought. As a final point about sustaining neutrality, we should note that if it is indeed the case that Esperanto is being used as a native language, then 'Babelisation' (or in more linguistic terms, 'drift', see Chapter 1) in relation to both structural change and ideological divergence will be well under way and beyond the institutional control of organisations such as the Esperanto Academy. Such developments in native Esperanto will doubtless impact on the use and associations of auxiliary Esperanto, but at the moment it remains to be seen how this might unfold.

We will revisit Esperanto in Section 7.5, but turn now to consideration of a language deliberately constructed not with neutrality but bias in mind: Láadan.

7.4 Case study: Láadan

As mentioned in Section 7.2, Suzette Haden Elgin constructed Láadan with a view to providing women (specifically, we should note, English-speaking women, particularly in the USA)[10] with a language able to clearly and unambiguously express in their own terms their particular perceptions, experiences and world views. Elgin's 'experiment' was catalysed by contemporary feminist linguistic debates on and about the relative sociopolitical status of men and women (primarily in the Western world) and how this was sustained through cultural and linguistic systems. To better understand the themes Elgin explored in the creation of Láadan and her real-world aims for the language, we therefore need to first briefly consider the theoretical context which fed its creation.[11]

Elgin (1999) states that she wrote *Native Tongue* in order to test four interrelated hypotheses:

> (1) that the weak form of the linguistic relativity hypothesis is true (that is, that human languages structure human perception in significant ways); (2) that Goedel's Theorem applies to language, so that there are changes you could not introduce into a language without destroying it and languages you could not introduce into a culture without destroying it; (3) that change in language brings about social change, rather than the contrary; and (4) that if women were offered a women's language one of two things would happen – they would welcome and nurture it, or it would at minimum motivate them to replace it with a better women's language of their own construction.

Hypothesis (1) states the overarching theoretical context for Elgin's work, and we will therefore take it as our starting point. *Linguistic relativity* is probably best known as part of the Sapir–Whorf hypothesis, which essentially postulates that language and world view are symbiotically related. Sapir and Whorf, anthropological linguists who worked extensively on Native American languages and cultures during the early decades of the twentieth century, were extremely interested in why perceptions of what we might term universal phenomena (such as of time and space) differed significantly between their ancestral (Western European) cultures and those in which they were observers. Sapir and Whorf argued that differences in perception were caused ultimately by the *encodings* of individual languages, which had inevitably been shaped over centuries by the extralinguistic, cultural experiences of their respective speech communities. This meant, therefore, that languages were not equivalent systems of communication (an assumption we touched on earlier in relation to Esperanto and translation), but were instead *relative* to the cultures they respectively gave expression to. Furthermore, the perceptions each language embodied profoundly but subconsciously affected the ways in which their speakers viewed the world around them (*linguistic determinism*). Thus, as Sapir stated:

> Human beings . . . are very much at the mercy of the particular language
> which has become the medium of expression for their society. . . . The
> fact of the matter is that the 'real world' is to a large extent
> unconsciously built up on the language habits of the group. No two
> languages are ever sufficiently similar to be considered as representing
> the same social reality. The worlds in which different societies live are
> different worlds, not the same world with different labels attached.
>
> (Sapir 1929; in Mandelbaum 1958: 162)

We will not pursue discussion of the Sapir–Whorf hypothesis further here,[12] but note instead Cameron's (1992: 135) assertion that the ideas of relativity and determinism informed feminist linguistic work, which argued that sexism against women was a 'background' feature encoded in many languages and, as a consequence, either determined (the 'strong' interpretation) or influenced (the 'weak' interpretation) cultural perceptions of gender and gender roles. More specifically, work in this area postulated that the sexist foundations of some languages were not only inevitably and unconsciously perpetuated by speakers (thus reinforcing sexist perceptions) but were also, by their very 'background' nature, extremely difficult or even impossible to challenge and change.

This deterministic view of sexism *in* language went hand in hand with an assumption of male control *over* language; an assumption actually rooted in 'a more general discourse of twentieth century Western culture about the abuse of language as a coercive political instrument' (Cameron 1992: 138). Such discourse surfaced, for example, in the post-Second World War writings of George Orwell, which explored the role of language (and propaganda) in the rise of totalitarian regimes. Indeed, Orwell's concerns about the power of language to control thought and behaviour formed the central theme of his novel *Nineteen Eighty-Four*, a hellish imagining of a totalitarian society in which a regulated and carefully crafted language, Newspeak, prevails. As a medium of language- and thought-policing, Newspeak represents the darkest realisation of linguistic determinism: its speakers (who, to paraphrase Sapir (1933: 157), have not learnt to fight the implications of their language) cannot really step outside the reality it constructs. As Cameron (1992: 139) notes, this is not a society in which sociopolitical dissent, for instance, is censored or punished, but rather one in which it is practically impossible because it simply cannot be expressed: 'there is no way even to think subversive thoughts'. Language therefore becomes a powerful instrument in the maintenance of the community's authoritarian regime.

This particular notion of linguistic thought control has surfaced in debates on sexist language. Indeed, Cameron (1992: 140) points out that 'radical feminist theories of language have determinism and (male) control as their twin foundation stones'. It is not necessary for us to explore such work in detail here and the questions and issues they have raised,[13] but we should note their firm grounding in the assumption that language constructs 'reality' and specifically, the 'reality' of a dominant, controlling group. In relation to sexist language, feminist linguists have argued that in systems such as English, where dominant discourses have been shaped by the socio-politically powerful male group, 'the reality turns out to be androcentric and indeed misogynistic' (Cameron 1992: 157). Importantly, speakers generally remain unaware of this 'background' bias which, if unquestioned and unchallenged, lives on through generations of language transmission and continues to significantly influence (or in some perspectives, determine) other cultural manifestations of sexism.

These perspectives inevitably raise the question of whether women can escape the deterministic influence of the androcentric language they are born into, and find linguistic expression of their particular reality. For proponents of weaker forms of the determinism and control theories, change could be effected by increasing awareness of the biases inherent in language and so paving the way for more careful usage in both speech and writing. Cameron (1992: 152) states that for the radical feminist theorists, however, who held strong deterministic views, such a solution has been inadequate: if a language was fundamentally androcentric (as many were judged to be), then that basic principle could not be changed, regardless of careful usage. The only answer, therefore, lay in creating gynocentric systems, such as entirely new languages in which the common experience of women could find expression.

It is within this real-world theoretical context that Elgin decided to experiment with Láadan, in order to test not only the ideas of determinism and control, but also that of active, non-violent resistance for women through the creation of a common language (cf. hypotheses (1)–(4)). Unlike the other language inventors we have discussed here, Elgin chose to first 'release' her creation in the realm of fiction, stating that 'science fiction is our best and most powerful resource for trying out social changes before we make them, to find out what their consequences might be' (cited in Squier and Vedder 2000: 305). However, like her creative counterparts, she also believed that only an invented language could supersede the 'flaws' of natural language (in this case, androcentricity) and provide an appropriate and adequate lingua franca: 'women are distressed' she stated, 'because existing human languages are inadequate to express their perceptions' (Elgin 1999). Elgin set a limit of ten years on her experiment (1984–94) in order to conduct a viable assessment of the real-world impact of Láadan, as well as of the validity of her hypotheses. We will return to the question of Láadan's fortunes later in this section.

Elgin's laboratory, *Native Tongue*, simulates a possible dystopian future (set in America) in which androcentricity rules unchallenged. The civil rights of women have been revoked, and they exist for the most part as subservient housewives and baby machines. The only women who have some small measure of autonomy are female linguists, whose services are necessary in trade negotiations between Earth and humanoid aliens and also, of course, in breeding future generations of the linguist families, known as the Lines.

When linguist women are no longer useful as either physical partners or translators, they are sent to communal, all-female *barren houses*. Within these enclaves a quiet revolution takes place. These linguists, now to all intents and purposes invisible in their physical removal from a world in which they did not ever really exist, resurrect practices of – and so reschool themselves in – a past in which women had control over their bodies and minds. To this end, they keep instruments for abortion and contraceptive drugs and, importantly, create a secret language, Láadan, whose *raison d'être* is to shape and express a female world view.

Elgin's female linguists are able language inventors and construct a system that is described as grammatically efficient and adequate. The aspect of invention that takes most thought, however, is that of *encoding* or, essentially, giving precise shape to, to paraphrase Whorf (in Gumperz and Levinson 1996: 21), the house of female consciousness which 'no known "man-made language" expresses except by endless, inexact and timewasting circumlocution' (Cameron 1992: 153). Through this process of defining and labelling, the female linguists construct a female 'reality' that is distinct from that perpetuated by the languages of men.

We now turn to a brief examination of Láadan itself which, unlike many fictional creations, is in fact relatively detailed in its construction;[14] partly because this was essential to its potential 'release' into real-world use, but also because the actual experience of construction itself (by a linguist) was integral to the veracity of the fictional storyline of invention. Elgin therefore created Láadan before writing the novel, thus making the latter both laboratory and showcase for the language and the ideology behind it.

Like many of the auxiliary languages of the nineteenth century, the corpus of Láadan is a posteriori, drawing on natural language features and processes that its creator found 'valuable and appropriate'. A summary of the main rules, and an excerpt of Láadan writing (adapted from Sperling 1996), is given below.

7.4.1 *Láadan sounds and phonology*

Láadan has five vowels and thirteen consonants, almost all of which possess phonetic qualities familiar to English speakers. For example, the five vowel notations and their phonetic realisations are *a, e, i, o, u* (/a/, /ɛ/, /ɪ/, /o/, /u/ respectively). The consonantal inventory includes *b* (/b/), *d* (/d/), *h* (/h/), *l* (/l/), *lh* (the sound of which is close to /x/), *m* (/m/), *n* (/n/), *r* (/r/), *sh* (/ʃ/), *th* (/θ/), *w* (/w/), *y* (/j/), *zh* (/ʒ/). The system also makes use of high tones, indicated in writing by an acute accent above the relevant vowel.

In general, Láadan prohibits a sequence of two consonants or two vowels; the only exception being a sequence of two identical vowels, in which case one carries high tone, as in *Láadan*. The constraint against CC or VV structure also applies in instances of affixation, where an epenthetic vowel *e* or consonant *h* is inserted to break up the offending cluster. Thus, root *nen* plus suffix *-th* results in *neneth*, and prefix *du-* plus root *ada* equals *duhada* (no glosses given).

7.4.2 *Láadan nouns*

Láadan nouns are not distinguished for number. Number marking for subject nouns in a sentence is signalled by a verb prefix *me-*, which indicates plurality. Otherwise, the hearer/reader disambiguates number on the basis of other structures such as anaphoric pronouns (which are differentiated as singular or plural), or where possible, quantifying modifiers such as *five*, *one* or *several*.

Láadan follows the pattern of various natural languages (and also of invented ones such as Esperanto) in incorporating a principle of 'gendered' affixation. Unusually but unsurprisingly, the gendered affix *-id* in Láadan denotes male/masculine, meaning that in relevant cases, the unmarked noun can be interpreted as female/feminine (as in *thul* '(female) parent', *thulid* 'male parent').

Nouns in Láadan carry case suffixes, apart from instances where they serve as subjects and subject complements. A noun in accusative case, for example, carries *-(e)th* (as in 'I ate *the apple*' > *doyeth*). Nouns in NPs which precede a postposition, however, take different suffixes according to the latter's function, as can be seen in the examples in 7.4.2.a (note that for convenience and ease of explanation, the English example sentences use prepositions with the relevant NPs):

7.4.2.a Láadan postposition functions and noun suffixes

Postpositional function	Suffix	Láadan noun
Source, as in 'She came from the house'	*-(e)de*	*belidede*
Goal, as in 'They went to school'	*-(e)di*, *-(e)dim*	*ulinedi, ulinedim*
Beneficiary, as in 'I worked for the scientist'	*-(e)da*: voluntarily	*eháda*
	-(e)dáa: obligatorily	*ehádáa*
	-(e)daá: accidentally	*ehádaá*
	-(e)dá: by force, against one's will	*ehádá*
Associate, as in 'The child played with the baby'	*-(e)den*: neutral form	*áwitheden*
	-(e)dan: with pleasure	*áwithedan*
Time, as in 'I worked on Monday'	*-(e)ya*	*henesháaleya*
Place, as in 'I played in the room'	*-(e)ha*	*shodeha*
Instrument, as in 'She wrote with a pencil'	*-(e)nan*	*dalethodiwanenan*
Cause, as in 'She cried because of pain'	*-(e)wan*: purpose, in order to	*heyiwan*
	-(e)wáan: reason, because of	*heyiwáan*

Possession is also expressed through a range of affixes, depending on the sense intended by the speaker/writer (7.4.2.b):

7.4.2.b Possession
The child's hands > *háawith* + *-(e)tha* (by reason of birth) = *háawithetha*
> *háawith* + *-(e)thi* (by reason of chance) = *háawithethi*
> *háawith* + *-(e)the* (for unknown/unacknowledged reasons) = *háawithethe*

7.4.3 Pronouns

Láadan pronouns are not differentiated for gender or case, but for person and number (with a plural subdivision). Elgin appears to have also drawn on the solidarity/status differentiation present in the *tu/vous* distinction of natural languages, but reshaped her cline to reflect particular degrees of emotional relationship, as can be seen in 7.4.3.a:

7.4.3.a Láadan pronouns

Person	Regarded as	Singular	Plural (2–4)	Plural (5+)
First person	neutral	*le*	*lezh*	*len*
	beloved	*la*	*lazh*	*lan*
	honoured	*li*	*lizh*	*lin*
	despised	*lhele*	*lhelezh*	*lhelen*
Second person	neutral	*ne*	*nezh*	*nen*
	beloved	*na*	*nazh*	*nan*
	honoured	*ni*	*nizh*	*nin*
	despised	*lhene*	*lhenezh*	*lhenen*
Third person	neutral	*be*	*bezh*	*ben*
	beloved	*ba*	*bazh*	*ban*
	honoured	*bi*	*bizh*	*bin*
	despised	*lhebe*	*lhebezh*	*lheben*

Reflexives are formed through the addition of suffix *-yóo* to the relevant singular pronoun. To pluralise, *-zh* or *-n* are further added (as in *be* > *beyóo* > *beyóozh/ beyóon*.

7.4.4 Verbs

As indicated in Section 7.4.2, Láadan verbs are marked only for the plural number of their subjects through the addition of *me-*, as in *le radama* ('I refrain from touching') > *bin meradama* ('They refrain from touching').[15] The *me-* prefix always precedes other verb affixes, so will be placed before the prefix *nó-* ('to cease to X') for example, as in *menóradama*. Láadan also makes use of an alternate form of *me-* with verbs beginning with /d/; namely syllabic /n/ ([ŋ]), as in *dashobin* 'to chew' > *len ndashobin* 'we chew'. This violates the prohibition on CC structures, but is counted as a permissible exception. Finally, Láadan verbs are also used as adjectives.

7.4.5 Adverbs

In Láadan, adverbs can be derived from nouns, verbs/adjectives and pronouns through suffixation of *-(e)nal* 'in the manner of', as can be seen in 7.4.5.a:

7.4.5.a Adverb formation

ehá 'scientist' (noun)   + *-(e)nal* = *ehánal* 'in the manner of a scientist'
rile 'silence' (noun)   + *-(e)nal* = *rilenal* 'silently'
thal 'to be good' (verb) + *-(e)nal* = *thalenal* 'in a good manner; well'

7.4.6 Syntax

As mentioned earlier, Láadan makes use of postpositions, as in *shodeha nil*, 'the room inside' > 'inside the room'. Basic word order is VSO, but sentences also include what are termed *speech act* and *evidence act* morphemes. Speech act morphemes (SAMs) are placed at the beginning of each sentence (although if a sequence of sentences is likely to have the same SAM, then it may only occur in the initial sentence). In general, SAMs tell the hearer/ reader whether the sentence to follow is declarative, interrogative or imperative, and also indicate promise or warning, as can be seen in the list in 7.4.6.a:

7.4.6.a Láadan speech act morphemes

Speech act morpheme	Function
bíi	opens a declarative sentence
báa	opens a question
bó	opens a command (rarely used)
bóo	opens a request (usual 'polite command' form)
bé	opens a promise
bée	opens a warning

Evidence act morphemes (EAMs), on the other hand, end sentences and indicate the basis on which information in the preceding sentence has been presented, as can be seen in 7.4.6.b.

No EAM is used in question structures, since the latter express requests for information, rather than presenting it. Finally, negation is achieved by the addition of the negative particle *ra*, which is placed after the verb. *Ra* appears to have also been used as a negative prefix on nouns and verbs/ adjectives: witness our previous example *radama* 'to non-touch', *radona*

7.4.6.b Láadan evidence act morphemes

Evidence act morpheme	Function
wa	known to speaker because perceived by him/her
wi	known to speaker because self-evident
we	perceived by speaker in a dream
wáa	assumed true by speaker because speaker trusts source
waá	assumed false by speaker because speaker distrusts source; if evil intent by the source is also assumed, the form is *waálh*
wo	imagined or invented by speaker, hypothetical
wóo	used to indicate that the speaker states a total lack of knowledge as to the validity of the matter

'unfriendliness for foolish reasons', *rarulh* 'non-synergy; that which when combined only makes things worse'.

On the basis of such rules, passages such as that in 7.4.6.c have been generated (note too that Elgin created a lexicon of over one thousand words):

7.4.6.c 'The Frog's Jewel'
Láadan
Bíide eríli oóbemid wo. Thi be thedath omeha nil. Oth be thedawáan. Nadelishe oóbemid. Memime thul betha, 'Báa delishe ne bebáawáan?'
Di oóbemid, 'Bíiya delishe le bróo bre aril thi le ebahideth, ébre wam le theda letha bróo aril be heth wa! Id aril nóhoth le!
Medi thul, 'Izh, bíidi bre thi with ebahideth, ébre edeláad ra rawith oth behé wi.'

English
Once upon a time, there was a frog who had had a jewel in her head since her birth. The jewel gave her importance. One day, the frog began to cry.
Her parents asked her, 'Why are you crying?'
The frog said, fearfully, 'I am crying because if I get a husband, then I will lose my jewel because it will be the dowry! And then I will stop being important.'
Her parents said, in teaching, 'But, as everyone knows, if a woman has a husband, then no one believes that she is important anyway.'

(from Sperling 1996)

At the end of *Native Tongue*, Láadan begins to be used as an auxiliary language among adult women and to be passed on to younger female generations who will eventually acquire native-speaker fluency. In this dual process, it starts to move beyond its artificial beginnings into the realm of 'naturalness' in language: Susannah, one of Láadan's inventors, comments that the language is changing rapidly as it is used, particularly by the younger speakers who are forming intuitions about what 'feels right' in it. In addition, and as would be expected within a deterministic perspective, the 'reality' of the linguist women begins to change, as is manifested in turn by a behavioural change; namely, the emergence of easy and relatively detached dealings with their menfolk. As Elgin (undated interview with Kim Wells) states, through the use of Láadan,

> the women were released from the constant tension and frustration that comes of not having words for the things you want to say, and of not being listened to when you try to talk about those things anyway; they were spared the suffering that comes of deciding that talking about those things is utterly impossible and giving up trying.

The reality, however, has been quite different. Elgin's fourth hypothesis appears to have been proved false: Láadan was neither adopted nor used as a springboard for new gynocentric invention by women in the real world. As Elgin herself points out, this has brought the language experiment to a standstill, since testing of the first three hypotheses could only proceed once the new language had been accepted into widespread use. Indeed, Elgin wrote this real-world failure into a subsequent novel, *Earthsong* (1994), in which the linguist women are forced to acknowledge that their attempt to promote Láadan beyond the Lines is a failure. As she states, 'this reflects what happened in the real world . . . women did not welcome and nurture the language either in the novel or outside of the novel' (undated interview with Kim Wells).

The reasons cited for Láadan's failure are various. Elgin implies that no place has been given to a female language in an androcentric world (a strongly deterministic view) and, in support of this, points to the unprecedented popularity of another invented language initially introduced in a fictional setting, Klingon: 'Klingon, a language of war designed to express the perceptions of warriors – the doing battle kind of warriors – has been wildly popular . . . Láadan, a language of harmony designed to express the perceptions of women, has been largely ignored' (Elgin, undated interview with Kim Wells).

There is, however, another dimension to this. Klingon has had, in language planning terms, tremendous status planning success in its inclusion in the *Star Trek* series, and proponents and planners of the language now enjoy benefits of real-world acknowledgement, such as funding, an Academy and university accreditation. Elgin, on the other hand, states that she was disinclined to actively promote her language, since this was not the way in which 'languages live or die in the real world' (Elgin, undated interview with Kim Wells). This is of course, not entirely true: as our discussions of revitalisation (Chapter 5) and revival (Chapter 6) have shown, deliberate intervention and promotion can make a significant difference to the fate of a language. It is arguable that such intervention is even more necessary for an invented language: as a system that lived in the pages of a fictional novel with a fictional speech community, it is perhaps unlikely that Láadan would become established (either in actual use or as a point of critical departure) in the real-world without active, sustained promotion. The question of whether it would 'live or die' therefore remains moot until acquisition by a real-world speech community occurs.

As with Volapük and Esperanto, explanations of the real-world failure of Láadan could also conceivably focus on the flaws of the corpus (again in relation to expectations of both invented and natural systems). For instance, although the language is a posteriori in character, it has an a priori flavour in that decisions on linguistic value and appropriateness have been made on the grounds of logical conceptions personal to the creator, which are some-what opaque to outsiders. It is not clear, for instance, what the benefit of certain rules are, such as the prohibition of CC and VV structure, or the specification that preverbal *me-* > *n* before initial [d]. Similarly, it is difficult to understand the purpose of Láadan high tones which, unlike their coun-terparts in natural languages, exist here independently of a contextualising system of meaningful contrasts. Overall, the impression created of Láadan is that of a language put together with what we might term a sense of the *Cafeteria Principle*.[16] In other words, it seems that Elgin has combined various features and processes from different languages into a system that does not seem intuitively 'right'. For instance, as we have seen, Láadan nouns remain uninflected for plural number – a feature that in fact occurs in many natural languages. This, however, seems at odds with the system of intricately nuanced, carefully differentiated noun affixes in 7.4.a, since we might expect that if a language morphologically distinguishes between four different types of 'beneficiary', for instance, it would also morphologically mark a cross-linguistically salient feature such as plurality. In addition, it appears out of kilter with the Láadan pronoun system, in which degrees of plurality are painstakingly differentiated. One feels compelled to ask not only why five is a cut-off point that merits a distinct pronoun but also, what the *point* is of such differentiation when it has not been built into the noun word class with which pronouns exist so closely.

Interestingly, Láadan is also, in syntactic typological terms, inconsistent: it has V(S)O structure, but makes use of postpositions and adjective + noun structures (see Chapter 1). While such 'irregularities' may have no conscious validity for speakers, it is interesting to note that recent research into the structure of grammars suggests that certain inconsistencies, or combinations of certain inconsistent constructions, may in fact result in processing dif-ficulties (see Hawkins 2004).

Finally, Láadan words are not as transparent as those in Esperanto for example, which, as we have seen, are largely recognisable to speakers of Indo-European languages. Elgin seems to have built her roots *ex novo* from Láadan syllables and, as such, her creations bear no resemblance to words in natural languages – perhaps the ultimate expression of difference and distance from man-made languages but, simultaneously, a possible alienating factor for potential real-world speakers.

These specifics of the corpus are not, however, the only problematic aspect of Láadan. A major issue, in our opinion, lies with Elgin's fundamental aim of constructing a woman's language – an undertaking for which there are no objective linguistic criteria. The end result is therefore a system in which gynocentricity is most obviously expressed (and indeed most easily achieved) in the lexis but is transparently evident nowhere else. How do features such as VSO structure, for example, or the use of postpositions, or speech act and evidence act morphemes help generate a language better suited to women's experiences and perspectives? Of course, there is no theoretical reason why they should not, nor any reason why Elgin should not have experimented with such structures. Our point is that, from the perspective of a potential real-world speaker, the encodings might be seen to have some merit but the rest of the structural rules, as comparatively difficult and perhaps even unnecessary (given that the lexis could be borrowed into natural languages). But encodings alone do not a language make, and it is arguable that Elgin's experiment may have had a better rate of success if it had been actively promoted as a 'women's vocabulary'.

Finally, we would like to note that in this section we have used phrases such as 'women's experience/perception/language/vocabulary' with a measure of uneasiness, particularly in the preceding paragraph. This is not only because of the structural issues referred to above but also because it is not at all clear whether such generalised conceptions are in fact salient. In other words, is there really a separate (from men), common (to women) reality to express and give linguistic shape to? As Cameron (1992: 156) states:

> Is it really the case that all women share perceptions and experiences to the degree that one language would capture 'women's reality'? Or is this a false universalising of the varied experience of women? Does the 'dream of a common language' depend on our accepting a lie the powerful have always told about their powerless Others: 'they're all the same?'. And does it depend also on our 'essentialising' certain so-called 'female qualities' (nurturance, non-violence, love of nature and so on) when we ought to be challenging these restrictive views of femininity?

Theoretical perspectives on such questions have shifted considerably in the past few decades and, as a result, the notion of 'shared experience or global sisterhood' (Cameron 1992: 156–7) has, to a large extent, fallen by the wayside. Feminists have become increasingly reluctant to make generalisations about women's perceptions, natures and experiences even if, as Elgin stipulated for *Native Tongue*, those women share a cultural system and a language. As Cameron (1992: 157) notes, *Native Tongue*'s ideal of a common language, which in 'an earlier phase of feminism' would have been regarded as an appealing fantasy, would now very likely be regarded by many women as a 'totalitarian nightmare'.

7.5 Discussion

As we have seen in this chapter, language invention has been undertaken, in instances such as those exemplified by Volapük, Esperanto and Láadan, as viable and, indeed, ideal alternatives to natural languages which, by virtue of their 'flawed' nature, either catalyse, contribute to, or at the very least do not help, wider social and sociopolitical problems. In the perception of invention for real-world use as a language planning strategy, such linguistic creation essentially works towards the achievement of at least one of three aims; namely, the creation of a common language, a 'perfect' system and a practical medium of communication. Indeed, Esperanto and Láadan may be evaluated in these terms: both were invented for practical, auxiliary use by particular speech communities, and the creator of each strove towards a linguistic a posteriori ideal. Both have also involved status and corpus planning – elements, which as we have already seen in Chapter 5, need to be co-ordinated successfully if planning measures are to have any real effect.

As we also saw in Chapter 5, however, language planning strategies are not always as successful as might be hoped, for a variety of reasons. For instance, planners may not, or may not be able to, carry out effective status planning measures to promote the use of the system in question. In the case of invented languages, this would seem to be absolutely crucial, given that, as Sapir (1925; see Section 7.2) stated, the important choice for potential speakers lies not between different invented systems, but between natural and invented systems. Target audiences therefore have to be convinced of the benefits and advantages of using a language which, at least initially, has no real-world frame of reference – neither established traditions of usage nor speech communities – and which, to all intents and purposes, is essentially untried and untested. As a case in point, Esperanto appears to have benefited greatly from sustained and well-funded promotion, whereas the lack of such support has probably not helped the cause of Láadan.

In Chapter 5, we also saw that corpus planning for natural languages has to be handled carefully in order to gain acceptance in the relevant speech community. This is also an issue for language inventors, who have to convince potential speakers not only of the appropriateness of their corpora but also of their comparative 'superiority' (typically in terms of our three aims of commonality, practicality and perfection; see Section 7.2) in relation to the resources of natural languages. This is an extremely tall order, since to claim such for an invented system is to immediately invite both comparison with natural features and processes and evaluation against ideals of linguistic invention. And as we have seen, invented systems are often found wanting in both areas: Volapük, Esperanto and Láadan have all been critiqued for possessing, to varying degrees, 'imperfections' or flawed systems. Volapük's heavy dependence on a priori principles has been claimed to make it difficult to learn, and therefore both impractical and a poor candidate for a common language; Láadan's 'cafeteria construction' appears to have created a linguistic mix that in many ways seems extremely complicated, counter-intuitive and therefore 'impractical' as it stands; Esperanto has been pointed out to be not as universally representative as supporters have claimed. Finally, the ideological assumption of a common women's language which underlies Láadan may well be problematic.

On the whole, it would seem that language invention does not generally meet with a significant degree of real-world success, possibly because the decontextualised processes and rarefied air of invention generates unrealistic expectations of both inventors and their creations. The attempt to create a linguistically 'perfect' system, for instance, is inherently problematic in that perfection is ultimately not an objectively defined and evaluated criterion but instead a personal, subjective notion. 'Perfection' is therefore a quality shared only at the ideological level – each invention is in fact shaped by (and therefore reflects) what its individual creator considers 'perfect'. Paradoxically, this means that inventors more often than not create systems as 'imperfect' and as opaque as the natural ones they seek to improve on.

Assumptions of 'perfection' create other problematic issues for inventors and their languages, such as the fact that these creations seem to be expected to function fully in the real world but to remain untouched by it. We noted such assumptions earlier in Schleyer's and Zamenhof's reluctance to let their creations undergo processes of both deliberate reform and subconscious 'natural' language change, and to attempt to prevent – or at the very least control – such processes through both prescriptive codes (such as Zamenhof's *Fundamento*) and their authoritarian enforcers such as language academies. Indeed, in their determination to constrain change, Schleyer and Zamenhof were not unlike the scholars of eighteenth-century Europe, who sought to 'ascertain and fix' (Swift 1712; see Chapter 1) 'correct' (or 'perfect', perhaps?) forms of the vernacular tongues, in order to essentially prevent the 'Babelisation' of communication. Interestingly, Elgin has been, in this respect, the least conservative of the three inventors discussed here in her belief that unregulated change was absolutely essential to Láadan's survival in the real-world: 'from the very beginning, every chance I got, I made it clear that I was not only willing to have other people do things to the language, I encouraged it. Nobody has to have my permission; nobody has to clear what they do with me, or report to me or anything like that' (Elgin 2002b). However, as we have seen, the fact that Láadan has not been widely popular has meant that such potential 'naturalisation' of the language has not been realised.

Despite her liberal attitude to structural change, Elgin nonetheless appears to share with inventors such as Zamenhof an ideological conservatism in assuming that the fundamental philosophies of their languages – in this case, gynocentricity and neutrality respectively – will also remain intact in the real world. This, however, is as unlikely as the possibility that structural change will not occur once speakers adopt and adapt such systems for real-world use. Thus, while ongoing change on every level can in many cases be taken as a sign of the 'success' of a natural language, it is inevitably seen as the kiss of death for one generated by the desire for a common, unifying tongue, unfettered by real-world politics and introduced in as 'perfect' a state as possible. As Cameron (1992: 156) states, this ideal is unfeasible in practice – it is simply impossible to '[seal] language . . . in an imaginary plastic bubble forever' and assume that it will remain impervious to the culture it operates within and the speakers it exists for. Overall, the sanguine resistance to change on any or some level(s) through real-world use is perhaps one of the most flawed and 'flaw-retaining' principles of the language invention movement.

And, of course, one of the consequences of existence and use in the real world is competition with natural languages, which are typically entrenched in the domains in which it is hoped that respective invented systems will succeed. Languages such as Volapük and Esperanto, for instance, have to compete with English on the international auxiliary language front: a battle which will be difficult (if not impossible) to win despite, in the case of Esperanto, not insignificant support. As Sapir (1925) implied, natural languages have a tremendous psychological advantage over invented tongues: shaped with us and through us through the centuries, they already encode and express a great deal about who we are historically, culturally and individually, and have the potential to continue adapting in this respect without conscious and deliberate interference. Inventions such as those considered in this chapter on the other hand, are, to all intents and purposes, unilateral (emerging from one mind instead of the myriad interacting ones of a speech community) and importantly, ahistorical and acultural, which we speakers are not. While such traits have the potential to disappear through 'naturalisation', they may well present the initial, psychologically based obstacles to widespread acceptance of invented tongues.

Our approach throughout this chapter has been critical, but this should not detract from the fact that, as a linguistic exercise, the processes of invention, as well as its concomitant problems and issues, have the potential to complement our general understanding of how human language functions as successfully as it does. Nor do we intend to devalue the altruistic spirit that motivates invention in a quest for social solidarity and unity, nor to invalidate the very salient issues about natural language use (such as ideological bias) that consideration of such a process raises. Indeed, it is vital that such respective objectives and concerns continue to be addressed and considered. Our point, however, is that while 'starting from linguistic scratch' is a theoretically appealing and easily justified prospect in the context of the search for social unity, social and linguistic 'equality' and easy and efficient communication, it is not actually the straightforward solution that it might appear. As Cameron (1992: 156) argues, 'everything we create has to take its chances with history'. Invented languages are no exception.

Notes

1 Internally motivated change

1 The Neogrammarians (also known as *Jungrammatiker* 'young grammarians') were a group of late nineteenth-century scholars who studied relationships between Indo-European languages and the phenomenon of language change.

2 As mentioned in Chapter 2, not all linguists in the historical tradition have adopted this perspective. Schuchardt (1884), for example, consistently maintained that contact had played an integral role in language change.

3 The actuation problem first surfaces in Weinreich, Labov and Herzog (1968).

4 *Creativity* is a term used in linguistics to refer to the ability of language users to produce and understand an infinite number of well-formed original utterances. We are using it here to refer generally to the ability of language users to consistently produce new pronunciations, meanings, words and structures, many of which become adopted into actual usage.

5 Neogrammarian theory distinguished between *regular* and *sporadic* sound changes. The former occur in accordance with certain rules and are therefore predictable (as in assimilation), and the latter take place in isolated cases (as in the reordering of segments through metathesis (OE *brid* > *bird*)). Importantly, the Neogrammarians also developed the *regularity hypothesis*, which essentially states that changes affecting a particular sound or sounds in a particular phonetic environment, at a given point in time and within a specific speech community, will operate regularly and admit no exception that cannot be explained by reference to other laws (see McMahon 1994: 19–21).

6 McMahon (1994: 20) describes *analogy* as a process which 'clears up' after a sound change has operated. Analogy, however, occurs sporadically: it does not operate after every sound change and when it does, does not affect all relevant items. Thus, English still retains plurals such as *feet* and *mice* (which are the result of a regular sound change known as *i-mutation*), but the sporadic application of analogy has resulted in a noun such as *book* (OE *bōc*), which originally underwent the same method of plural formation as *foot* and *mouse* (hence OE plural *bēc*), gaining the more productive -*s* plural inflection; hence modern *books*. The relationship between sound change and analogy is summed up in Sturtevant's Paradox: sound change is regular but creates irregularity, whereas analogy is irregular but creates regularity.

7 The interested reader might consult Harris (1988) *Language, Saussure and Wittgenstein*.

8 It is worth noting that the question of whether the Shift was in fact a 'unified phenomenon' remains a matter of debate. The interested reader might consult, for instance, Lass (1976) and Stockwell and Minkova (1988) who respectively argue for and against the Shift having comprised a single, composite change.

9 *Functional load* refers to the amount of 'work' oppositions do in a system. Thus the opposition between /t/ and /d/, which is a meaningful distinction for many words, has a high functional load in English, whereas /n/ and /ŋ/ does not. Vowels can also carry high functional loads.

10 *Unmarked* order is typically that which occurs in, for example, simple declarative sentences and ideally is the most frequently occurring clausal order in the sentence. However, this is sometimes difficult to determine: some Australian languages, such as Dyirbal and Warlpiri, have no fixed basic clausal order (McMahon 1994: 140).

11 'Normal' here refers to children who have not been incapacitated neurally and who grow up in an environment where interaction with other speakers is the norm.

12 See Traugott (1982), which discusses the semantic-pragmatic effects of grammaticalisation, and Lehmann (1985), which explores the processes through which an element undergoing grammaticalisation loses *autonomy*. See also Hopper and Traugott (1993).

13 *Editor* and *sculptor* were originally borrowed from Latin and *burglar*, from Norman French.

14 Cambourne, a new village on the outskirts of Cambridge, England, has a Quidditch Lane.

15 This is a somewhat surprising perspective. As DeGraff (2001: 65) notes, we know that processes of language contact do not preclude morphological (re)analysis. For example, English makes use of derivational affixes which originally entered the language in loanwords, but which have since been 'extracted' and become productive in its morphology. Examples include Old French *-ese* (*journalese*, *computerese*), Greek *-ize* (*harmonize*, *criticize*) and Latin *-ician* (*beautician*, *statistician*). Yet these are not considered 'pseudo-Latin/Greek/French' constructions on the part of hypercorrecting English speakers but instead, as examples of their lexico-morphological creativity. That this propensity for (re)analysis is celebrated in a language like English but denigrated in a language like HFC therefore seems to be based more on ideological assumption than on linguistic fact.

2 Externally motivated change

1 Jersey Norman French is the dialect spoken on the Island of Jersey. It is called 'Jèrriais' by its speakers and, for this reason, will be referred to as 'Jèrriais' in this book.

2 Looking in a German dictionary under *p* will give you a good idea of how many loanwords there are in German, as strictly speaking one would expect them all to begin *pf-*.

3 In Classical Latin, the infinitive of the verb 'to want' was *velle*. *Volere* is a regularised form that arose in Vulgar Latin.

4 We have seen that in historical linguistics, the term *convergence* is used to refer to bi- or multi-directional structural influence between two or more languages where no single language is dominant. However, the notion of convergence has been subject to some reassessment. For example, Campbell (in press) (also downloadable from <http://www.linguistics.utah.edu/Faculty/campbell/research.html>) asks whether using the term *convergence* as an overarching label for change of this kind actually gets in the way of our understanding of individual contact-induced changes. The term has also recently become extended to apply to other instances of language change. Watson (2002) uses the term in a highly innovative way to refer to the interlinguistic interference occurring during 'contact' between two languages in the brain of primary bilinguals when those

two languages become more alike than they are for comparable monolinguals. Wright (2002) applies the concept to the writing system in her examination of the business writing of medieval England, where the economics of trade caused Anglo-Norman and English on the one hand, and medieval Latin and English on the other, to become mixed together in an orderly, systematic way, resulting in a contact-induced script with its own system-internal principles. These newer uses of the term will not (and are not intended to) supplant the well-established, primary meaning of convergence within historical linguistics, but they do reveal interesting extensions of current thinking within the framework of this topic.

5 However, this claim is made with the proviso that phonological integration may be incomplete (see Sankoff, Poplack and Vanniarajan 1990: 73; Muysken 2000: 7). Poplack, Sankoff and Miller (1988) also state that phonological integration is not completely reliable as a criterion to distinguish between code-switched forms and borrowings.

6 The study of code-switching has gained in prominence during the past twenty years. Key studies of its different aspects include Myers-Scotton (1993a), Blom and Gumperz (1972) and Gumperz and Hernández-Chavez (1975) (all of which focus on its social motivation) and Myers-Scotton (1993b, 2002), Muysken (2000), Poplack (1980), Pfaff (1979) and Gumperz (1982) (which consider its mechanics and syntactic workings).

3 Language birth

1 Leith (1983), however, suggests that contact played a major role in this particular case of language birth, postulating that French, for instance, is ultimately descended from contact between Latin and Frankish, and Spanish from that between Latin and Gothic.

2 Gimbutas, for instance, has argued for three successive waves of aggressive migration from a growing Kurgan/PIE population (in 4400–4200 BC, 3400–3200 BC, 3000–2800 BC), while Renfrew has posited instead movement through peaceful farming dispersal.

3 Renfrew (1987: 150–1) has postulated that as PIE farming communities spread into new environments, they sometimes encountered earlier hunter-gatherer populations. Where these were sparse in number, they are likely to have assimilated linguistically to the more numerous Indo-European farmers. However, where non-Indo-European communities were denser and integrated, as is thought to have been the case in areas of western Europe, the non-Indo-European languages may have impacted on the development of the relevant Indo-European daughters. Renfrew (1987: 151) also theorises that if these stronger communities adopted farming techniques, then they too would have experienced an increase in population, which may have strengthened the chances of survival for their native languages; hence the continued existence of languages such as Basque.

4 See, for instance, Bailey and Maroldt (1977), Thomason and Kaufman (1988), Watts and Trudgill (2002).

5 For detailed discussions of Tok Pisin, see Mühlhäusler (1982), Romaine (1988).

6 Reinecke (1937), however, hypothesised that the birthplace of MPE was New Caledonia, the area from which the majority of the first indentured servants on the Queensland plantations were drawn. Holm (1989: 528) points out that while a contact language based on English was indeed spoken in this area, it was more likely to be a 'Beach-la-mar pre-pidgin' than an early form of MPE.

7 Mühlhäusler (1982: 447) has referred to the use of the pidgin outside of plantation settings as a process of *nativisation*, in that it comes to be used in interaction between indigenous speakers rather than colonisers and the colonised. Note,

however, that this sense of *nativisation* is different from that used in the traditional *pidgin > creole life-cycle*.

8 It is worth noting, however, that positions such as Görlach's may be based primarily on a consideration of Scottish Standard English (SSE), whose points of difference from other standard Englishes (such as that used in England) lie, as is stated later in this chapter, mainly in the areas of phonology and (to a limited extent) lexis. This is not necessarily the case for non-standard dialects of Scots, which may differ significantly from English (standard and otherwise) not only phonologically and lexically, but also morphologically and syntactically (see Beal 1997 for instance).

9 See the Scots Leid Associe web site, <http://www.lallans.co.uk/index.html>, for discussions and opinions on this particular issue.

4 Language death

1 We would like to thank Oxford University Press for allowing us to draw on parts of M.C. Jones (1998) *Language Obsolescence and Revitalisation* in this chapter and Chapter 6.

2 However, it should be remembered that in any given locality the process of obsolescence is typically swifter. For example, Fisherfolk Gaelic will have died out within the typical two-to three-generational span in East Sutherland, even though the Scots Gaelic language will have taken much longer to die out in the region overall (Dorian, in personal communication with Jones).

3 See Aitchison (1991: 198–208) for discussion of these two terms.

4 Here, the soft mutation of Welsh causes the nasal stop /m/ to become the fricative /v/ and voiceless stop /t/ to voice to /d/.

5 As Legère points out, in obsolescent languages, code-switching is more likely to occur when modern topics, such as the world of business or politics are discussed, rather than traditional issues such as narrating stories from the past (1992: 110–11). The fact that a word might not exist in the obsolescent language for a technical term or concept incurs the necessity to borrow, which in turn may act as a trigger for the code-switch. However, it should also be pointed out that code-switching will not necessarily be triggered by modern topics in all obsolescent languages. For example, as we saw in Chapter 2, in East Sutherland Gaelic topic accounts for virtually no switches (Dorian 1981: 80).

6 Lenition is defined as 'A term used in phonology to refer to a weakening in the overall strength of a sound' (Crystal 1991: 197).

5 Language planning and revitalisation

1 We would like to thank Blackwell for allowing us to draw on parts of M.C. Jones (2001) *Jersey Norman French* in this chapter.

2 For a more detailed account of the setting up of the Académie française, see Cooper (1989: 3–11).

3 The *Pages Jersiaises* may be found at < http://www.societe-jersiaise.org/geraint/jerriais.html>.

4 *Crapaud*, 'toad', is a soubriquet given to the inhabitants of Jersey by the other Channel Islanders.

5 As seen in Chapter 4 the basis of standard Welsh goes back to the bardic schools of the medieval period and its 'common core' nature was not the result of a decision taken as part of a language planning initiative. However, as it turns out, standardisation according to this model has proved highly beneficial for the revitalisation of Welsh (see Jones 1998: Chapter 4).

6 Language revival

1 Clearly, if language revival is successful, the reviving tongue may later acquire native speakers.
2 The different roles of men and women in the Jewish religion meant that, at this time, Hebrew was not known to many Jewish women.
3 For highly readable accounts, see Fellman (1973) and Nahir (1988).
4 At least, this is the year in which the last recorded native speaker of Cornish died.
5 Before the death of the last native speaker of Manx (1974) extensive recordings were made of the language. Unlike the case of Cornish, therefore, records are available of the pronunciation of Manx.
6 For a discussion of this, see Fishman (1991: 300).
7 It seems likely that large parts of Pryce's work are drawn from Lhuyd (1707).
8 The fact that the Gorseth was only established in the twentieth century was of little cultural consequence, given that the Welsh and Breton institutions on which it was modelled were themselves modern inventions.
9 Price has subsequently abandoned the term 'Cornic' due to the fact that it gave rise to some offence in certain Cornish circles (Price 1998: 191), but both his 1984 point and the reaction it caused remain interesting matters for reflection.

7 Language invention

1 We should note, however, that such 'games' can also have great pedagogical benefit. *The Language Construction kit* (at <http://www.zompist.com/kit.html>), for instance, increases the conlanger's awareness of linguistic structures and patterns through its descriptions of 'natural' languages, which are used as models. In addition, in 2004, the BBC reported that a primary school in London has paved the way to introducing French by first teaching their pupils a currently popular language, Elvish.
2 The notion of the relationship between 'false speech' and 'false thought' found expression in the work of seventeenth-century scholars such as Hobbes who, in *Leviathan* (1651: IV) wrote for example that 'abuses' of speech occurred 'when men register their thoughts wrong, by the inconstancy of the signification of their words . . . when they use words metaphorically . . . [and] when by words they declare that to be their will, which is not.'
3 See Couturat and Leau (1903) *Histoire de la langue universelle* (Paris: Hachette) for detailed discussion of a priori systems.
4 Latin is often referred to as dead, but has in fact metamorphosed into its modern Romance descendants (see Chapter 1).
5 Jacob (1947) makes a distinction made between extreme and modified a priorism and a posteriorism. Extreme a priorism has no reference at all to existing languages, while its modified counterpart is one in which logic, rather than analogy with natural languages, is a shaping force. Languages which demonstrate extreme a posteriorism are essentially natural languages with slight modifications of forms or processes (such as Interlingua or Latino Sine Flexione), while modified a posteriorism describes systems that make use of features drawn from natural languages but in which they are functionally different (such as Esperanto and Ido).
6 The Délégation was formed in 1901 for the purpose of ascertaining and promoting one of the nineteenth-century inventions as an IAL.
7 Eco (1995: 325) mentions, for instance, that Esperanto speakers were victimised in Tsarist Russia and also in various Nazi-occupied territories.
8 For a more detailed discussion see Harlow (1995) 'The Sixteen Rules of Esperanto Grammar' (<http://www.webcom.com/~donh/Esperanto/rules.html>)

from which the examples in 7.3.a are adapted. Thanks to Don Harlow for permission to use these data.

9 The UEA claim that there are as many as 1,000 native speakers of Esperanto but we have been unable to corroborate this.

10 In many of her interviews, Elgin is at pains to point out that she does not claim to speak for and about all men and women, but instead about 'tendencies, and majorities, and the typical' in the USA.

11 Quotations from Elgin, unless otherwise indicated, are taken from her web pages at <http://www.sfwa.org/members/elgin/>. We have used the posting dates as dates of publication but because of the nature of the web format, are unable to provide page numbers.

12 Interested readers might consult Carroll (1956), Mandelbaum (1958) and, in this particular association with feminist linguistics, Cameron (1992).

13 See Cameron (1992) for a detailed and interesting discussion. Cameron (1998) also usefully collates various papers on sexist language and discourse.

14 Linguistic invention in fiction typically serves a simultaneous dual purpose: the signification of otherness and the plausible construction of a different world and/ or world view, as can be seen in (to take a few Western examples) the fragments of Huttese in the *Star Wars* series, the highly developed Klingon of *Star Trek*, the Sindarin and Quenya of *The Lord of the Rings* trilogy and the Nasdat utterances of *A Clockwork Orange*.

15 Tense is apparently carried in auxiliaries, although there are no examples available.

16 The *Cafeteria Principle* was a term coined by Dillard (1970) initially to refer to the tendency of some creole scholars to arbitrarily attribute certain features in Atlantic English-based creoles to a superstratal ancestry in various English dialects. It has come to be used more generally to refer to the allegedly random focusing on a particular feature in a creole and the superficial citation of a plausible (but unproved) ancestral source. We have used the term here with primary reference to its connotations of the random selection of linguistic features.

Bibliography

ADEA (Association for the Development of Education in Africa) (1999) *The Major Developments in Education in the Seychelles 1977–1998*. Republic of Seychelles: Ministry of Education.

Aikhenvald, A.Y. (1996) 'Areal Diffusion in Northwest Amazonia: The Case of Tariana'. *Anthropological Linguistics* 38, 1, 73–116.

Aitchison, J. (1991) *Language Change: Progress or Decay?* 2nd edn. Cambridge: Cambridge University Press.

Allen, W.S. (1950) 'Notes on the Phonetics of an Eastern Armenian Speaker'. *Transactions of the Philological Society* (1950), 180–206.

Andersen, R. (1988) *The Power and the Word*. London: Paladin.

Appel, R. and P. Muysken (1993) *Language Contact and Bilingualism*. London: Arnold.

Arends, J., P. Muysken and N. Smith (eds) (1995) *Pidgins and Creoles: An Introduction*. Amsterdam: John Benjamins.

Bailey, C.-J.N. and K. Maroldt (1977) 'The French Lineage of English'. In J.M. Meisel (ed.) (1977) *Langues en Contact: Pidgins, Creoles*. Tubingen: TBL Verlag Narr, pp. 21–53.

Bakker, P. and M. Mous (eds) (1994) *Mixed Languages: 15 Case Studies in Language Intertwining*. Amsterdam/Dordrecht: IFOTT/Foris.

Ballart, J. (1996) 'Language Planning in Catalonia'. In M. Nic Craith (ed.) (1996) *Watching One's Tongue: Aspects of Romance and Celtic Languages*. Liverpool Studies in Regional Cultures 5. Liverpool: Liverpool University Press, pp. 7–19.

Barber, C. (1993) *The English Language: A Historical Introduction*. Cambridge: Cambridge University Press.

Bartens, A. (2001) 'The Rocky Road to Education in Creole.' *Estudios de Sociolingüística* 2, 2, 27–56.

Bavin, E.L. (1989) 'Some Lexical and Morphological Changes in Warlpiri'. In N.C. Dorian (ed.) (1989) *Investigating Obsolescence*. Cambridge: Cambridge University Press, pp. 267–86.

Beal, J. (1997) 'Syntax and Morphology'. In C. Jones (ed.) (1997) *The Edinburgh History of the Scots Language*. Edinburgh: Edinburgh University Press, pp. 335–77.

Bentahila, A. and E.E. Davies (1993) 'Language Revival: Restoration or Transformation?' *Journal of Multilingual and Multicultural Development* 14, 5, 355–73.

Bickerton, D. (1981) *Roots of Language*. Ann Arbor, Mich.: Karoma.

—— (1988) 'Instead of the Cult of Personality . . .'. *The Carrier Pidgin* 16, 3, 2–3.

Birt, P. (1985) *Lé Jèrriais Pour Tous. A Complete Course on the Jersey Language.* Jersey: Don Balleine.

Blackman, M.B. (1989) *Sadie Brower Neakok: An Iñupiaq Woman.* Seattle, Wash. and Vancouver: University of Washington Press/Douglas & McIntyre.

Blom, J.P and J.J. Gumperz (1972) 'Social Meaning in Structure: Code-switching in Norway'. In J.J. Gumperz and D. Hymes (eds) (1972) *Directions in Socio-linguistics: The Ethnography of Communication.* New York: Holt, Rinehart & Winston, pp. 407–34.

Bradley, D. (1989) 'The Disappearance of Ugong in Thailand'. In N.C. Dorian (ed.) (1989) *Investigating Obsolescence.* Cambridge: Cambridge University Press, pp. 33–40.

Brathwaite, E.K. (1984). *History of the Voice: The Development of Nation Language in Anglophone Caribbean Poetry.* London and Port of Spain: New Beacon Press.

Brenzinger, M. (1992) 'Lexical Retention in Language Shift: Yaaku/Mukogodo-Maasai and Elmolo/Elmolo-Samburu'. In M. Brenzinger (ed.) (1992) *Language Death: Factual and Theoretical Explorations with Special Reference to East Africa.* Berlin and New York: Mouton de Gruyter, pp. 213–54.

Britain, D. and A. Sudbury (2002) 'There's Sheep and There's Penguins: Con-vergence, "Drift" and "Slant" in New Zealand and Falkland Island English'. In M.C. Jones and E. Esch (eds) (2002) *Language Change: The Interplay of Internal, External and Extra-Linguistic Factors.* Berlin and New York: Mouton de Gruyter, pp. 209–40.

Brosnahan, L.F. (1961) *The Sounds of Language: An Inquiry into the Role of Genetic Factors in the Development of Sound Systems.* Cambridge: Heffers.

Brown, W. (1984) *A Grammar of Modern Cornish*, 1st edn. Saltash: Cornish Language Board.

—— (2001) *A Grammar of Modern Cornish*, 3rd edn. Callington: Cornish Language Board.

Bugarski, R. (1992) 'Language Situation and General Policy'. In R. Bugarski and C. Hawkesworth (eds) (1992) *Language Planning in Yugoslavia.* Columbus, Ohio: Slavica, pp. 10–26.

Butt, M. and W. Geuder (2003) 'Light Verbs in Urdu and Grammaticalisation'. In R. Eckardt, K. v. Heusinger and C. Schwarze (eds) (2003) *Words in Time: Dia-chronic Semantics from Different Points of View.* Berlin: Mouton de Gruyter, pp. 295–350. Available online at <http://ling.uni-konstanz.de/pages/home/butt/lv-gramm.pdf> pp. 1–38. Accessed December 2004.

Bynon, T. (1990) *Historical Linguistics.* Cambridge: Cambridge University Press.

Cameron, D. (1992) *Feminism and Linguistic Theory.* London: Routledge.

—— (1995) *Verbal Hygiene.* London: Routledge.

—— (ed.) (1998) *The Feminist Critique of Language: A Reader.* London: Routledge.

Campbell, L. (1998) *Historical Linguistics: An Introduction.* Edinburgh: Edinburgh University Press.

—— (in press) 'Areal Linguistics: The Problem to the Answer'. In A. McMahon, N. Vincent and Y. Matras (eds) *Language Contact and Areal Linguistics.*

Campbell, L. and M.C. Muntzel (1989) 'The Structural Consequences of Language Death'. In N.C. Dorian (ed.) (1989) *Investigating Obsolescence*. Cambridge: Cambridge University Press, pp. 181–96.

Carroll, J.B. (ed.) (1956) *Language, Mind and Reality: Selected Writings of Benjamin Lee Whorf*. Cambridge, Mass.: MIT Press.

Cazden, C. and C.E. Snow (eds) (1990). 'English Plus: Issues in Bilingual Education'. *The Annals of the American Academy of Political and Social Science* 508 (special edition).

Chandler, J. (1997) 'Esperanto (1887) by L.L. Zamenhof: A Critique'. Available online at <http://www.geocities.com/athens/forum/5037/Esp.html>. Accessed May 2004.

Childe, V.G. (1926) *The Aryans: A Study of Indo-European Origins*. New York: Alfred A. Knopf.

Chomsky, N. (1986) *Knowledge of Language*. New York: Praeger Special Studies.

Climo-Thompson, A. (2001) *Kernuak Es: Cornish the Easy Way. A Beginner's Course in Everyday Cornish*. [s.l.]: Kernuak Es.

Cobarrubias, J. (1983) 'Ethical Issues in Status Planning'. In J. Cobarrubias and J.A. Fishman (eds) (1983) *Progress in Language Planning: International Perspectives*. Berlin and New York: Mouton, pp. 41–84.

Cooper, R.L. (1989) *Language Planning and Social Change*. Cambridge: Cambridge University Press.

Coteanu, I. (1957) *Cum dispare o limba (istroromana)*. Bucharest: Societatea distiinte istorice si filologice din RPR.

Couturat, L. and L. Leau (1903) *Histoire de la langue universelle*. Paris: Hachette.

—— (1907) *Les Nouvelles Langues Internationales*. Paris: Hachette.

Crawford, J. (1992) *Language Loyalties: A Social History of the Spanish-Speaking Californians, 1846–1890*. Berkeley, Calif.: University of California Press.

—— (2002) 'The Bilingual Education Act 1968–2002'. Available online at <http://ourworld.compuserve.com/homepages/JWCRAWFORD/T7obit.htm>. Accessed June 2005.

Cremona, J. (2002) 'Latin and Arabic Evolutionary Processes: Some Reflections'. In M.C. Jones and E. Esch (eds) (2002) *Language Change: The Interplay of Internal, External and Extra-Linguistic Factors*. Berlin and New York: Mouton de Gruyter, pp. 201–8.

Crystal, D. (1991) *A Dictionary of Linguistics and Phonetics*, 3rd edn. Oxford: Blackwell.

—— (1999) 'Death Sentence'. *Guardian*, 25 October, pp. 2–3.

Csató, E.A. (2002) 'Karaim: A High-Copying Language'. In M.C. Jones and E. Esch (eds) (2002) *Language Change: The Interplay of Internal, External and Extra-Linguistic Factors*. Berlin and New York: Mouton de Gruyter, pp. 315–27.

D'Ans, A.-M. (1968) *Le Créole Français d'Haïti*. The Hague: Mouton.

Daoust, D. (1997) 'Language Planning and Language Reform.' In F. Coulmas (ed.) (1997) *The Handbook of Sociolinguistics*. Oxford: Blackwell, pp. 437–55.

DeGraff, M. (2001) 'Morphology in Creole Genesis: Linguistics and Ideology'. In M. Kenstowicz (ed.) (2001) *Ken Hale: A Life in Language*. Cambridge, Mass.: MIT Press, pp. 53–121.

Delsing, L.-O. (2000) 'From OV to VO in Swedish'. In S. Pintzuk, G. Tsoulas and A. Warner (eds) (2000) *Diachronic Syntax: Models and Mechanisms*. Oxford: Oxford University Press, pp. 255–74.

Denison, N. (1977) 'Language Death or Language Suicide? *International Journal of the Sociology of Language* 12, 13–22.

Deshpande, M.M. (1979) 'Genesis of Rgvedic Retroflexion: A Historical and Socio-linguistic Investigation'. In M.M. Deshpande and P.E. Hook (eds) (1979) *Aryan and Non-Aryan in India*. Ann Arbor, Mich.: Karoma, pp. 235–315.

Dillard, J.L. (1970) 'Principles in the History of American English: Paradox, Virginity, and Cafeteria'. *Florida Foreign Language Reporter* 8, 32–3.

Dimmendaal, G. (1992) 'Reduction in Kore Reconsidered'. In M. Brenzinger, (ed.) (1992) *Language Death: Factual and Theoretical Explorations with Special Reference to East Africa*. Berlin and New York: Mouton de Gruyter, pp. 117–35.

Dixon, R.M.W. (1991) 'The Endangered Languages of Australia, Indonesia and Oceania'. In E.M. Uhlenbeck and R.H. Robins (eds) (1991) *Endangered Languages*. Oxford: Berg, pp. 229–55.

Dorian, N.C. (1978a) 'The Fate of Morphological Complexity in Language Death: Evidence from ESG'. *Language* 54, 590–609.

—— (1978b) 'The Dying Dialect and the Role of the Schools: East Sutherland Gaelic and Pennsylvanian Dutch'. In J.E. Alatis (ed.) (1978) *International Dimensions of Bilingual Education*. Washington, DC: Georgetown University Press, pp. 646–56.

—— (1981) *Language Death: The Life Cycle of a Scottish Gaelic Dialect*. Philadelphia, Pa.: University of Pennsylvania Press.

—— (1987) 'The Value of Language-Maintenance Efforts which are Unlikely to Succeed'. *International Journal of the Sociology of Language* 68, 57–61.

—— (1993) 'Internally and Externally Motivated Change in Language Contact Settings: Doubts about Dichotomy'. In C. Jones (ed.) (1993) *Historical Linguistics: Problems and Perspectives*. Harlow: Longman, pp. 131–55.

—— (1994a) 'Purism vs. Compromise in Language Revitalisation and Language Revival'. *Language* 23, 479–94.

—— (1994b) 'Stylistic Variation in a Language Restricted to Private-Sphere Use'. In D. Biber and E. Finegan (eds) (1994) *Sociolinguistic Perspectives on Register*. Oxford: Oxford University Press, pp. 217–32.

Eco, U. (1995) *The Search for the Perfect Language*. Oxford: Blackwell.

Elgin, S.H. (1984) *Native Tongue*. New York: The Feminist Press.

—— (1994) *Earthsong: Native Tongue III*. New York: Daw Books.

—— (1999) 'Láadan, the Constructed Language in *Native Tongue*'. Available online at <http://sfwa.org/members/elgin/laadan.html>. Accessed September 2002.

—— (2002a) 'Láadan Made Easier'. Available online at <http://sfwa.org/members/elgin/LaadanLessons/index.html>. Accessed September 2002.

—— (2002b) 'The Láadan Language: Frequently Asked Questions'. Available online at <http://sfwa.org/members/elgin/nativetongue/laadan_FAQ.html>. Accessed September 2002.

—— (2002c) 'A Láadan Sampler'. Available online at <http://sfwa.org/members/elgin/nativetongue/laadansampler.html>. Accessed September 2002.

Elliott, F. (2002) 'Kernewk re be grontys dewhelans' [Cornish has been Granted a Comeback]. *Sunday Telegraph*, 17 November, p. 3.

Ellis, P. Berresford and S. Mac a'Ghobhainn (1971) *The Problem of Language Revival*. Inverness: Club Leabhar.

Elmendorf, W.E. (1981) 'Last Speakers and Language Change: Two Californian Cases'. *Anthropological Linguistics* 23, 1, 36–49.

Emeneau, M.B. (1956) 'India as a Linguistic Area'. *Linguistics* 32, 3–16.

Fasold, R. (1984) *The Sociolinguistics of Society*. Oxford: Blackwell.

Fellman, J. (1973) *The Revival of a Classical Tongue*. The Hague: Mouton.

Fennell, B. (2001) *A History of English: A Sociolinguistic Approach*. Oxford: Blackwell.

Fennell, D. (1981) 'Can a Shrinking Linguistic Minority be Saved? Lessons from the Irish Experience'. In E. Haugen, J.D. McClure and D.S. Thomson (eds) (1981) *Minority Languages Today*. Edinburgh: Edinburgh University Press, pp. 32–9.

Ferguson, C.A. (1959) 'Diglossia'. *Word* 15, 325–40.

Fishman, J.A. (1972) 'Language Maintenance and Language Shift as a Field of Inquiry: Revisited'. In A.S. Dil (ed.) (1972) *Language in Sociocultural Change: Essays by Joshua A. Fishman*. Stanford, Calif.: Stanford University Press, pp. 76–134.

—— (1991), *Reversing Language Shift: Theoretical and Empirical Foundations of Assistance to Threatened Languages*. Clevedon, UK: Multilingual Matters.

Fishman, J.A., R.L. Cooper, R. Ma et al. (eds) (1971) *Bilingualism in the Barrio*. The Hague: Mouton.

Fowkes, R.A. (1945) 'English Idiom in Modern Welsh.' *Word* 1, 239–48.

Fudge, C. (1982), *The Life of Cornish*. Redruth: Truran.

Gal, S. (1979) *Language Shift: Social Determinants of Linguistic Change in Bilingual Austria*. New York and London: Academic Press.

Gamkrelidze, T. V. and V.V. Ivanov (1990) 'The Early History of Indo-European Languages.' *Scientific American* (March), 110–16.

Garzon, S. (1992) 'The Process of Language Death in a Mayan Community in Southern Mexico'. *International Journal of the Sociology of Language* 9, 53–66.

Gendall, R. (1997) *A Practical Dictionary of Modern Cornish. Part I*. Liskeard: Teere Ha Tavaz.

—— (1998) *A Practical Dictionary of Modern Cornish. Part II*. Liskeard: Teere Ha Tavaz.

George, K. (1986) *The Pronunciation and Spelling of Revived Cornish*. [s.l.]: Cornish Language Board.

—— (2001) 'Changes in the Verbal System in the Subjunctive Mood in Cornish'. *Agan Yeth* 3, 6–33.

George, K. and P. Dunbar (1997) *Kernewek Kemmyn. Cornish for the Twenty-First Century*. Hale: Cornish Language Board.

Giacalone Ramat, A. (1979) 'Language Function and Language Change in Minority Languages'. *Journal of Italian Linguistics* 4, 2, 141–62.

—— (1992) 'The Pairing of Structure and Function in Syntactic Development'. In M. Gerritsen and D. Stein (eds) (1992) *Internal and External Factors in Syntactic Change*. Berlin and New York: Mouton de Gruyter, pp. 316–39.

Gimbutas, M. (1970) 'Proto-Indo-European Culture: The Kurgan Culture during the Fifth, Fourth and Third Millennia BC'. In G. Cardona, H.M. Hoeningswald and A. Senn (eds) (1970) *Indo-Europe and Indo-Europeans*. Philadelphia, Pa.: University of Pennsylvania Press, pp. 159–60.

Gleason, P. (1980) 'American Identity and Americanisation'. In S. Thernstrom, A. Orlov and O. Handlin (eds) (1980) *Harvard Encylopaedia of American Ethnic Groups*. Cambridge, Mass.: Harvard University Press, pp. 31–58.

Görlach, M. (1991) *Introduction to Early Modern English*. Cambridge: Cambridge University Press.

Gorman, T.P. (1973) 'Language Allocation and Language Planning in a Developing Nation'. In J. Rubin and R. Shuy (eds) (1973) *Language Planning: Current Issues and Research*. Washington DC: Georgetown University Press.

Greenberg, J.H. (1963) 'Some Universals of Grammar with Particular Reference to the Order of Meaningful Elements'. In J.H. Greenberg (ed.) (1963) *Universals of Language*. Cambridge, Mass.: MIT Press, pp. 73–113.

Guiraud, P. (1965) *Les Mots Etrangers*. Paris: Presses Universitaires de France.

Gumperz, J.J. (1982) *Discourse Strategies*. Cambridge: Cambridge University Press.

Gumperz, J.J. and E. Hernández-Chavez (1975) 'Cognitive Aspects of Bilingual Communication'. In E. Hernández-Chavez, A.D. Cohen and Anthony F. Beltramo (eds) (1975) *El Lenguaje de Los Chicanos: Regional and Social Characteristics used by Mexican Americans*, pp. 54–64.

Gumperz, J.J. and R. Wilson (1971) 'Convergence and Creolisation: A Case from the Indo-Aryan/Dravidian border'. In D. Hymes (ed.) (1971) *Pidginisation and Creolisation of Language*. Cambridge: Cambridge University Press, pp. 151–68.

Gumperz, J.J. and S.C. Levinson (1996) *Rethinking Linguistic Relativity*. Cambridge: Cambridge University Press.

Guthrie, M. (1967–71) *Comparative Bantu*, 4 vols. London: Gregg Press.

Hale, A. (1999) 'A History of the Cornish Revival'. In T. Saunders (ed.) (1999) *The Wheel. An Anthology of Modern Poetry in Cornish, 1850–1980*. London: Francis Boutle, pp. 19–27.

Hall, R.A., Jr. (1953) *Haitian Creole: Grammar, Texts, Vocabulary. The American Anthropologist. Memoir 74*. Washington DC: American Anthropological Association.

—— (1966) *Pidgin and Creole Languages*. Ithaca, NY: Cornell University Press.

Hamer, R. (1970) *A Choice of Anglo-Saxon Verse*. London: Faber & Faber.

Harlow, D. (1995) 'The Sixteen Rules of Esperanto Grammar'. Available online at <http://www.webcom.com/~donh/Esperanto/rules.html>). Accessed July 2004.

Harris, R. (1988) *Language, Saussure and Wittgenstein*. London: Routledge.

Haugen, E. (1950) 'The Analysis of Linguistic Borrowing'. *Language* 26, 210–32.

—— (1966) *Language Conflict and Language Planning: The Case of Modern Norwegian*. Cambridge, Mass.: Harvard University Press.

Hawkins, J. (2004) *Efficiency and Complexity in Grammars*. Oxford: Oxford University Press.

Heath, S.B. and F. Mandabach (1983) 'Language Status Decisions and the Law in the United States'. In J. Cobarrubias and J.A. Fishman (eds) (1983) *Progress in Language Planning: International Perspectives*. Berlin and New York: Mouton, pp. 87–105.

Henderson, E.J.A. (1956) 'The Topography of Certain Phonetic and Morphological Characteristics of South-East Asia Languages'. *Lingua* 15, 400–34.

Hewitt, S. (1977) 'The Degree of Acceptability of Modern Literary Breton to Native Breton Speakers'. Unpublished Diploma of Linguistics dissertation, University of Cambridge.

Hill, J.H. and K. Hill (1977) 'Language Death and Relexification in Tlaxcalan Nahuatl'. *International Journal of the Sociology of Language* 12, 55–69.

Hindley, R. (1990) *The Death of Irish*. London: Routledge.

Hobbes, T. (1651) *Leviathan* (edited by Richard Tuck 1996). Cambridge: Cambridge University Press.

Hock, H.H. (1991) *Principles of Historical Linguistics*, 2nd edn. Berlin and New York: Mouton de Gruyter.

Hock, H.H. and B.D. Joseph (1996) *Language History, Language Change, and Language Relationship: An Introduction to Historical and Comparative Linguistics*. Berlin: Mouton de Gruyter.

Hodge, P. (1997) *The Cornish Dialect and the Cornish Language*. Kernow: Cornish Language Board.

Holm, J. (1988) *Pidgins and Creoles. Volume I: Theory and Structure*. Cambridge: Cambridge University Press.

—— (1989) *Pidgins and Creoles. Volume II: Reference Survey*. Cambridge: Cambridge University Press.

Hopper, P.J. and E. Traugott (1993) *Grammaticalisation*. Cambridge: Cambridge University Press.

Hornberger, N.H. (1989) 'Bilingual Education and Indigenous Languages in the Light of Language Planning'. *International Journal of the Sociology of Language* 77, 5–9.

—— (1990) 'Bilingual Education and English-Only: A Language Planning Framework'. *Annals of the American Academy of Political and Social Science* 508, 12–26.

Hornberger, N.H. and K.A. King (1996) 'Language Revitalisation in the Andes: Can Schools Reverse Language Shift?' *Journal of Multilingual and Multicultural Development* 17, 6, 427–41.

Hróarsdóttir, T. (1995) 'Setningafrœðilegar breytingar á 19. öld; þróun þriggja málbreytinga'. Master's thesis. University of Iceland, Reykjavík.

—— (1996) 'The Decline of OV Word Order in the Icelandic VP: A Diachronic Study'. *Working Papers in Scandinavian Syntax* 57, 91–141.

—— (2001) *Word Order Change in Icelandic: From OV to VO*. Amsterdam: John Benjamins.

Huffines, M.L. (1980) 'Pennsylvania German: Maintenance and Shift'. *International Journal of the Sociology of Language* 25, 43–57.

—— (1989) 'Case Usage among the Pennsylvanian German Sectarians and Non-sectarians'. In N.C. Dorian (ed.) (1989) *Investigating Obsolescence*. Cambridge: Cambridge University Press, pp. 211–26.

—— (1991) 'Pennsylvania German: Convergence and Change as Strategies of Discourse'. In H.W. Seliger and R.M. Vago (eds) (1991) *First Language Attrition*. Cambridge: Cambridge University Press, pp. 125–37.

Jacob, H. (1947) *A Planned Auxiliary Language*. London: Dobson.

Jeffers, R.J. and I. Lehiste (1979) *Principles and Methods for Historical Linguistics*. Cambridge, Mass.: MIT Press.

Jenner, H. (1904) *A Handbook of the Cornish Language*. London: David Nutt.

Jespersen, O. (1918) 'Artificial Languages after the War'. *Two Papers on International Language in English and Ido*. Available online at <http://www.geocities.com/athens/forum/5037/AL.html>. Accessed May 2004.

—— (1931) 'Interlinguistics'. *International Communication*. London: Kegan Paul. Available online at <http://www.geocities.com/athens/forum/5037/Il.html>. Accessed May 2004.

Jones, M.C. (1995) 'At What Price Language Maintenance? Standardisation in Modern Breton'. *French Studies* 49, 4, 424–38.

—— (1996) 'The Role of the Speaker in Language Obsolescence: The Case of Breton in Plougastel-Daoulas'. *Journal of French Language Studies* 6, 1, 45–73.

—— (1998) *Language Obsolescence and Revitalisation: Linguistic Change in Two Sociolinguistically Contrasting Welsh Communities*. Oxford: Clarendon Press.

—— (2001) *Jersey Norman French: A Linguistic Study of an Obsolescent Dialect*. Oxford: Blackwell.

—— (2002) 'Mette a haout dauve la grippe des Angllaïs: Convergence on the Island of Guernsey'. In M.C. Jones and E. Esch (eds.) (2002) *Language Change: The Interplay of Internal, External and Extra-Linguistic Factors*. Berlin and New York: Mouton de Gruyter, pp. 143–68.

Jones, W. (1786) 'The Third Anniversary Discourse, on the Hindus'. Published 1788 *Asiatick Researches* 1, 415–31.

Joseph, B.D. (1983) *The Synchrony and Diachrony of the Balkan Infinitive*. Cambridge: Cambridge University Press.

Keller, R.E. (1961) *German Dialects*. Manchester: Manchester University Press.

King, K.A. (1999) 'Inspecting the Unexpected: Language Status and Corpus Shifts as Aspects of Quechua Language Revitalisation'. *Language Problems and Language Planning* 23, 2, 109–32.

Kloss, H. (1969) *Research Possibilities on Group Bilingualism: A Report*. Quebec: International Center for Research on Bilingualism.

—— (1977) *The American Bilingual Tradition*. Rowley, Mass.: Newbury House.

Koerner, K. (ed.) (1983) *Linguistics and Evolutionary Theory: Three Essays by August Schleicher, Ernst Haeckel and Wilhelm Bleek*. Amsterdam: John Benjamins.

Krauss, M. (1992) 'The World's Languages in Crisis'. *Language* 68, 4–10.

Kroskrity, P.V. (1993) *Language, History and Identity: Ethnolinguistic Studies of the Arizona Tewa*. Tucson, Ariz.: University of Arizona Press.

Kuter, L. (1989a) 'Breton vs. French: Language and the Opposition of Political, Economic, Social and Cultural Values. In N.C. Dorian (ed.) (1989) *Investigating Obsolescence*. Cambridge: Cambridge University Press, pp. 75–90.

—— (1989b) 'A Note from the Editor.' *Bro Nevez* 32, 40.

Labov, W. (1972) *Language in the Inner City*. Philadelphia, Pa.: University of Pennsylvania Press.

Lakoff, R. (1972) 'Another Look at Drift'. In R.P. Stockwell and R.K.S. Macaulay (eds) (1972) *Linguistic Change and Generative Theory*. Bloomington, Ind.: Indiana University Press, pp. 172–98.

Lass, R. (1976) *English Phonology and Phonological Theory: Synchronic and Diachronic Studies*. Cambridge: Cambridge University Press.

—— (1987) *The Shape of English: Structure and History*. London: Dent.

—— (1997) *Historical Linguistics and Language Change*. Cambridge: Cambridge University Press.

Leap, W.L. (1992) 'American Indian English'. In J. Reyhner (ed.) (1992) *Teaching American Indian Students*. Norman, Okla.: University of Oklahoma Press, pp. 143–56.

LeFebvre, C. (1998) *Creole Genesis and the Acquisition of Grammar: The Case of Haitian Creole*. Cambridge: Cambridge University Press.

Legère, K. (1992) 'Language Shift in Tanzania'. In M. Brenzinger (ed.) (1992) *Language Death: Factual and Theoretical Explorations with Special Reference to East Africa*. Berlin and New York: Mouton de Gruyter, pp. 99–115.

Lehmann, C. (1985) 'Grammaticalisation: Synchronic Variation and Diachronic Change'. *Lingua e Stile* 20, 3, 303–18.

Lehmann, W. (1973) 'A Structural Principle of Language and its Implications'. *Language* 49, 47–66.

Leibowitz, A.H. (1969) 'English Literacy: Legal Sanction for Discrimination'. *Notre Dame Lawyer* 45, 7, 7–67.

Leith, D. (1983) *A Social History of English*. London: Routledge and Kegan Paul.

Le Maistre, F. (1947) 'The Jersey Language in its Present State. The Passing of a Norman Heritage'. Paper read before the Jersey Society in London, 8 July 1947. London: Jersey Society.

—— (1966) *Dictionnaire Jersiais–Français*. Jersey: Don Balleine.

Lewy, E. (1964) *Der Bau der Europäischen Sprachen*, 2nd edn. Tübingen: Niemeyer.

Lhuyd, E. (1707) *Archaeologia Britannica*. Oxford: Printed for the author and sold by Mr Bateman in London and Jeremiah Pepyat bookseller in Dublin.

Lightfoot, D. (1979) *Principles of Diachronic Syntax*. Cambridge: Cambridge University Press.

Lippi-Green, R. (1997) *English with an Accent: Language, Ideology, and Discrimination in the United States*. London and New York: Routledge.

Lodge, R.A. (1993) *French from Dialect to Standard*. London and New York: Routledge.

Lorenz, R. (1910) 'The Relationship of the International Language to Science'. In L. Couturat, O. Jespersen, R. Lorenz, W. Ostwald, L. Pfaundler (1910) *International Language and Science: Considerations on the Introduction of an International Language into Science*. Trans. by F.G. Donnan. London: Constable, Chapter V. Available online at <http://www.geocities.com/athens/forum/5037/ILS5.html>. Accessed February 2004.

Lyons, J.J. (1990) 'The Past and Future Directions of Federal Bilingual-Education Policy'. *Annals of the American Academy of Political and Social Science* 508, 66–80.

Ma, R. and E. Herasimchuk (1971) 'The Linguistic Dimensions of a Bilingual Neighborhood'. In J.A. Fishman, R.L. Cooper, R. Ma et al. (eds) (1971) *Bilingualism in the Barrio*. The Hague: Mouton, pp. 347–464.

McCrum, R., W. Cran and R. MacNeil (1992) *The Story of English*. London: Faber & Faber and BBC Books.

McDonald, M. (1989) *We Are Not French!* London and New York: Routledge.

MacKaye, S.D.A. (1990) 'California Proposition 63: Language Attitudes Reflected in the Public Debate'. *Annals of the American Academy of Political and Social Science* 508, 135–46.

MacKinnon, K. (1982) 'Scottish Opinion on Gaelic'. *Social Sciences Reports Series* 14.

McMahon, A.M.S. (1994) *Understanding Language Change*. Cambridge: Cambridge University Press.

Macnamara, J. (1971) 'Successes and Failures in the Movement for the Restoration of Irish'. In B.H. Jernudd and J. Rubin (eds) (1971) *Can Language be Planned? Sociolinguistic Theory and Practice for Developing Nations*. Honolulu: University Press of Hawai'i, pp. 65–94.

Madrid, A. (1990) 'Official English: A False Policy Issue'. *Annals of the American Academy of Political and Social Science* 508, 62–5.

Mahapatra, B.P. (1991) 'An Appraisal Of Indian Languages'. In E.M. Uhlenbeck and R.H. Robins (eds) (1991) *Endangered Languages*. Oxford: Berg, pp. 177–88.

Mahoune, J.-C. (2002) 'Seychellois Creole: Development and Evolution'. IIAS Newsletter Online 22, 1–4. Available at <http://www.iias.nl/iiasn/22/regions/22ISA1.html>. Accessed July 2003.

Martinet, A. (1952) 'Function, Structure and Sound Change'. *Word* 8, 1–32.

—— (1991) 'Sur quelques questions d'interlinguistique. Une interview de François Lo Jacomo et Detlev Blanke'. *Zeitschrift für Phonetik, Sprach- und Kommunikations-wissenschaft* 44, 6, 675–87.

Matras, Y and P. Bakker (eds) (2003) *The Mixed Language Debate*. Berlin: Mouton de Gruyter.

Meillet, A. (1912) 'L'évolution des formes grammaticales'. In A. Meillet (1912) *Linguistique historique et linguistique générale*. Paris: Champion, pp. 131–48.

—— (1918) *Les Language dans l'Europe Nouvelle*. Paris: Payot.

Meyer, H. (1901) 'Über den Ursprung der Germanischen Lautverschiebung'. *Zeitschrift für deutsches Alterum und deutsches Litteratur* 45, 101–28.

Miller, W.R. (1971) 'The Death of a Language, or Serendipity Among the Shoshoni'. *Anthropological Linguistics* 13, 114–20.

Milroy, J. and L. Milroy (1999) *Authority in Language*, 3rd edn. London: Routledge.

Mougeon, R. and E. Beniak, (1991) *Linguistic Consequences of Language Contact and Restriction: The Case of French in Ontario, Canada*. Oxford: Clarendon Press.

Mufwene, S. (2001) *The Ecology of Language Evolution*. Cambridge: Cambridge University Press.

Mühlhäusler, P. (1974) *Pidginisation and Simplification of Language*. Series B, Vol. 26. Canberra: Pacific Linguistics.

—— (1976) 'Samoan Plantation Pidgin English and the Origin of New Guinea: An Introduction'. *Journal of Pacific History* 11, 2, 122–5.

—— (1980) 'Structural Expansion and the Process of Creolisation'. In A. Valdman and A. Highfield (eds) (1980) *Theoretical Orientations in Creole Studies*. New York and London: Academic Press, pp. 19–55.

—— (1982) 'Tok Pisin in Papua New Guinea'. In R.W. Bailey and M. Görlach (eds) (1982) *English as a World Language*. Ann Arbor, Mich.: University of Michigan Press, pp. 439–66.

Müller, M. (1861) *Lectures on the Science of Language*. London: Longman.

Muysken, P. (1981) 'Halfway between Quechua and Spanish: The Case for Relexification'. In A. Highfield and A. Valdman (eds) (1981) *Historicity and Variation in Creole Studies*. Ann Arbor, Mich.: Karoma, pp. 52–78.

—— (2000) *Bilingual Speech: A Typology of Code-Mixing*. Cambridge: Cambridge University Press.

Myers-Scotton, C. (1993a) *Social Motivations for Code-switching. Evidence from Africa*. Oxford: Clarendon Press.

—— (1993b) *Duelling Languages. Grammatical Structure in Code-switching*. Oxford: Clarendon Press.

—— (2002) *Contact Linguistics: Bilingual Encounters and Grammatical Outcomes*. Oxford: Oxford University Press.

Myers-Scotton, C. and J.L. Jake (2001) 'Explaining Aspects of Code-switching and their Implications'. In J. Nicol (ed.) (2001) *One Mind, Two Languages: Bilingual Language Processing*. Oxford: Blackwell, pp. 84–116.

Nahir, M. (1984) 'Language Planning Goals: A Classification'. *Language Problems and Language Planning* 8,3, 294–327.

—— (1988) 'Language Planning and Language Acquisition: The 'Great Leap' in the Hebrew Revival'. In C.B. Paulston (ed.) (1988) *International Handbook of Bilingualism and Bilingual Education*. New York: Greenwood, pp. 275–95.

Nance, R.M. (1929) *Cornish For All: A Guide to Unified Cornish*. St Ives: James Lanham.

—— (1938) *A New Cornish–English Dictionary*. St Ives: Federation of Old Cornish Societies.

Nurse, D. and M. Walsh, (1992), 'Chifundi and Vumba: Partial Shift, No Death'. In M. Brenzinger (ed.) (1992) *Language Death: Factual and Theoretical Explorations with Special Reference to East Africa*. Berlin and New York: Mouton de Gruyter, pp. 181–212.

Payton, P. (2000) 'Cornish'. In G. Price (ed.) (2000) *Encyclopedia of the Languages of Europe*. Oxford: Blackwell, pp. 99–103.

Petrovici, E. (1957) *Kann das Phonemsystem einer Sprache durch fremden Einfluss umgestaltet werden? Zum slawischen Einfluss auf das rumänisce Lautsystem*. The Hague: Mouton.

Pfaff, C. W. (1979) 'Constraints on Language Mixing: Intrasentential Code-Switching and Borrowing in Spanish/English'. *Language* 55, 291–318.

Phillipson, R. (2003) *English-Only Europe? Challenging Language Policy*. London: Routledge.

Picoche, J. and C. Marchello-Nizia (1991) *Histoire de la langue française*. Paris: Nathan.

Pool, J. (1979) 'Language Planning and Identity Planning'. *International Journal of the Sociology of Language* 20, 5–21.

Pool, P.A.S. (1975). *The Death of Cornish*. Penzance: Wordens of Cornwall.

Poplack, S. (1980) ' "Sometimes I'll start a sentence in Spanish y termino en español": Toward a Typology of Code-switching'. *Linguistics* 18, 581–618.

—— (1988). 'Contrasting Patterns of Code-switching in Two Communities'. In M. Heller (ed.) (1988) *Code-switching*. Berlin and New York: Mouton de Gruyter, pp. 215–44.

Poplack, S. and M. Meechan (1998) 'How, Languages Fit Together in Code-mixing'. *International Journal of Bilingualism* 2, 2, 127–38.

Poplack, S., D. Sankoff and C. Miller (1988) 'The Social Correlates and Linguistic Processes of Lexical Borrowing and Assimilation'. *Linguistics* 26, 47–104.

Price, G. (1984) *The Languages of Britain*. London: Edward Arnold.

—— (1998) 'Modern Cornish in Context'. *Cornish Studies* 6, 187–93.

Pryce, W. (1790) *Archeologica Cornu-Britannica or, an Essay to Preserve the Ancient Cornish Language*. Sherbourne.

Rabin, C. (1971) 'Spelling Reform – Israel 1968'. In B.H. Jernudd and J. Rubin (eds) (1970) *Can Language be Planned?* Honolulu: University Press of Hawai'i, pp. 95–121.

Ravel, J.-L and P. Thomas (1985) *État de la Réforme de l'Enseignement aux Seychelles (1981–1985)*. Paris: Ministre des Relations Extérieures, Coopération et Développement.

Reinecke, J.E. (1937) 'Marginal Languages: A Sociological Survey of the Creole Languages and Trade Jargons'. Ph.D. dissertation, Yale University. Ann Arbor, Mich.: University Microfilms International.

Renfrew, C. (1987) *Archaeology and Language*. London: Jonathan Cape.

Richards, J.B. (1989) 'Language Planning in Guatemala'. *International Journal of the Sociology of Language* 77, 93–115.

Rickford, J. (1992) 'Grammatical Variation and Divergence in Vernacular Black English'. In M. Gerritsen and D. Stein (eds) (1992) *Internal and External Factors in Syntactic Change*. Berlin and New York: Mouton de Gruyter, pp. 175–200.

Romaine, S. (1988) *Pidgin and Creole Languages*. London: Longman.

Rögnvaldsson, E. (1994) *Word Order Variation in the VP in Old Icelandic*. Available online at <http://www.hi.is/~eirikur/wordord.pdf>, pp. 1–32. Accessed April 2004.

Rouchdy, A. (1989a), ' "Persistence" or "Tip" in Egyptian Nubian'. In N.C. Dorian (ed.) (1989) *Investigating Obsolescence*. Cambridge: Cambridge University Press, pp. 91–102.

——(1989b), 'Urban and Non-Urban Egyptian Nubian: Is There a Reduction in Language Skill?'. In N.C. Dorian (ed.) (1989) *Investigating Obsolescence*. Cambridge: Cambridge University Press, pp. 259–66.

Sandercock, G. (1996) *A Very Brief History of the Cornish Language*. Hayle: Cornish Language Board.

Sandfeld, K. (1930) *Linguistique balkanique: problèmes et resultants*. Paris: Société de Linguistique.

Sankoff, D., S. Poplack and S. Vanniarajan (1990) 'The Case of the Nonce Loan in Tamil'. *Language Variation and Change* 2, 71–101.

Sapir, E. (1921) *Language: An Introduction to the Study of Speech*. New York: Harcourt, Brace. Published April 2000 by Bartleby.com. Available online at <http://www.bartleby.com/186>. Accessed April 2004.

——(1925) 'The Function of an International Auxiliary Language'. In H.N. Shenton, E. Sapir and O. Jespersen (1931) *International Communication: A Symposium on the Language Problem*. London: Kegan Paul, pp. 65–94. Available online at <http://www.geocities.com/Athens/Forum/5037/sapir.html>. Accessed May 2004.

——(1929) 'The Status of Linguistics as a Science'. *Language* 5, 207–14. Reprinted in D. G. Mandelbaum (ed.) (1958) *The Selected Writings of Edward Sapir in Language, Culture, and Personality*. Berkeley, Calif.: University of California Press, pp. 160–6.

——(1933) 'Language'. *Encyclopaedia of the Social Sciences* 9, 155–69.

Sasse, H.-J. (1992) 'Language Decay and Contact-Induced Change: Similarities and Differences'. In M. Brenzinger (ed.) (1992) *Language Death: Factual and Theoretical Explorations with Special Reference to East Africa*. Berlin and New York: Mouton de Gruyter, pp. 59–80.

Saussure, F. de (1974) *Course in General Linguistics*. Translated by C. Baltaxe. London: Fontana.

Schiffman, H.F. (1996) *Linguistic Culture and Language Policy*. New York and London: Routledge.

Schleicher, A. (1863) *Die Darwinsche Theorie und die Sprachwissenschaft – offenes Sendschreiben an Herrn Dr. Ernst Haeckel*. Weimar: H. Boehlau.

Schlichter, M.-A. (1976) 'English Yuki Vocabulary'. Unpublished MA thesis, University of California, Berkeley.

Schlieben-Lange, B. (1977) 'The Language Situation in Southern France', *International Journal of the Sociology of Language* 12, 101–7.

Schmidt, A. (1985) *Young People's Dyirbal*. Cambridge: Cambridge University Press.

Schuchardt, H. (1884) *Slawo-deutches und Slawo-italienisches*. Graz: Leuschner and Lubensky.

Sebba, M. (1997) *Contact Languages: Pidgins and Creoles*. London: Macmillan.

Seuren, P. and H. Wekker (1986) 'Semantic Transparency as a Factor in Creole Genesis'. In P. Muysken and N. Smith (eds) (1986) *Substrate vs. Universals in Creole Genesis*. Amsterdam: John Benjamins, pp. 56–70.

Shield, Lesley E. (1984) 'Unified Cornish: Fiction or Fact?', *Journal of Multilingual and Multicultural Development* 5, 3–4, 329–37.

Siegel, J. (1999) 'Creoles and Minority Dialects in Education: An Overview'. *Journal of Multilingual and Multicultural Development* 20, 6, 508–31.

—— (undated) *Tok Pisin*. Available online at <http://www.une.edu.au/langnet/tokpisin.htm>. Accessed December 2004.

Sigurðsson, H.A. (1988) 'From OV to VO: Evidence from Old Icelandic'. *Working Papers in Scandinavian Syntax* 34, 1–42.

Singh, I. (2000) *Pidgins and Creoles: An Introduction*. London: Arnold.

—— (2005) *The History of English: A Student's Guide*. London: Arnold.

Smith, A.S.D. (1947) *The Story of the Cornish Language: Its Extinction and Revival*, Camborne: Camborne Printing and Stationery Company.

Smith, J. (1996) *An Historical Study of English*. London: Routledge.

Sperling, K. (1996) *Learning Láadan*. Available online at <http://members.rogers.com/kmsperling/laadan/history.html>. Accessed September 2002.

Squier, S. and J. Vedder (2000) 'Afterword: Encoding a Woman's Language'. In S.H. Elgin (1984) *Native Tongue*. New York: The Feminist Press, pp. 305–24.

Stockwell, R.P. and D. Minkova (1988) 'The English Vowel Shift: Problems of Coherence and Explanation'. In D. Kastovsky, G. Bauer and J. Fisiak (1988) *Luick Revisited*. Tübingen: Gunter Narr, pp. 355–94.

Swadesh, M. (1948) 'Sociologic Notes on Obsolescent Languages'. *International Journal of American Linguistics* 14, 226–35.

Swift, J. (1712) *A Proposal for Correcting, Improving, and Ascertaining the English Tongue*. Available online at <http://etext.library.adelaide.edu.au/s/s97p>. Accessed June 2005.

The English Company UK Ltd. 'This Year's New Words' (25 July 2003). *Global English Newsletter*, <http://www.engcool.com/GEN/archive.php>. Accessed June 2004.

Thomas, C. (1973) *The Importance of Being Cornish*. Redruth: Institute of Cornish Studies.

Thomason, S.G. and T. Kaufman (1988) *Language Contact, Creolization and Genetic Linguistics*. Berkeley, Calif.: University of California Press.

Thomason, S.G. (2001) *Language Contact*. Washington DC: Georgetown University Press.

Timm, L.A. (1975) 'Spanish–English code-switching: Porque y How-Not-To'. *Romance Philology* 28, 473–82.

—— (1980) 'Bilingualism, Diglossia and Language Shift in Brittany'. *International Journal of the Sociology of Language* 25, 29–41.

Tomlinson, H. (1981) 'Le Guernésiais: étude grammaticale et lexicale du parler normand de l'île de Guernesey'. Unpublished Ph.D. thesis, University of Edinburgh.

Trask, R.L. (1996) *Historical Linguistics*. London: Arnold.

Traugott, E. (1982) 'From Propositional to Textual and Expressive Meanings: Some Semantic-Pragmatic Aspects of Grammaticalization'. In W. Lehmann and Y. Malkiel (eds) (1982) *Perspectives on Historical Linguistics*. Amsterdam: John Benjamins, pp. 245–71.

Trudgill, P. (1983a) 'Language Contact and Language Change. On the Rise of the Creoloid'. In P. Trudgill (ed.) (1983) *On Dialect: Social and Geographical Perspectives*. Oxford: Blackwell, pp. 102–7.

—— (1983b), 'Language Contact, Language Shift and Identity'. In P. Trudgill (ed.) (1983) *On Dialect: Social and Geographical Perspectives*. Oxford: Blackwell, pp. 127–40.

—— (1983c) *Sociolinguistics: An Introduction to Language and Society*, 2nd edn. Hamondsworth: Penguin.

United Nations Department of Public Information (undated) *Universal Declaration of Human Rights*. Available online at <http://www.unhchr.ch/udhr/lang/eng.htm>. Accessed December 2004.

Université Populaire Normande du Coutançais (1995) *Essai de grammaire de la langue normande*. Périers: Garlan.

UEA (Universala Esperanto Asocio) (undated) 'An Update on Esperanto'. Available online at <http://www.uea.org/info/angle/an_ghisdatigo.html>. Accessed May 2004.

(Untitled) (undated) 'A Quick Look at Volapük'. Available online at <http://web.onetel.net.uk/~rmidgley/VpIntroTo.doc>. Accessed September 2002.

(Untitled) 'Seychelles Welcomes First Indian Ocean Creole New Testament'. *United Bible Society Newsletter*, 1 September 2000. Available online at <http://www.biblesociety.org/latestnews/latest112.html#Seychelles>. Accessed July 2002.

Unz, R.K. and G.M. Tuchman (1997) *The Unz Initiative*. Available online at <http://www.catesol.org/unztext.html>. Accessed July 2002.

US English (2002a) <http:// www.us-english.org/foundation>. Accessed June 2002.

—— (2002b) <http:// www.us-english.org/inc>. Accessed June 2002.

Valdman, A. (1978) *Le Créole: structure, statut et origine*. Paris: Editions Klinksieck.

—— (1988) 'Diglossia and Language Conflict in Haiti'. *International Journal of the Sociology of Language* 71, 67–80.

Velupillai, V. (2003) *Hawai'i Creole English: A Typological Analysis of the Tense-Mood-Aspect System*. Basingstoke: Palgrave Macmillan.

Vennemann, T. (1974) 'Topics, Subjects and Word Order: From SXV to SVX via TVX'. In J.M. Anderson and C.J. Jones (eds) (1974) *Historical Linguistics. Volume 1: Syntax, Morphology, Internal and Comparative Reconstruction*. Amsterdam: North-Holland, pp. 339–76.

—— (1975) 'An Explanation of Drift'. In C.N. Li (ed.) (1975) *Word Order and Word Change*. Austin, Tex.: University of Texas Press, pp. 269–305.

Voegelin, C.F. and F.M. Voegelin (1977) 'Is Tübatulabal De-Acquisition Relevant to Theories of Language Acquisition?' *International Journal of American Linguistics* 43, 4, 333–8.

Ward, A.W., A.R. Waller, W.P. Trent, J. Erskine, S.P. Sherman and C. Van Doren (eds) (2000) *The Cambridge History of English and American Literature*. New York:

G.P. Putnam's Sons, 1907–21. Available online at <http://www.bartleby.com/cambridge>. Accessed 2004.

Watson, I. (2002) 'Convergence in the Brain: The Leakiness of Bilinguals' Sound Systems'. In M.C. Jones and E. Esch (eds) (2002) *Language Change: The Interplay of Internal, External and Extra-Linguistic Factors*. Berlin and New York: Mouton de Gruyter, pp. 243–66.

Watts, R. and P. Trudgill (eds) (2002) *Alternative Histories of English*. London: Routledge.

Weinreich, U. (1953) *Languages in Contact: Findings and Problems*. The Hague: Mouton.

Weinreich, U., W. Labov and M.I. Herzog (1968) 'Empirical Foundations for a Theory of Language Change'. In W. Lehmann and Y. Malkiel (eds) (1968) *Perspectives on Historical Linguistics*. Amsterdam: John Benjamins, pp. 95–195.

Wells, K. (undated) 'Suzette Haden Elgin: An Interview'. Available online at <http://www.womenwriters.net/editorials/hadenelgin.htm>. Accessed December 2003.

Welmers, W.E. (1970) 'Language Change and Language Relationships in Africa'. *Language Sciences* 12, 1–8.

Whitney, W.D. (1867) *Language and the Study of Language*. London: N. Trübner & Co.

—— (1881) 'On Mixture in Language'. *Transactions of the American Philosophical Association* 12, 1–26.

Williams, N.J.A. (1990), 'A Problem in Cornish Phonology'. In M.J. Ball, J. Fife, E. Poppe and J. Rowland (eds) (1990) *A Festschrift for T. Arwyn Watkins*. Amsterdam: John Benjamins, pp. 241–74.

—— (1995) *Cornish Today: An Examination of the Revived Language*. Sutton Coldfield: Kernewek Dre Lyther.

Winford, D. (2003) *An Introduction to Contact Linguistics*. Malden, Mass.: Blackwell.

Winsboro, B.L. and I.D. Solomon (1990) 'Standard English vs. "the American dream"'. *Education Digest* 56, 4, 51–2.

Wmffre, I. (1998) *Late Cornish*. Munich: Lincom Europa.

Wright, L. (2002) 'Standard English and the Lexicon: Why so Many Different Spellings?' In M.C. Jones and E. Esch (eds) (2002) *Language Change: The Interplay of Internal, External and Extra-Linguistic Factors*. Berlin and New York: Mouton de Gruyter, pp. 181–200.

Wurm, S.A. (1966) 'Pidgin: A National Language'. *New Guinea and Australia, the Pacific and South-East Asia Quarterly* 7, 49–54.

—— (1977) 'The Nature of New Guinea Pidgin'. In S.A. Wurm (ed.) (1977) *New Guinea Area Languages and Language Study, Volume III*. Pacific Linguistics Series C, no. 40. Canberra: Australian National University, Research School of Pacific Studies, pp. 511–32.

—— (1991) 'Language Death and Disappearance: Causes and Circumstances'. In E.M. Uhlenbeck and R.H. Robins (eds) (1991) *Endangered Languages*. Oxford: Berg, pp. 1–18.

Yamanaka, L.-A. (1993) *Saturday Night at the Pahala Theatre*. Honolulu: Bamboo Ridge Press.

Useful web sites

Chapter 2: External change
Code-switching Bibliography database:
<http://ccat.sas.upenn.edu/plc/codeswitching>. Accessed June 2005.

Summer Institute of Linguists Languages in Contact web site:
<http://www.ethnologue.com/show_subject.asp?code=LIC>. Accessed June 2005.

Chapter 3: Language birth
Learning and Teaching Scotland (information on educational curricula):
<http://www.ltscotland.org.uk>. Accessed June 2005.

The Scots Leid Associe:
<http://www.lallans.co.uk/index.html>. Accessed June 2005.

Tok Pisin:
<http://www.une.edu.au/langnet/tokpisin.htm>. Accessed June 2005.

Chapter 4: Language death
The Foundation for endangered languages:
<http://www.ogmios.org/home.htm>. Accessed June 2005.

Chapter 5: Language planning
US English:
<http://www.us-english.org/foundation>. Accessed June 2005.
<http://www.us-english.org/inc>. Accessed June 2005.

US Language legislation archives:
<http://www.humnet.ucla.edu/humnet/linguistics/people/grads/macswan/leg-arc.htm>.
Accessed June 2005.

Issues in US language policy:
<http://ourworld.compuserve.com/homepages/jwcrawford/langleg.htm>. Accessed
June 2005.

For policy and planning in Jersey:
<http://jerriais.ifrance.com/jerriais/>. Accessed June 2005.
<http://www.societe-jersiaise.org/geraint/jerriais/>. Accessed June 2005.

For educational policy in the Seychelles:
<http://www.ibe.unesco.org/International/ICE47/English/Natreps/reports/seychelles_scan.pdf>. Accessed June 2005.
<http://www.tmc.waikato.ac.nz/english/ETPC/article/pdf/2004v3n1art4.pdf>. Accessed June 2005.

Chapter 6: Language revival
The Cornish Language web site:
<http://members.ozemail.com.au/~kevrenor/kevren.html>. Accessed June 2005.

The Cornish Language Fellowship web site:
<http://www.cornish-language.org>. Accessed June 2005.

The Jewish Language Research web site:
<http://www.jewish-languages.org/hebrew.html>. Accessed June 2005.

Chapter 7: Language invention
The Conlangs web site:
<http://www.langmaker.con/conlangs.htm>. Accessed June 2005.

General index

Index of people

Schuchardt, H. 3n2, 29
Scott, W. 73
Sebba, M. 75
Seuren, P. 23
Sherman, S.P. 70–1
Shield, L. 143
Siegel, J. 67, 127
Sigurðsson, H.A. 11, 13
Singh, I. ix, 58, 65, 75, 129, 130
Smith, A.S.D. 140, 142
Smith, J. 27–28
Smith, N. 107, 124, 128
Snow, C.E. 111, 112
Solomon, I.D. 114
Sperling, K. 172, 176
Squier, S. 171
Stockwell, R.P. 7n8
Sudbury, A. 47–8
Swadesh, M. 78, 81–2
Swift, J. 1, 181

Thomas, C. 144
Thomas, P. 127
Thomason, S.G. 2, 3, 26, 29, 36, 38, 51,
    54, 64n4, 88
Timm, L.A. 50, 90, 138
Tolkien, J.R.R. 153
Tolstoy, L. 164
Tomlinson, H. 52
Trask, R.L. 56
Traugott, E. 15n12
Tregear, J. 142
Trent, W.P. 70–1
Trudgill, P. 42, 64n4, 83, 88
Tuchman, G.M. 115

Unz, R. 114, 115

Valdman, A. 23, 24
Van Doren, C. 70–1
Vanniarajan, S. 49n5
Vaugelas, C. F. de 101
Vedder, J. 171
Velupillai, V. 15–16
Vennemann, T. 10, 27
Victor, P. 127
Vidal, E.T. 156
Voegelin, C.F. 78–9
Voegelin, F.M. 78–9

Waller, A.R. 70–1
Walsh, M. 87
Ward, A.W. 70–1
Watson, I. 48n4
Watts, R. 64n4
Weinreich, U. 3, 4n3, 30, 39, 44
Wekker, H. 23
Wells, K. 177
Welmers, W.E. 3
Welsh, I. 73
Whitney, W.D. 29, 36
Whorf, B.L. 169–70, 172
Wilkins, J. 156
Williams, N.J.A. 142, 144
Wilson, R. 46
Winford, D. 29
Winsboro, B.L. 114
Wmffre, I. 140
Wright, L. 48n4
Wurm, S.A. 66, 68, 85, 86

Yamanaka, L.-A. 15

Zamenhof, L.L. 160, 161, 163–4, 167,
    181